Mortuary Feasting on New Ireland

Mortuary Feasting on New Ireland

The Activation of Matriliny Among the Sursurunga

Alexander H. Bolyanatz

Bergin & Garvey
Westport, Connecticut • London

Library of Congress Cataloging-in-Publication Data

Bolyanatz, Alexander H., 1956–
    Mortuary feasting on New Ireland : the activation of matriliny among the Sursurunga /
Alexander H. Bolyanatz.
        p.   cm.
    Includes bibliographical references and index.
    ISBN 0–89789–721–8 (alk. paper)
        1. Sursurunga (Papua New Guinea people)—Funeral customs and rites.   2. Sursurunga
(Papua New Guinea people)—Kinship.   3. Matrilineal kinship—Papua New Guinea—New
Ireland Province.   I. Title.
DU740.42.B65   2000
393—dc21   99–059735

British Library Cataloguing in Publication Data is available.

Library of Congress Catalog Card Number: 99–059735
ISBN: 0–89789–721–8

First published in 2000

Bergin & Garvey, 88 Post Road West, Westport, CT 06881
An imprint of Greenwood Publishing Group, Inc.
www.greenwood.com

Printed in the United States of America

The paper used in this book complies with the
Permanent Paper Standard issued by the National
Information Standards Organization (Z39.48–1984).

10 9 8 7 6 5 4 3 2 1

In Memory of Robert D. Kvasnica

1946–1998

Contents

A photo essay follows Chapter 4.

Illustrations

Preface

I first arrived on New Ireland in November of 1989. Through the kindness of Don and Sharon Hutchisson of the Summer Institute of Linguistics, my family and I found suitable accommodations at Tekedan village, in the midst of the Sursurunga language area. My debt to the Hutchisson family is profound. The research site, Tekedan, is inhabited by 128 people and is renowned for its clear, cool river. Much of 1990 and 1991 were spent at Tekedan, and we departed in February of 1992. I returned for a shorter period in the summer of 1998.

Most people on New Ireland know about anthropologists and have some idea of what they do, and it was not uncommon to hear stories about Roy Wagner, Bob Foster, or Steve Albert. It was therefore relatively effortless for me to establish myself in and use the local idea of "anthropologist." This made my work much easier than it might have been otherwise. Toward the end of 1991, University of Virginia graduate student Steve Jackson and his spouse, Susan, and young son Sam arrived just down the road at Nokon. I have been informed about a number of aspects of Sursurunga social life by conversations with Steve and by reading his dissertation, and I appreciate the work he put into his research.

Anthropological fieldwork requires the ability to know when one is seeing anomalous behavior and when one is seeing typical behavior. Not long after my family and I first settled at Tekedan village, I found myself begining to make generalizations about what I saw and heard. Here is a passage from my journal that I wrote less than five months after I arrived:

In many aspects of Sursurunga life, a rigid distinction is made between males and females. In general, this distinction appears most acutely in ritual contexts, and seems to be less prominent in everyday contexts. The sexual division of labor is strongest in the areas of the procurement of food (only men fish and hunt) and the provision of shelter (only men build houses). Men have been observed preparing and cooking food, harvesting from gardens, and washing clothes. To be sure, these are all considered women's tasks, but there seems to be no proscription against these chores for men.

Women, for their part, can and do participate in public meetings, build themselves a *pal* or kitchen, own land and other property (such as trees), and even head lineages, "if," according to one male informant, "all of us lineage men were ne'er-do-wells."

That description now seems to me to be rather austere and lifeless—a stick figure in a world of paintings by Raphael or Titian. Later, I penned the following:

There are many behaviors which seem to be at odds with matrilineal descent understandings. The behavior of individuals may even contradict what those individuals verbalized during interviews. For example, Toateli's bridewealth payment at Tekedan village was made on his behalf by his father, rather than by his enates. This occurred not long after he had mentioned to me that a young man like himself was dependent on older enates for such things. When I pointed out the discrepancy to him, he shrugged and said that his mother's brother was a bit short of cash (the payment was K100 and two strands of *reu* shell money), his father had had it, and he was keen to marry. Neither Toateli, his father, nor his mother's brother intended to undermine matrilineal descent understandings. He wished to marry, and the others agreed that he ought to do so. Toateli did allow that he wished to reciprocate his father's help with a pig at some point in the future, not to reinforce matrilineal descent understandings (although this would probably be an unintended consequence should he do so), but because it was consistent with his views about the complexion of his relationship with his father. It is, then, not unusual to find actors engaged in social relations which seem inconsistent with matrilineal descent.

This later passage is a more richly textured description, I think. It makes one wonder: how much better would the description be if I had spent even more time on New Ireland? How does an ethnographer know when she or he has spent enough time at a place to be able to write cogently about the people there? Then there is the prior question of what makes an ethnographer believe that she or he even has the right to make public the lives of other people.

I worry about the invasion of privacy. I fretted about it on New Ireland when a keening woman collapsed at a mortuary feast and the people from Tekedan urged me to snap photographs of her sobbing in the fetal position on the ground. And I fret about it now when I have to decide whether to use pseudonyms. For the most part I have not used pseudonyms except when, in my view, it would reflect badly on a person. I am guessing that most people would be pleased to see their names in print, so unless otherwise indicated, pseudonyms are not used.

I began my research armed with information about the "matrilineal puzzle" and the ways in which matrilineal descent engenders certain "stresses" and "strains" in society. My interest was to test the validity of the notion of the "matrilineal puzzle" at two levels: (1) how do these "strains" occur structurally—that is, what specific local institutions are at cross-purposes? and, of greater interest to me, (2) are these stresses and strains found not only at the structural level, but intrapsychically as well? In other words, do individuals—both male and female—experience stress and tension by virtue of being members of a matrilineal descent group?

My results did not support the hypothesis that matriliny is replete with "strain," either structurally or individually. Socio-structural and individual tensions do exist among the Sursurunga, but I found nothing to indicate that these tensions exist as either the direct or indirect result of the presence of matrilineal descent understandings and matrilineal descent groups.

As it happened, most of my Sursurunga informants were much more interested in talking about mortuary feasting than about the emotional aspects of the "matrilineal puzzle." Matrilineal descent theory predicts that matriliny breaks down when the transmission of property—especially land—ceases to pass through the matriline and is transferred patrifilially. To test this hypothesis, I gathered information on hundreds of different land transactions and found that, in fact, the Sursurunga do transfer land patrifilially now much more than in the past. But the expected concomitant erosion of matrilineal descent ideology has not occurred. I became more and more interested in this theoretical quandary. Simply put, I found that the salience of matrilineal descent understandings among the Sursurunga is retained in the mortuary feasting complex, a finding that has implications for the theory of the demise of matriliny, and for descent group theory in general.

It occurred to me that a matrilineal descent group was in some ways like an anthropology course. Students are members of a class even on a Sunday evening, but the class exists in quite a different way on Monday morning at the eight o'clock lecture hour. Students are no less members of the class on Sunday than they are on Monday, but the difference between the import of class membership on Sunday and on Monday is quite palpable. That difference exists, I think, for all groups, whether an anthropology course at an undergraduate institution in North America or a matrilineal descent group on New Ireland.

To tell all of the ways in which all of the aspects of life fit together—as they do in real life—on New Ireland would be impossible. I do not purport to tell all there is to know about the Sursurunga; rather, I have isolated particular social dynamics and described them. The realities of social life forced the necessity of an artificial framework to explicate some of Sursurunga life in a coherent way. I hope that the following account succeeds.

My research and writing were made possible by grants from the Office of Graduate Studies and Research at the University of California, San Diego, the Institute for Intercultural Studies, a Kenneth and Dorothy Hill Fellowship, and the Wheaton College Alumni Office.

In Papua New Guinea, the people of Tekedan village had the kindness to welcome interlopers into their midst. I especially appreciate, for the goodwill shown to my family and me: Eriel, Gideon Toateli, the late Kaminiel Ladi, Mati Puspalai, the late Misidoris Tobung, Mosili Tokbol, Rodi, the late Sam Milen, the late Sam Tovina, Sokip, Taitus Siantokbol, Tinamel, and Toateli.

I was also assisted by the kindnesses of the National Museum of Papua New Guinea, the National Archives of Papua New Guinea, the New Ireland Provincial Government, and the Summer Institute of Linguistics. Mark Busse and

Claudia Gross, Bob and Linda Kvasnica, and Tim and Denise Sieges provided countless ways of supporting my family and me while we were in Papua New Guinea.

My thinking about the issues presented in this book—as well as issues that go beyond the book—has benefited by my interactions with Kevin Birth, Roy D'Andrade, Dan Fessler, David Jordan, Ken Kroesen, Fitz John Poole, Mel Spiro, Marc Swartz, Elizabeth Throop, Donald Tuzin, and James Wilce. The remaining errors are mine.

My greatest debt is to my family—my spouse Pam and our children: Lexi, Mari, and Zander—who not only accepted the rigors of fieldwork, but were unflaggingly supportive, and their presence on New Ireland with me constitutes a cherished chapter in the chronicle of our household.

The book is dedicated to Bob Kvasnica, who died in 1998 of complications from malaria that he contracted while in Papua New Guinea. Bob was in Papua New Guinea because he sought to serve God and humanity—especially children. He succeeded.

A Note About Language

The most authoritative corpus of materials on the Sursurunga language is the product of Don Hutchisson (1984, 1986, and a number of unpublished materials). The Sursurunga language has six vowels, /á/, /a/, /e/, /i/, /o/, and /u/. The final five sound very much like Spanish vowels. The /á/ represents the schwa sound, the vocoid in the English words "but" or "cut." Consonants are also given Spanish values, except for the stops, in which prenasalization is especially pronounced. The same is true of the local version of Neo-Melanesian (Pidgin English).

Sursurunga and Neo-Melanesian words are in italics throughout. This is opposed to the convention of using italics for the first appearance only of a word. My reason for declining to use the convention is that some Neo-Melanesian and Sursurunga words are homomorphic with English. For example, the Sursurunga *bang* and *him* ("men's house" and "work," respectively), were they not italicized, might be confusing. The same problem applies in Neo-Melanesian, as in *as* ("source" or "root"), which may be misconstrued as a conjunction.

Throughout the text, foreign words should be understood to be Sursurunga unless otherwise identified as Neo-Melanesian words. A glossary of Sursurunga and Neo-Melanesian terms used can be found toward the end of the book.

Chapter 1

Introduction

This book is about a series of mortuary feasts (so named because they take place in honor of deceased individuals) conducted by people known as the Sursurunga who live toward the southern end of the island of New Ireland, Papua New Guinea. Since Bateson's *Naven*, focusing on a specific ritual aspect of social life has been a convention of ethnographic description, and I treat Sursurunga mortuary feasting in this way. One possible pitfall of such an approach is that the resulting portrait may overstate the importance of a particular institution in the lives of the people who are described, the purported centrality being more of a literary convenience than an ethnographic reality. This is a risk I am willing to take since there are, everywhere anthropologists have been, social institutions that serve as key features of social life and around which a disproportionately large amount of time, energy, and resources get expended. Mortuary feasting among the Sursurunga is such an institution.[1] By referring to the centrality of the traditional mortuary feasting complex, I mean to emphasize the fact that for many individuals, mortuary feasting is a means to multiple ends—that is, people meet more than one objective by participating in mortuary feasting.

These feasts are analyzed using the distinction between "causes" and "effects."[2] This distinction is important because it provides a better understanding

---

1. Recent work by Albert (1987), Jackson (1995), Wagner (1986), and Foster (1988, 1990a, 1990b, 1995) makes unequivocally clear the centrality of mortuary feasting throughout southern New Ireland Province.

2. My use of quotation marks here is to acknowledge that I do not view social analysis as social physics—that is, as an approach in which clear-cut variables can always be seen to have the same results. On the other hand, social life is not random; there are patterns to why people do what they do, and the explication of these patterns is, in my

of the object under scrutiny (in this case mortuary feasting), and because consequences (effects) cannot necessarily be construed to be the reasons (causes) for an individual's performance of an action. The approach I employ can be expressed in the diagram below, in which ritual mortuary feasting among the Sursurunga can be seen as an effect (the outcome of x) and as a cause (the precipitator of y):

$x \rightarrow$ SURSURUNGA MORTUARY FEAST SEQUENCE $\rightarrow y$

As in the mathematical use of symbols such as x and y, x and y could be, but are not necessarily, the same thing. In the book I present a number of phenomena that are related to Sursurunga mortuary feasting as x, and also a (smaller) number of things that fit in the y slot. One of the things that operates vis-à-vis mortuary feasting as both x and y is matrilineal descent. For Sursurunga speakers in and around Tekedan village on the southeast coast of New Ireland, matrilineal descent is one reason for participation in the sequence of mortuary feasts. And matrilineal descent is one of the outcomes of the mortuary feasting complex.[3] When I speak of matriliny as an effect of behavior, I mean an increased relevance or salience of matrilineal descent understandings and of the statuses that those understandings inform that result from mortuary feasting. As Foster (1995:67) reports for nearby Tanga: "the 'groupiness' of Tangan matrilineages becomes salient."

In short, the constitution of matrilineal descent groups will be shown to be a largely unintended consequence of mortuary feasting (that is, matriliny as a y), and that matrilineal descent is but one of a number of reasons (an x) for participation in mortuary feasting. This seems like an innocuous enough claim, but it turns out that the question of whether, how, or to what degree an ideology of descent might be related to behavior such as that found in mortuary ritual has been rather controversial. Here is a brief recap of that controversy and some of the implications.

STRUCTURE AND PROCESS

Fifty years ago, much of anthropology took the relationship between mental processes and behavior to be largely unidirectional: what people thought and felt generated or caused their behavior. What people felt was relegated to psychology, and the task of anthropology was to construct an articulation of the beliefs and understandings that were behind observable actions.

That was then; this is now. As Ortner (1984) has shown, anthropology has since shifted to a perspective that attends primarily to the outcomes or effects of

view, the job of the social sciences. Even though I do not use the quotation marks for the rest of the book, they should be understood to be implicit reminders of what I say here.

3. The mortuary feasting sequence involves the three feasts that I describe subsequently. The mortuary feasting complex or institution is not only the feasting sequence, but also the understandings and social relations that surround mortuary ritual.

behavior—what Ortner calls "practice." Beliefs and understandings are still important in anthropology, but they are no longer seen exclusively as the determinants of behavior, but also now as, in important ways, the products of behavior. Indeed, the trend has gone ever further: it has stressed that the only way to understand culture is to see it as the outcome of practice. One outcome of such a view is that not only are 50- (and more)-year-old anthropological descriptions under fire for their oversimplifications, but now even the nomenclature is suspect. As a result, it is not uncommon to see terms such as "clan" branded as anachronistic and unsophisticated. In such a view, not only does clan membership cause behavior, but there are no clans; there are only people behaving in ways that *used* to be called clans by anthropologists who should have known better.

I think this overdoing a good thing. The overdue recognition that we had failed to give adequate attention to the effects of human behavior does not mean that attention to the causes is and always has been misguided. Yes, there is more to people's behavior than a set of rules that look something like, "I am a member of clan X. Clan X is sponsoring a feast next week. Therefore I sponsor a feast." But it is also inaccurate to imagine that the idea of a group that can be called a "clan" is merely an ethnographer's convenient fiction, with little or no meaning to a local person. More to the point, a matrilineal descent group can be seen as an effect of mortuary feasting among the Sursurunga without necessarily rejecting it as a cause of feasting.

One way to think of the difference between the two ways of seeing matrilineal descent and mortuary feasting is to see recent, processual analyses as representing a "you are what you do" way of looking at human behavior: if you act like a lineage member, then you *are* a lineage member. These processual analyses eschew the structural idea that individuals have a set of rules to follow, which result in participation in groups—a "you do what you are" approach: you act like a lineage member because you are one. This difference is worthy of our attention because it is the case that members of Sursurunga matrilineal descent groups do not always behave as members of such groups. Furthermore, there are times when membership in a matrilineal descent group is not a conspicuous driving force behind a person's behavior.

An ancillary argument is that (foreshadowing a later discussion), contrary to conventional anthropological understandings, matrilineal descent groups need not always be wealth- or land-transmitting groups, but can be principally feast-sponsoring groups. I make this point about matrilineal descent and mortuary ritual because it shows that the erosion or disintegration of matrilineal descent is not necessarily connected to a change from the matrilineal transmission of rights to land (Gough 1961). Earlier analyses of matriliny relied on a notion that cultural understandings and values can be inferred from behavior (Bolyanatz 1996). It is for this reason that Gough wrote of the disintegration of matrilineal descent *groups* and derived from this some doubts about the "survival of the matrilineal *principle*" (1961:638; emphasis added). Although it is not wrong to infer understandings from behavior, it is fallacious to infer the absence of particular (matrilineal) understandings from the absence of a particular behavior (matrilineal transmission of land). What is at stake is not the existence of ideas *about* behavior, but behavior, and the ideas that generate it. In the end, an accurate appraisal of matriliny has to rely on a determination of how understandings about filiation, descent, and the values connected to those understandings inform and are informed by social relations.

It has long been known that in the analysis of descent groups, it is necessary to distinguish between descent constructs and the functions of the group, or what I call activated social relations: behaviors at least partly effecting an actor's sense of membership in a descent group—lineage, clan, or moiety—are salient. An individual might be conscious of the salience of descent group membership, but this is to be distinguished from conspicuous behavior: behavior that is in part a product of the salience of the status of group membership. Sursurunga matrilineages are activated by individuals' combined participation in feasting events. Individuals' reasons for participating in feasts vary, and often have little to do with matrilineal group membership. The unintended outcome, however, of certain overdetermined behaviors is the existence and perpetuation of activated matrilineal descent groups.

I have used three terms in the foregoing that I want to highlight and define with some precision because they are the concepts that I use in much of my analysis. The terms are "status salience," "group membership," and "activated groups."

The Salience of Social Statuses

A Sursurunga person, like persons everywhere, occupies a number of different social statuses. An analysis of Sursurunga behavior, then, must take into consideration the fact that, for example, men who are members of matrilineal descent groups will at times act as fathers/husbands and at other times act as brothers/uncles. Cultural and sociological analyses that do not attend to the variable relevance of social statuses cannot adequately portray social life. This variable relevance is a result of the fact that social statuses have, as part of their cultural construction, what Swartz (1990:117; 1991:10–11) calls "salience understandings." These understandings "concern which status or statuses (vis-à-vis others) properly serve as a guide for behavior in particular situations and, when more than one status is involved, which ones are appropriate with what relative importance in guiding behavior" (Swartz 1991:102).

"Salience" thus refers to the conscious awareness of membership in a social status or set of statuses. Note that the cognitive salience of a social status is a prerequisite for behavior but is not itself behavior. Membership in, for example, a matrilineal descent group might be salient, but behaving according to that understanding is something else. Status salience is a motivator of behavior, but it is behavior itself that makes an individual's group membership manifest or conspicuous, and when two or more individuals collaborate or cooperate in their conspicuous group membership, we can say that a social group is activated.

Conspicuous Group Membership

I have referred to conspicuous group membership as an instance in which an individual's behavior manifests her or his occupancy of a social status. This is behavior in which a social status is seen as particularly salient, even if the behavior is not performed in a social context. For example, a Sursurunga person may go to her or his garden alone to gather some provisions for a feast that her or his matrigroup is sponsoring. Going to a garden alone is not social behavior in the sense that sociality is present, but it is social behavior in the sense that the awareness of one's relationships vis-à-vis others (one's own matrikin, the guests of the upcoming feast, and so on) is part of the reason for heading to the garden. It is this difference that makes the analytical distinction between conspicuous group membership and an activated social group (which I discuss shortly) worth making. Much of human behavior is social, but much social behavior takes place outside the presence of other people—or at least other people whose own statuses are relevant.[4]

Conspicuous or manifest group membership is behavior that may have a number of different antecedents, and status salience may not be the most keenly experienced one, or it may not be cognized at all. It is furthermore the case that conspicuous group membership cannot take place without status salience, which makes status salience a necessary but not sufficient condition of manifest action or conspicuous group membership. This means that conspicuous group membership itself has the same necessary-but-not-sufficient-condition relationship to activated groups.

Activated Groups

Houseman and White note that with regard to kinship, "it is not the existence of kinship ties but their activation or inactivation that is significant" (1998:60). My concept of the activation of ties to a group is derived from the work of New Ireland ethnographers Clay (1992:722) and Foster (1995:10). In this processual way of understanding a group, a group's activation is the evincement of a relationship or relational sphere through behavior. An activated group exists, then, as a result of the agency of actors. In a narrow sense, I differ somewhat in my use of the term in that for Clay and Foster, activated groups are those in which the relationships and the social statuses that order them do not exist until invoked. In my use, the relationships encoded in social statuses do exist, but they do not matter until invoked. (At least one reason for the slightly different take that I have on activated groups is that Clay would disagree with the idea

---

4. By this distinction I mean that a person who goes to the garden alone to gather provisions for an upcoming feast is analytically no different from the person who is accompanied by an anthropologist. The garden owner is not alone, but the anthropologist status of her or his companion may make little or no difference in terms of matrilineal group status salience.

of "the individual as a self-contained entity" (1992:722), a concept that would be required for the use of the concept of social statuses. I address the concept of "the individual" toward the end of the chapter.) By definition, a single person cannot constitute an activated social group. When, however, two or more people act conspicuously as group members in concert, then we can say that a group is activated.

Consider the following example, which makes more clear the relationship between terms such as "salience," "conspicuous group membership," and "activated groups." One of the social statuses that I occupy by virtue of having children is "father." I am no less an occupant of the "father" category when I am at my office not thinking about my children than I am when I am at a birthday dinner for one of them. When, however, I am in my office thinking about what birthday gift to buy, the "father" status is salient. When I leave my office early to stop at a store and buy a present, my status as "father" is still salient for me, but because my behavior is affected by that salience, we can say that my membership in a particular group ("family," of which my status as "father" is a part) is *conspicuous*. Finally, when I actually engage in social relations (eating together, taking photographs) with others whose statuses ("child," "spouse") are salient and whose membership in the group ("family") are conspicuous, then we can say that the group—the nuclear family—is *activated*. Note that my family does not cease to exist if we are all apart, nor if it is not salient for us; indeed, we can all be engaged in conspicuous group-membership behavior—that is, we can be operating as a nuclear family—on our own, isolated from each other. In short, status salience, conspicuous behavior, and group activation are different phenomena, and they must be distinguished in social analysis.

The example in the preceding paragraph implies that status salience, conspicuous group membership, and activated social groups are sequential steps. This is often the case, but it is not always the case, nor is it required to be so. Imagine another example in which you and a colleague are planning an event for a third colleague, who is retiring. You encounter her in the hallway, and all within a second or two, you recall that you need to discuss some detail of the event with her, use a facial expression to indicate that you'd like to talk, and open a conversation about the event that the two of you—an ad hoc social group, but a social group nonetheless—are planning. In this case, status salience, conspicuous group membership, and the activation of the group are analytically indistinguishable; all three are there and are identifiable, but unlike the birthday example above, it is sometimes difficult to know at what point, say, the activated group appears.

The progression of status salience, conspicuous group membership, and an activated social group can be thought of as a kind of *epidemiological* understanding of behavior—that is, it provides an account of the factors that go into the behavior of social actors (Sperber 1985:30–31; 1996:*passim*). In other words, an epidemiological analysis of Sursurunga mortuary ritual feasting is an analysis that attends to cause as I outlined above; among other things, it regards status salience as an x in the $x \rightarrow$ SURSURUNGA MORTUARY FEAST SEQUENCE equation.

But there is also the SURSURUNGA MORTUARY FEAST SEQUENCE $\rightarrow y$ equation to consider, and here we see that the progression of salience, membership, and activated group can be reversed such that the salience of a social status can also be thought of as y, or an outcome. Thus, in my earlier discussion of seeing Sursurunga ritual feasting as both effect and cause, and seeing matriliny as both cause and effect, it is the salience of a matrilineally informed social status (for example, a person's sense of the salience of her or his membership in the Malai matrimoiety, or in the Sahwon matriclan) that is in focus.

For most Sursurunga, enatically based social statuses are not salient or activated very often or for very long outside of the mortuary feasting complex. Women, for example, interact with their children much more as mothers than as older enates,[5] and men may interact with the people they like *qua* friends irrespective of descent group membership. It is most often in the context of mortuary feasting that matrilineal group membership becomes emphasized. Matrilineal descent group membership is not created in the performance of mortuary ritual, it is only made salient.

In the Sursurunga case, for example, men and women design and execute plans of action according to their statuses as members of many different groups, including matrilineages, churches, villages, households, men's cults, and so on. But not all of, say, a Sursurunga man's activities can be attributed to his membership in a matrilineal descent group. Even when membership in his matrilineage is not cognized, he is no less a member of that group than when awareness of membership is prominent and serves as a basis for action. It is this action as a group member that makes the matrilineal descent group activated. The matrilineage exists abstractly all of the time; it exists conspicuously when its members are behaving in ways that are influenced by their awareness of their membership in the group. The group is also activated when members behave as a group for non-group-related reasons. The behaviors of individual social actors activate the group even if they have disparate purposes for doing so. To speak of a group conducting a certain action can be to lose sight of the individuals who have made, for various reasons, the choice to participate in behavior that activates a group. This leads to the two main points about groups—specifically matrilineal descent groups—among the Sursurunga: (1) matrilineal descent groups do not sponsor feasts; individuals do; and (2) matrilineal descent groups do not provide guidelines for behavior; an individual's understandings about the salience of entailments of membership in the group do.

Foster, on nearby Tanga, notes that mortuary ritual analogous to that among the Sursurunga is "an instance of deliberate collective action through which agents define relations of similarity among themselves—[i.e.,] bound themselves

---

5. I will be following the convention of using *enate* and *enatic* to describe matrilineal relationships in the same way that *agnate* and *agnatic* have been used to describe analogous patrilineal relationships.

as a group" (1995:12). Foster attends in his study to the outcome of mortuary ritual, an analysis with which I agree in the Sursurunga case: individuals "make themselves appear as a matrilineage almost solely in connection with hosting mortuary feasts" (1995:67). My attention, however, will be less on the matriliny-making outcomes of feasting and more on those things that impel participation in mortuary ritual in the first place. My concern, then, is with the part of the equation that attends to the bases of participation in mortuary feasting; I explicate what Foster calls "deliberate action." A study of Sursurunga mortuary feasting shows that the analysis of groups—in this case, matrilineal descent groups—is best conducted by attention to the reasons that the individuals who make up those groups act as they do.

The salience of group membership cannot be seen as simply the blueprint for social life, but, importantly, also as the outcome of social life. A processual analysis of Sursurunga mortuary feasting (one in which status salience is seen as an outcome of group action) can provide useful insights. Foster, for example, understands mortuary ritual on Tanga "as a form of collective action that constructs collective individuals—matrilineages in this case" (Foster 1995:11). In this way, my analysis is consistent with Foster's: I agree that matrilineages are not simply static monolithic structures that dominate the landscape of the behavioral environment; it is important to recognize that matriliny is constituted through ritual. My analysis is intended to amplify and extend Foster's in that I describe the nature of and what is behind the unintended, emergent aspects of Foster's "construction." To the degree, however, that Foster sees this process as the intention of social actors, we diverge, either on ethnographic grounds in that feasting on Tanga is not like feasting among the Sursurunga, or on analytical grounds in that we disagree on how this process of "constructing" actually works. In fact, as I discussed earlier, I am looking largely at what is behind mortuary feasting, whereas Foster attends primarily to the outcome of mortuary feasting.

For all his attention to the processual construction of Tanga matrilineages, Foster does not follow the processual perspective to its reductio ad absurdum; he notes, for example, that "Tangan sociality is not a directionless flow" (Foster 1995:12). In other words, Foster allows that some structure *is* inherent in social systems. But just how far does one go before stopping short of an entirely structure-less, process-ful analytical perspective? And how does one know when one gets there? My answer is that in the analysis of Sursurunga mortuary feasting, the decision-making individual is impelled by various sorts of presses to engage in mortuary ritual behavior. And these presses are themselves the result of some structures; seeing structure as both cause and effect, then, provides a balanced social analysis. Foster does not say that Tangans *intentionally* try to accomplish social reproduction (1995:*passim*); this means that there is still the question of why mortuary feasting occurs in southern New Ireland in the first place.

The issue, then, is not the arbitrary degree to which the reality of a "social structure" exists, but the degree to which social statuses are experienced by individuals as salient in a given context. In the terms of this study, the balance that Foster resolves to strike is best achieved by attention to the realities of a social structure that is composed of social statuses occupied by social actors. These statuses, and, importantly, the social relations—that is, activated groups—in which these statuses are expressed, can be seen as "process" in the waxing and waning of their salience for individual actors.

Two implications for anthropological theory emerge from the analysis of the relationship between matrilineal descent and Sursurunga mortuary feasting. The first addresses what is called "The New Melanesian Ethnography." The second is the effort to rethink a century of anthropological attention to the nature of kinship, descent, and descent groups, and has been called "The New Kinship." Both of these "New" trends in anthropology share the idea that, until recently, anthropological analyses and description have been twisted by unreflective assumptions. Specifically, constructs such as "lineage" have come to be challenged along the lines that the label obscures more than it illuminates. The New Kinship advocates a view that eschews biology as a starting point for the analysis of kinship systems. Likewise, The New Melanesian Anthropology eschews ideas such as "groups." In both cases, I think that there has been an unwarranted dismissal of preexisting realities, and that recent insights into processual social analysis should not fail to take the volition of actors into account; my concern is with the readiness to dismiss, a priori, the notion that actors may have ideas like the reality of parent-child relationships, and other relationships, in mind as the basis for their behavior.

The bulk of the remainder of this chapter addresses The New Melanesian Anthropology and The New Kinship along with one that is mentioned above: the matter of whether there is such a thing, for purposes of social analyses, "an individual."

THE NEW MELANESIAN ANTHROPOLOGY

"The New Model Anthropology" (Carrier 1992:1) and "The New Melanesian Ethnography" (Josephides 1991[6]) are recent labels that are intended by their creators to indicate that recent anthropological work in Melanesia is qualitatively different from earlier work. James Carrier, in *History and Tradition in Melanesian Anthropology*, characterizes one who engages in New Model Anthropology is as "a facilitator, the recorder of divergent voices and viewpoints" (Carrier 1992:1), rather than a scientist who presents ethnographic information as chunks of evidence in support of and as a means of explicating explanations of human behavior. A New Melanesian Ethnographer, like a New Model Anthropologist, is one who takes the processual approach, which does away with structural notions such as "clan," or "moiety"—and even the a priori assumption of something that can be called "society." Such a view prefers instead the dynamic of

---

6. Josephides coined this term as a means of describing Barth (1987), Mimica (1988), J. Weiner (1988), and Strathern (1988).

"sociality" (Josephides 1991:158).   Both are intended to be antiessentialist strategies: the New Model Anthropology aims to avoid the homogenizing that results from the lumping of inhabitants of the anthropologist's natural laboratory into a generic category called Other. The New Melanesian Ethnography is also antiessentialist in its goal of encouraging the fieldworker to be an information-gathering tabula rasa for whom nothing, except perhaps the existence of the people with whom she or he lives, is taken for granted.

As I argued earlier, I think this can be overdone—not only in terms of analytic utility but also in terms of experiential integrity—when it breaks down the individual as the unit of analysis. In my view, the individual is irreducible as a unit of inquiry.[7] Understandings, statuses, choice, and the logic of the situation (to use a phrase that I will discuss later) are all important components of the individual and are worthy of study in their own right, as long as it is understood that the individual is more than the sum of her or his understandings, statuses, choices, and logics. The Sursurunga data show that the fundamental anthropological question, "Why do people do what they do?" is best answered by construing "people" as individuals rather than as a group.

The following analysis of Sursurunga mortuary feasting is New Melanesian Anthropology in that I attend more to the process of descent group activation than the causal effects of descent group structure. It *is* important to be aware that social life is better understood not by staid patterns to which most people mostly conform, but by the dynamic formation and reformation of relationships by social actors. Foster describes the theoretical flight from structure to process, "the purpose of which is to enable a reconceptualization of 'the social order' in terms other than those or relationships between 'individuals' and between 'individuals' and 'groups.' Put differently, the conceptual aim of the New Melanesian Ethnography is to displace the static, morphological notion of 'society' with the alternative notion of 'sociality'" (Foster 1995:8).

Although I do not share the need to renounce terms such as "society," "individual," and "group," I am in agreement with the need to understand process rather than be concerned only with discrete packages of rights and obligations. So, although I am a New Melanesian Anthropologist in this way, I am a jaded one because I see these things as causal, too.

KINSHIP AND DESCENT

Schneider's well-known essay on the dynamics of matrilineal descent groups (1961) represents part of the foundation for his landmark *Critique of the Study of Kinship* (1984) on the anthropological analysis of kinship systems.[8] In his analy-

---

7. That is, the individual is irreducible as a unit of inquiry *for social anthropology*. The unanswered questions in genetics and neuroscience make me unwilling to assert that intraindividual variables are unimportant.

8. Indeed, Schneider himself dates the beginning of his thinking that became the Critique to 1941 (1995:221).

sis of matriliny, Schneider abandons the parent-child relationship—filiation. In his *Critique*, Schneider attributes the skewed nature of anthropological analyses of kinship systems to the assumption of the universal import of filiation when he asserts that anthropologists have long had the preconceived idea that "blood is thicker than water" (Schneider 1984:165–177). In Schneider's characterization, "blood" means the parent-child relationship, along with its corollaries, such as shared parent-child relationships, or siblingship. Schneider's view takes him to the conclusion that terms such as "lineage" and "clan" are just anthropological constructs that may—but probably do not—reflect the cultural realities of a particular person or group. In other words, "a culture which is chopped up with a Z-shaped instrument yields Z-shaped parts" (Schneider 1984:198).

Schneider asserts that, *"the first task of anthropology, **prerequisite to all others**, is to understand and formulate the symbols and meanings and their configuration that a particular culture consists of"* (1984:196; emphases in original). This study of the Sursurunga mortuary feasting provides a counterpunctual analysis in that I do not eschew terms and concepts such as "lineage" or "clan." This is because these terms serve the purpose of describing large segments of Sursurunga understandings and behavior in a concise fashion. The Sursurunga *do* think and act in terms of constructs such as lineage and moiety. This is not because I say so, or because I have been blinded to alternatives. It just is. If I had rejected ideas such as lineage and moiety before learning about the Sursurunga, and had I been operating as a strict Schneiderian, I would have been forced to reject Sursurunga descriptions of lineagelike and moiety-like groups on the grounds that they were recognizable to me, a non-Sursurunga, and therefore not authentically Sursurunga constructs. The Schneiderian idea that reference to concepts such as "lineage" or "moiety" is due to the presence of preconceptions such as "blood is thicker than water" is grounded in a logical fallacy. Consider the following use of formal logic:

When one begins with an acceptable premise, certain inferences can and cannot be made. For example, one acceptable premise is, "If the car starts, then the car has fuel." If the antecedent ("the car starts") is labeled **p** (according to convention) and the consequent ("the car has fuel") is labeled **q** (again, according to convention), then we have the following four possible cases:

1. **p** (the car starts)
2. **not p** (the car does not start)
3. **q** (the car has fuel)
4. **not q** (the car does not have fuel)

Only in the first and fourth cases are we allowed—indeed, compelled—to make inferences. In the first, we can be certain that if the car starts, it must have fuel (*modus ponens*), and in the fourth, we know that if the car does not have fuel, it cannot start (*modus tollens*). In the second case, the car's failure to start does not necessarily tell us anything about the fuel supply (the problem could be, say, inadequate compression). And in the third case, an adequate fuel supply does not necessarily tell us whether the car will start or not (again, some other problem could be the cause). For any acceptable premise, cases two and three (**not p** and **q**, respectively) *never* compel or require an entailed inference.

Consider now the following premise, which is Schneider's claim above:

IF A SOCIETY IS ANALYZED USING A Z-SHAPED INSTRUMENT,
THEN Z-SHAPED PARTS OF THE SOCIETY WILL BE REPORTED.

In other words, if an anthropologist walks into a field site expecting unilineal descent groups as they appear in an introductory textbook, then she or he will necessarily interpret certain kinds of behavior as being grounded in such groups, and record the presence of them. This premise, it seems to me, cannot be disputed. Let us consider, then, the premise in terms of logical conditional statements, in which the belief in the antecedent—using a Z-shaped instrument—can be denoted (again, following conventional logical practice) **p**. The consequent, the reporting of Z-shaped parts, is symbolized as **q**. We have the following four outcomes:

1. **p:** A SOCIETY IS ANALYZED USING A Z-SHAPED INSTRUMENT. If an anthropologist uses procrustean analytical constructs such as lineage, clan, or moiety (**p**), then it logically follows that she or he will report those phenomena (**q**). In other words, if blood is assumed to be thicker than water, then that conclusion is inescapable.
2. **not p:** A SOCIETY IS **NOT** ANALYZED USING A Z-SHAPED INSTRUMENT. If an anthropologist were to dispense with concepts such as lineage, clan, and moiety, then it is a logical fallacy to conclude that she or he must necessarily end up reporting the absence of lineages, clans, and moieties (**not q**). I call this fallacy the Epistemological Relativism Fallacy: the idea that we cannot know anything outside of our own (cultural) assumptions.
3. **q:** Z-SHAPED PARTS OF THE SOCIETY WILL BE REPORTED. If an anthropologist returns from the field making the claim that she or he observed "classic" lineages, clans, and moieties (**q**), then it is also a logical fallacy—based on an affirmation of the consequent—to conclude that they can only be the result of a priori assumptions about the presence of such social phenomena (**p**). I call this fallacy the Social Constructionist Fallacy: the idea that the world as we perceive it exists only in our minds.
4. **not q:** Z-SHAPED PARTS OF THE SOCIETY ARE **NOT** REPORTED. Finally, if our anthropologist describes a set of people for whom the likes of lineages, clans, and moieties are utterly absent (**not q**), then it logically follows that we can be quite sure that she or he did not walk in with that particular paradigm (**not p**).

The two fallacies described above (cases 2 and 3) afflict the extreme versions of processual models. Reporting lineages does not necessarily mean that an ethnographer is naïve, nor does an a priori expectation that they do not exist necessarily mean that they are not there.

Mistaken assumptions can skew anthropological descriptions, no question. But not all assumptions skew equally, and any particular conclusion cannot necessarily be attributed to skewing. What, then, is the basis for the rejection of a priori analytical constructs? Yanigasako and Collier offer a rationale: "Both gender and kinship studies, we suggest, have foundered on the unquestioned assumption that the biologically given difference in the roles of men and women in sexual reproduction lies at the core of the cultural organization of gender, even as it constitutes the genealogical grid at the core of kinship studies" (1987:49).

For Yanigasako and Collier, social facts are all too often confused with natural facts (1987:14–15), and "there are no 'facts,' biological or material, that have social consequences and cultural meanings in and of themselves" (1987:39). Only an unregenerate positivist would argue that facts speak for themselves, but if biological or material facts are universally addressed in commensurate and comparable ways across human groups, then it must be concluded that cultural constructions cannot always be the starting point of analysis. Yanigasako and Collier state that "there are not material 'facts' that can be treated as precultural givens" (1987:39). On the other hand, Godelier suggests that kinship systems may even have preceded articulate hominid speech (1998:412). Clearly, there is a difference of opinion here. Nevertheless, the facts of, for example, genotypic relatedness and phenotypic similarity *can* be treated as precultural givens, since there is no known cultural system that separates these biological facts from cultural elaborations that rely on a concept of filiation. [9]

Still, it must be kept in mind as a caveat that the rubric "matrilineal" does not always describe a singular set of social features. Goody, for example, points out that "the presence of a genealogical structure of a unilineal kind signifies little in itself" (1990:53). Indeed, if matriliny can vary so much and if we take seriously the perspective proffered by Yanigasako and Collier, then can we say that there really is such a thing as matriliny? The question is perhaps better phrased with more precision as, Is there something that is called matriliny that is recognizable, commensurate, and comparable across societies?

As I showed above, a Yes answer to this question does not necessarily mean that I have foolishly allowed myself to conclude my assumptions. The fact that we anthropologists consistently cite comparative studies in our bibliographies, and that we can use—successfully—labels such as "matrilineal descent" on search engines suggests matriliny does have an ontological existence at some level. Even more compelling to me, however, is the fact that matrifiliation never, in the ethnographic record, goes unembellished. The mother-child rela-

---

9. This may be an appropriate place to be reminded of the cogent critique of Tooby and Cosmides (1992) of what they call the Standard Social Science Model, exemplified by Yanigasako and Collier, which is like

some nightmarish short story Borges might have written, where scientists are condemned by their unexamined assumptions to study the nature of mirrors only by cataloging and investigating everything that mirrors can reflect. It is an endless process that never makes progress, that never reaches closure, that generates endless debate between those who have seen different reflected images, and who enduring product is voluminous descriptions of particular phenomena. (1992:42) tionship is always given some cultural import, and when that import includes default rights to membership in a certain kind of group, there is little reason not to think of that cultural import as matriliny. The point is not that matriliny is structurally (that is, in the relation of genealogy to group membership) or functionally (that is, in the social relations of individuals *qua* group members) equivalent wherever it is found. Rather, we see that matrifiliation is given meanings that are recognizable, commensurate, and comparable in different places around the globe.

Filiation—and especially matrifiliation—among the Sursurunga functions in certain ways, one of which is matrilineal descent group membership. The salience of descent understandings can be an outcome of an actor's behavior as well as a precipitator of an actor's behavior, as I have said. Membership in a social group has, since Durkheim, been seen to involve a cluster of rights and responsibilities that impel and constrain the group's members. In so saying, I imply a theoretical position that does not see the Western sense of the self as "peculiar" (Spiro 1993) while recognizing that the way in which individuals negotiate and construe relationships with other, similar individuals varies cross-culturally.

THE INDIVIDUAL

In some ways, a defense of "the individual" is unnecessary, even though I rely on an analytical approach known as methodological individualism. One can take the approach of methodological individualism even if those whose behavior is being analyzed do not perceive of persons as discrete, bounded individuals. Nevertheless, Sursurunga-speaking people do see persons as individuals, so my reliance upon methodological individualism is not only an analytical convenience, but is also an approach commensurate with people's experiences of themselves (or, their "selves"). In short, "the individual" is an analytic construct, whereas "the person" is an emic construal.

What is at stake, then, in the well-known discussions about "dividuals" (Marriot 1976:111), "collective Man" (Dumont 1970:38), "partible persons" (Holy 1996:155–164), and "composite persons" (Foster 1995:9ff.)? Without recapitulating the arguments of Harris (1989) and Spiro (1993), it seems fair to say that if there is no commensurability between cultural constructions of "person" around the world, then all cross-cultural research is suspect.[10] But researchers *do* manage to convey the realities of life in other places. I take this to be prima facie evidence of what was once called the psychic unity of humanity. And part of this unity is overlapping perceptions of what human persons are worldwide (D. Brown 1991:135). The existence of first person pronouns in all languages should settle the question of the universality of certain components of the "person" construct cross-culturally; indeed, pronouns should probably have kept constructs such as "dividual" from ever emerging in the first place. There is

---

10. I do not mean to say that all ideas of the *internal* nature of a person are the same across cultures, as Busby (1997) shows.

simply no anthropological evidence (that I am aware of, anyway) that a phrase that can be glossed as something like "I have a knife" cannot be seen to mean something fundamentally the same to people who have quite different cultural or linguistic systems.

This does not mean, of course, that all people everywhere accord "persons" with the same primacy. The value of a person vis-à-vis other persons, groups, or objects varies within and across cultural systems. The point, however, is that cultural constructs of "person" share, if nothing else, a sense of a discrete "self." This is certainly true among the Sursurunga, who use the term *ninsin* to refer to a person's character/personality, and is the closest Sursurunga term to the English word "self."

In resisting the trend in anthropology today toward seeing "person" as a residue of behavior, I do not wish to imply that a concept such as "self" cannot also, like the salience of a status such as lineage member, be experienced in a more heightened or relevant way. Rather, there seems to be a point at which the processual approach loses its utility in seeing *all* of humanity and human affairs as social constructions.

Methodological Individualism

Methodological individualism provides a means of understanding social action in a way that the understandings, values, and motivations that underlie an actor's behavior cannot necessarily be inferred from the results of that behavior. In so saying, I mean that I attend primarily to the antecedents of mortuary ritual. But this is not necessarily a rejection of a processual perspective. The behavior of social actors must be seen as more than the sum total of the social statuses that they occupy within the social structure: sometimes, social structure is the outcome of individual choices made for reasons that may not be related to that structure. Bailey, in an example of this perspective, discussed political structures in Orissa, India, demonstrating that individual choice was the locus for understanding change in those structures (1960:243). Socio-cultural dynamics in Orissa were the net result, or vector sum, of the choices of particular individuals. Rather than an irresistible force shaping individual choice, social structure is, according to Bailey, better seen as "an abstraction, a set of generalizations abstracted from regularities of behavior or from statements about what ought to be regularities of behavior" (Bailey 1960:238). In short, what is taken as the set of normative rules that guides behavior should also be seen to emerge from behavior. In Bailey's terms, Sursurunga individuals make the choice to participate in the mortuary feasting complex, and out of the choices of a set of individuals, the structure of matriliny is abstracted. I do not mean to say that matrilineal structure does not exist until or unless the actions of individuals constitute it. The point is simply that when occupancy of a social status that has matrilineal membership criteria is relevant or cognized, matriliny exists as part of an actor's behavioral environment (Hallowell 1955) in a way that is quite different from when occupancy of that status is not cognized.

I am using "methodological individualism" in reference to Popper's position that "insists that the 'behavior' and the 'actions' of a collective, such as states or social groups, must be reduced to the behavior and to the actions of individuals" (1952:91). Popper rejects what he takes to be the extreme, "psychologistic" version of this position: that all individual behavior and action can be explained in terms of psychological phenomena and laws such as needs and drives (1952:98). Popper thus sees himself as the middle position between the psychological reductionist view and the "holists" (the term is Gellner's [1959]). Methodological holists view the idea of "wholes are made up of parts" (Gellner 1959:495) to be the tautological, and therefore chimerical, nucleus of the methodological individualism argument. Gellner, however, fails in his examples to recognize that holistic considerations are not causal if the individual(s) in question are not attending to their membership in the whole. But Popper makes a similar error in eschewing "psychologism." The logic of an actor's situation is the result of perception, cognition, and personality, including perceptions and cognitions about membership in social groups. And if group membership is not perceived or recognized, it cannot be part of an actor's social situational logic.[11]

Methodological individualism has the analytic advantage that it retains the distinction between an unintended sociological outcome and other intent-based individual actions; and it is one of the former—the unintended outcome of the salience of matriliny—that concerns us here. The distinction between intended outcomes and unintended outcomes is important. Jordan (1990:98–99), following Spiro (1961), points out that only the expected results—the intended functions or outcomes—of institutions can be seen as causal. This is because it is only what people perceive as the purpose for an action that can be said to impel people to conduct those actions. From this perspective, certain behaviors, such as providing support in mortuary feast sponsorship, proper comportment at mortuary events, and the giving and receiving of postfeast prestations of pork are the "actions taken by individuals according to the logic of their situations" (Tuzin 1976:xxvii; cf. Popper 1952:93), which result in, rather than only being the product of, matrilineal descent understandings. The matrilineal group is activated as an unintended result of feasting, but the matrilineal descent group need not be seen as the principal stimulus for participation in the mortuary feasting complex; a function is not a cause. In other words, for my purposes, the salience of matriliny may be only a small—or sometimes not a—part of Jordan's "intended functions" (1990:98), Popper's "logic" of a social actor's situation (1952:91), or Bailey's "individual and choice" (1960:251).

Implicit in this formulation is that most behavior is overdetermined; that is, multiple considerations are "funneled" (Swartz 1993) to constitute the logic of a particular actor's situation. This perspective contrasts with earlier matrilineal—indeed, socio-structural—theory in which matrilineal descent principles alone were viewed to be the sole salient basis for what I call activated matriliny, or

---

11. Tuzin (1976:xxv–xxx) has a clear discussion of methodological individualism from which I have borrowed.

conspicuous social relations. Matrilineal understandings, if they work in the same way that other cultural understandings work, certainly make up part of an actor's logic, but with equal certainty, do not comprise all of it. In other words, methodological individualism is not at odds with a processual perspective because it recognizes that the salience of matrilineal understandings can "arise as the result of conscious and intentional human actions," which means that such salience is *the indirect, the unintended and often the unwanted byproducts of such actions*" (Popper 1952:93; emphasis in original). Conspicuous matrilineal social relations—for example, accepting the position of "guest" and comporting oneself accordingly at a mortuary feast sponsored by a lineage of the other moiety—are the result of multiple and varied "funneled" understandings, not just a delimited set of understandings that involve descent. In fact, among the Sursurunga, matrilineal social relations—again, such as being a "guest"—are activated by understandings that may have little or nothing to do with descent at all. Methodological individualism allows matrilineally informed social statuses ("guest," "host") to be seen as activated through participation in the mortuary feasting sequence. In short, many people participate in mortuary feasting along matrilineal descent lines for many reasons (described in Chapter 6) that are not closely related to matrilineal descent understandings.

When a person's status as a member of her or his descent group is salient, and when that person actually utilizes the salient understanding of group membership as a guide for behavior in social relations, the group is activated. This, then, is the connection of methodological individualism to a structural perspective: the logic of an actor's social situation is importantly informed by understandings of the salience of the social statuses that she or he occupies. The salience of a social status must therefore be considered as part of the antecedent of behavior as well as part of the consequent—cause and effect. My concern in this monograph is more with status salience as consequent, but it is not absent in my discussion of the antecedents of Sursurunga ritual mortuary feasting.

OVERVIEW

Following this introductory chapter, the Sursurunga are introduced in Chapter 2 by means of a historical and ethnographic overview, using contact, Christianity, cash, and cultural context as touchstones.

Chapter 3 attends to land and matrilineal descent theory. I have already indicated that Gough's analysis of matriliny assumes that the status of matrilineal group membership is—or should be—always salient, and that the salience of any other social status as a guide for behavior constitutes the disintegration of matriliny. This view was consistent with understandings that dominated the analysis of matriliny as the outcome of certain specific social relations, namely, those involved in the mode of production. In such a view, land tenure is the principal factor in understanding matrilineal descent. Chapter 3 shows that land rights need not necessarily be seen as the primary raison d'être of matrilineal descent groups and that the salience of patrifilial relationships does not necessarily erode the integrity of matriliny even in cases where land tenure is transferred patrifil-ially.

This view of the social structure of matriliny and Schneider's (1961) analy-sis of the cultural logic of matrilineal descent groups both depend upon a pecu-liar understanding of the patrifilial link, as described in Chapter 4. This peculi-arity shows up in statements about matrilineal descent that do not conform to the ways in which matrilineal descent operates among the Sursurunga, where land is sometimes transferred patrifilially, and where fathers are not irrelevant.

Patrifiliation does not, in itself, undermine the matrilineal descent group. Schneider's theoretical statement about matriliny argues that the separation of loci of authority—fathers within the household and mother's brothers outside—means that fathers and husbands, being structurally powerless outside the do-mestic sphere, are logically not required for the maintenance of matrilineal de-scent groups. In fact, among the Sursurunga, many of the actions of many fa-thers actually support the integrity of the matrilineal descent group of their chil-dren and wives.

Chapter 5 is a description of mortuary ritual among the Sursurunga, and raises two questions: (1) Why is the mortuary feasting complex still extant among the Sursurunga—that is, what are the proximate causes of mortuary feasting? and (2) How does the mortuary feasting complex reinforce matriliny—that is, how does feasting cause the salience of matrilineally informed social statuses? The answer to the first question—elaborated in Chapter 6—is that certain aspects of Sursurunga culture and social relations impel individuals to participate in mortuary feasting. In addition to matrilineal descent salience, Sur-surunga understandings, social relations, and values relating to food and eating, leadership, affect, cognitive categories, and reciprocity generate the goal in most individuals to participate in the mortuary feasting complex.

Chapter 7 answers the second question, namely, how does the mortuary feasting complex reinforce matriliny? Matrilineal descent continues to be a prominent feature in the Sursurunga sociological landscape for reasons that are largely non kin- or descent-based reasons. Although matriliny flourishes in southern New Ireland indirectly due to a descent principle, it is the catalyst of ritual mortuary feasting that gives it dynamism.

Chapter 8, the concluding chapter, attends to the place of the Sursurunga data within the larger anthropological endeavor. Specifically, I return to my discussion of the New Kinship and the New Anthropology, in which some impli-cations of this study are articulated.

SUMMARY

Matriliny is a result of feasting activity. This means that Sursurunga ma-triliny, to be fully comprehended, has to be seen as a consequent, and not just as an antecedent, of mortuary feasting. Various understandings combine to gener-ate an antecedent logic that serves as the basis for individual social actors who engage in ritual feasting behavior. From the perspective of methodological indi-

vidualism, the resulting mortuary feast is conducive to "the equilibrium or preservation or development of the system" (Watkins 1962:511). The system that is
endowed with this "equilibrium, preservation, or development" is, in the case of
the Sursurunga, matrilineal descent. By putting on a proper mortuary feast,
those who sponsor the feast unintentionally activate the import of matrilineal
descent understandings and matrilineal group membership. In other words, they
unintentionally preserve the integrity of Sursurunga matriliny.

Sursurunga understandings, social relations, and values relating to food and
eating, leadership, affect, cognitive categories, and reciprocity are not solely
responsible for Sursurunga mortuary feasting. I do not deny that one important
component of the motivation to participate in mortuary feasting is the salience of
membership in a matrilineal descent group. But the way mortuary feasting operates in Sursurunga society cannot be understood if matrilineal goals are taken to
be the only, or even the most important, reasons that people are involved in
mortuary feasting. My interest is to articulate especially the non-descent-based
reasons that people participate, not because there are no other reasons, but because these reasons are too easily overlooked. Furthermore, an increase in the
salience of matrilineal descent-based social statuses is not the only consequent of
feasting. In sum, what I do in this book is show that the precipitators of feasting
and the outcome of feasting are not the same—that is, that the aspects of society
and culture that produce a set of behaviors are not the same aspects of society
and culture that are produced by those behaviors

This study is a description of the ways in which mortuary feasting is an outcome—a function—of a complex of understandings, values, and social relations.
Feasting also entails its own function: a constellation of understandings, values,
and social relations that utilize the matrifilial link in a particular way: matriliny.
To speak of "function" in this way is not to suggest that mortuary ritual is best
seen as a response to death. In this regard, I echo Metcalf and Huntington's essay on mortuary ritual, *Celebrations of Death*, in which the authors eschew a
"rigid version of functionalism" (1991:6) that takes mortuary ritual as the sociological remedy for death. My analysis of Sursurunga mortuary ritual is function-
alist in that I address the ways in which individuals accomplish certain objectives
through participation in mortuary feasting, along with the ways in which mortuary feasting makes salient and activates matriliny. This is not a teleological argument, in which actors perform mortuary feasting so that social solidarity in the
form of active or conspicuous matriliny is bolstered. In other words, it does not
develop the Radcliffe-Brownian notion that "all roads lead to preserving the social system" (Metcalf and Huntington 1991:47).[12] The analysis here does not
suggest that mortuary ritual exists to preserve a social system. Rather, the analysis here attends to the ways in which individuals are impelled to participate in a

---

12. Avruch, following Spiro, shows how Radcliffe-Brown's work confused function
with cause, resulting in an explanation of social solidarity rather than what he was trying
to explain: religion (Avruch 1990:37).

particular institution. Participation in mortuary feasting is looked at from the perspective of methodological individualism, and the resulting salience of ma-trilineally based social statuses is expressed as an outcome of mortuary feasting. Such an approach, then, attends to functions without being an exercise in func-tionalist reductionism.

Chapter 2

Sursurunga Historical and Ethnographic Milieux: Contact, Christianity, Cash, and Context

The nature of ethnographic description entails a careful assessment of the degree to which generalizations can be made. To provide a basis for making such an assessment, I offer a summary of the history and ethnology of the region. I do so because a similar history and ethnicity make me confident that what I have to say about life at Tekedan is also generally true for other Sursurunga-speaking villages. Also, for the same reasons, what is true about the Sursurunga area is largely true for other places in southern New Ireland. Finally, what is true about southern New Ireland is also mostly true for a wide swath of the Bismarck Archipelago. Each of these demarcations represents a decreasing level of reliability. In other words, one might imagine a series of concentric circles around Tekedan village, with what is said about Tekedan being more likely the case in other locales within the inner rings than within the outer rings. So, although this is largely a description of life in one village, the description is written—and should be read—with an eye to the world beyond Tekedan, although it is Tekedan and its historical and cultural context with the world beyond that is the focus of this chapter.

CONTACT

The first known episode of European-Sursurunga contact was in 1616, when a skirmish occurred between the crew of a Dutch vessel and Sursurunga speakers, probably near what is now Kápsál.[1] Today, no Sursurunga speaker that I have talked to recalls the incident, and the Europeans involved seem to have treated the episode as just one of many violent confrontations with indigenous peoples they encountered. By 1850, whaling vessels were calling somewhat

---

1. See Bolyanatz 1998b for a description and analysis of this episode.

regularly at the southern tip of New Ireland, which was also home to the site of the swindler Marquis De Ray's ill-conceived and disastrous attempt at a utopia (see Albert 1987). The Sursurunga have no oral accounts of contacts with these vessels or their crews.

Germany had annexed Neu Mecklenberg, as New Ireland was then known, and the rest of the Bismarck Archipelago in 1884, allowing the Neu Guinea Kompagnie to operate in North East New Guinea and the offshore islands (see Map 2.1). In 1899, the burden of administration of the region was shifted from the company to the German government. The first ethnographic work in southern New Ireland was performed under German colonial auspices. The work of Friederici at Nokon (1912), and others, such as Schlaginhaufen (1915–16, 1920–21), Schnee (1904), and Stephan and Graebner (1907) constitute the early ethnographic record of southern New Ireland.[2] Neu Mecklenberg was administered from Kawieng (Kavieng) at the northern end of the island. The distance from Kavieng to the southern part of the island (it is about 250 miles to New Ireland's southern tip) resulted in the south being not fully under German control and perhaps accounts for the relatively hostile reception received by a German patrol in the Sursurunga area in 1913. This German report suggests something of the tenor of German colonial philosophy:

The first steps towards the extension of the native organisation to the mountains in the southern part of the District were taken in the year covered by this Report, by traversing the island on two occasions. Contact was successfully established everywhere with the natives, who also served as carriers without any show of reluctance. The natives were told to expect a second visit, and that chiefs and *tultul* [administration-appointed local leaders] would be appointed. In answer to their inquiry they were also told that there were no plans to levy taxes on them for the present. [This was probably disingenuous since earlier in the same document, it was reported that taxes had been collected from more "organized" areas.] Further progress in the development of these areas was recently cut short by the attack by the mountain people on *Oberförster* Deininger's expedition. *Oberförster* Deininger, accompanied by *Fortassessor* Kempf, set out to cross the island and 11 of the [Namatanai] Station troopers had been assigned to him for his protection. On the second day of their march inland from the east coast, near Hilalon [a Sursurunga village], the expedition was unexpectedly attacked in the village of Poronzuan.[3] *Oberförster* Deininger was wounded, 5 troopers fell, and 4 carriers from the coastal village of Hilalon were also killed by the rebels. The bodies of those killed were consumed by the rebels.

The first punitive action was taken by the Station troop on the day after the attack, when three of the 9 rifles which had been captured were retaken as well as a large part of the stolen equipment of the Deininger expedition. Eight of the natives fell but the Station troop suffered no casualties. The expeditionary troop then took further punitive action against the rebels. The only results of their intervention reported to the Station have been

---

2. Others wrote useful depictions of life on southern New Ireland, including G. Brown (1910), and Parkinson (1887), but it was the Germans who conducted the first systematic field research projects there.

3. Poronzuan no longer exists, but its site can be visited by going inland several kilometers from the coastal village of Poronbus, about 12 kilometers north of Tekedan.

the shooting of many more natives. On hearing of the attack on the Deininger expedition, the mountain people also attacked the Chinese plantation Kamdaru on the west coast, robbing and looting the houses of the Chinese owner. No lives were lost. The expeditionary troop took punitive action for this attack.

The reason advanced for the attack is that the mountain people were against the introduction of the native organisation [presumably the *tultul* office and, most probably, taxation] and the attendant controls. The more powerful chiefs were afraid that the spread of the native organisation would put an end to the standing feuds and the associated cannibal practices and that their own influence would be weakened. As they had had scarcely any previous contact with Europeans, they believed that by wiping out an expedition they could dissuade the Europeans from visiting their mountain region. An attack had already been planned at the time of the crossing of the island by the District Officer. According to information obtained by the Station (no reports have been received on information obtained by the expeditionary troop) those taking part in the attack were the inhabitants of the inland area bounded in the north by a line drawn from Suralil to Cape Reis and in the south by a line from the mouth of the Mandaru to the mouth of the Danfu River [this would include present-day Tekedan and the bush territory of the ancestors of current Tekedan residents]. (Sack and Clark 1980:56–57)

There can be heard in Tekedan today stories of men who were killed by the Germans. Whether any of those accounts are accurate and whether those are the deaths mentioned in the "punitive" expeditions cannot be known. What can be derived from the report, as well as from local lore, is that the relationship with the German administration was a strained and violent one, even up until the last year of German control.

With the end of World War I in Europe, Germany lost control of its Pacific holdings, including New Ireland. Under a League of Nations mandate, Australia was accorded control of the Territory of New Guinea, which consisted of the northeastern quadrant of the island of New Guinea and offshore islands such as New Britain and New Ireland. Australia already had a colonial administration established in Papua to the south, so the arrangement seemed felicitous. German planters were allowed to stay and maintain their businesses, and the Australian administration was keen to see development throughout their Pacific holdings. Indeed, it was thought by many Australians that certainly Papua, and perhaps even New Guinea, might be annexed and become part of the state of Queensland. Many of the records of Australia's role in administering New Ireland and the rest of the New Guinea Territory (1920–1942) were kept at the territorial capital, Rabaul, on New Britain.

Rabaul was captured by Japanese forces in 1942, and remained in Japanese hands until near the end of the war. During that time, Allied bombing leveled much of the town, leaving little in the way of Japanese resistance or territorial records. The Japanese intrusion (1942–1945) had less impact on Tekedan than on other Sursurunga communities. A 30-minute walk away at Nokon village, for example, Japanese troops planted crops in Sursurunga cemeteries (Jackson 1995: 36–37). And just beyond Nokon at Huris, the Japanese constructed an airfield

Map 2.1

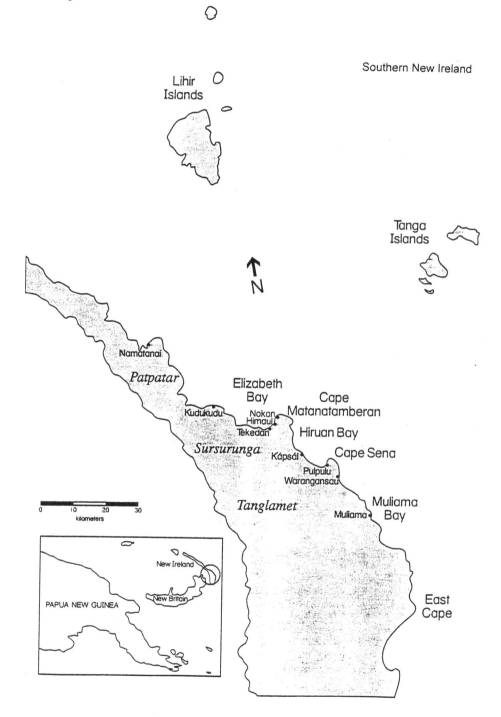

that housed a fighter squadron. Older individuals tell of forced labor, beatings, torture, and executions at the hands of the Japanese. It was a bad time, and many people tried to resume a semblance of normal life in the bush and leave the coast to the Japanese. After the war, people returned, over a period of a few years, to the beach. I will continue the narrative of resettlement in Chapter 3 when discussing land use and tenure. Now, I turn to the history of the United Church.

CHRISTIANITY

Even before the Germans, a permanent, but somewhat scattered, European contact with east coast Sursurunga speakers was first established in 1876 when the Reverend George Brown of the Wesleyan Methodist Mission arrived late one afternoon just outside of what is now known as the village of Kudukudu. The following morning, according to Brown and the descendants of those who greeted him, he entered Kudukudu and began a process of change that has arguably affected the Sursurunga more profoundly than any other: the Christian proselytization of southern New Ireland.

Originally from New Zealand, Brown and his spouse, Lydia, landed on neighboring New Britain in 1875 and rapidly went about their evangelistic work. Stations were established on the main island as well as at Port Hunter in the Duke of York group. Within a year, Brown had established a Fijian teacher on New Ireland at the west coast village of Kalil, which became the base of Methodist operations in New Ireland in those first days.

On 31 May 1876, Brown traversed New Ireland, departing from Kalil and arriving a bit north of present-day Kudukudu on the east coast. From Brown's autobiography:

Early on the following morning [1 June] we had a service with the people in the [Kudukudu] village square; we sang a hymn in Duke of York language; Elimotama [the Fijian teacher stationed on New Ireland's west coast] prayed in the Kalil dialect, which the people seemed to understand. . . . Sagina, the principal village chief there, was waiting to conduct us to his village, [and] we were soon on the way again. We walked along the coast to the south-east for about five miles, passing several small villages on our way.

The name of the chief, Sagina, means the Smeller or Smelling of ["stench" or "stink" may be a better gloss]; and he was so called because they said the smell of cooked meat, either of human bodies or of pig, was seldom absent from his village. (Brown 1908:163)

On 1 June 1991, a "Jubilee Celebration" was held at Kudukudu to commemorate Brown's arrival on the east coast as well as to dedicate the new Rev. George Brown Memorial United Church building at Kudukudu.[4] At this event, a banner proclaimed in Neo-Melanesian, "*Lait i Kamap Long Sangin 1.6.1876*" ("The Light Comes to Sangin 1 June 1876"). According to local informants,

---

4. See Errington and Gewertz (1994, 1995:77–106) for descriptions of an analogous event on the Duke of York Islands.

Brown gave Kudukudu its name, but the meaning and reason have been lost. The story of Sangin, or Sagina, however, lives on in that he was the carver of a post that overlooks the concrete slab that is the location of that early morning service in 1876.[5] A renowned killer and eater of men, modern-day stories of Sangin's conversion to Christianity (a conversion that is not recorded in Brown's autobiography) rival that of Saul on the road to Damascus in their emphasis on a dramatic and absolute change of heart. In any event, by all accounts, it was Sangin's conversion that led to the establishment of a Methodist station at Kudukudu. Kudukudu remained the administrative center for the mission until reorganization in 1911, when the head station was moved to Halis, a few miles south of the then recently established (1904) German administrative outpost of Namatanai.

In some areas, Wesleyan Methodism was, by all reports, eagerly accepted. In others, there was resistance; at Tekedan, for example, there was no church for many years after World War I,[6] largely because of leaders who were reluctant to welcome the interlopers. But Methodism eventually won out, and by 1940, the church was securely established in the area.

World War II was an especially difficult time for the Church, as many local pastors were incarcerated by the Japanese at Namatanai. One such man was the late Kaminiel Ladi, an evangelist and missionary for the church who spent his retirement at Nokon village. He reported that church leaders were viewed as

---

5. There is some confusion here. Contemporary Kudukudu is strung out along the coast for perhaps a half mile, so it is understandable that Brown would have walked some distance to Sangin/Sangina's house after the service that he mentions. But Brown notes that he walked about "five miles," which would have put him in present-day Balai. Older informants do tell of leaders whose authority was widespread, and Sangin is one of those mentioned. It is therefore possible that Sangin resided in or near today's Balai and was still the "chief" of Kudukudu. Yet Brown notes later in his autobiography that "Kudukudu, the town we visited, *where Sangina lived* . . . is now a flourishing station" (Brown 1908:171; emphasis added). In fact, Brown's memory—and, by extension, his record—is not without error. In his discussion of this same excursion, he loses a day by having two first of Junes (1908:163, 168). As a consequence, it is difficult to know with certainty about some of these events. The diary of Brown's colleague, the Reverend Benjamin Danks, does not clarify the matter. Like Brown, Danks fails to keep his days straight, and even locates Kudukudu on New Ireland's *west* coast (Danks 1933:249). Both Danks and Brown do agree, however, that it is a few miles—about an hour's walk—from the point at which they complete their crossing of New Ireland to Sangin's residence.

6. Tekedan village itself was not established until after the war. An older informant states that the river running through Tekedan made it a place claimed by more than one group, with the result that it would have been a very dangerous place to live. The best prewar German map of the area (Schnee 1904:nno) does not indicate the presence of a village anywhere near present-day Tekedan. The same informant suggests that "Lamarat," the former name of the parcel known as Kankapgam today, might appear on a German map, but I have not seen it. The earliest reference to Tekedan is a patrol report from 1934 (Territory of New Guinea 1933–34:12).

dangerous on two counts: (1) they had the power to influence public opinion, and (2) they were most likely to have strong allegiances to Christendom and the Allies. Ladi reports that many church leaders were killed at Namatanai, and that he himself was tortured by being beaten with cane on his bare buttocks.

After the war, the Methodists accelerated the indigenization of church leadership. Local pastors, trained at nearby (eastern New Britain) George Brown Theological College, were recruited from all over the Islands Region to minister. In general, these men were then and are now treated with deference and respect.

In 1968, the Methodists joined with the Papua Ekalesia (churches begun by the London Missionary Society) to form the United Church in Papua New Guinea and the Solomon Islands. Among most New Irelanders, George Brown is still revered as the founder of the United Church, and there is very little awareness of the affiliation with the Papua Ekalesia. The change from Methodist to United is generally viewed as an inconsequential, cosmetic change only.

Contemporary Sursurunga theology is richly informed by the presence of the Methodist/United Church, and represents a synthesis of traditional and Christian understandings. This synthesis is the reality of contemporary Sursurunga life in many aspects. An example of this blend of what might be seen as "old" and "new," but which is seen as neither by local people, is the following exegesis offered by a local well-respected United Church pastor. In his view, the origin of matrimoiety exogamy can be found in the sixth chapter of Genesis (verses 1–2, 4):

When men began to increase in number on the earth and daughters were born to them, the sons of God saw that the daughters of men were beautiful, and they married any of them they chose. . . . The Nephilim were on the earth in those days—and also afterward—when the sons of God went to the daughters of men and had children by them. They were the heroes of old, men of renown.

The explanation for matrimoiety exogamy rests on two points. The first, from verse 2, is that men "married any[one] they chose." The second, from verse 4, is the existence of another type of human being on earth—those descended from the Nephilim. From the context of the passage, it is clear that marrying just anyone that one chooses is brazen, sinful rebelliousness, and not pleasing to God, the implication being that there should be some sort of governing principle limiting who marries whom. Verse 4 lends itself to being the basis of that sort of principle since there are two kinds of people in the world, that is, those descended from the Nephilim and those not so descended—the origin of today's moieties.[7] The fact that modern Sursurunga view their marital choices as moral issues is not particularly surprising. What is, however, worthy of note is the way in which a Judeo-Christian idiom is used to legitimize a traditional aspect of the social order. In this example, it can be seen that the distinction

---

7. In this context, I asked why exogamy should be preferred over endogamy since both are restraining principles, or why the children of Nephilim male-human female unions should result in *matri*moieties. No one could say.

sometimes made between traditional and modern, old and new, aboriginal and alien, can be meaningless to local people, and occur only in the minds of outside observers (cf. Barker 1990, 1992; Carrier 1992; Errington and Gewertz 1995).

CASH

Elsewhere (Bolyanatz 1998a), I discuss the history of the copra-dominated cash crop industry in the Sursurunga area. One local version of that history is given below.

There was an old man who lived in a small village on the coast. One day he thought of his *koko* [sister's child, or younger lineage member; also mother's brother] who lived not too far away, about as far from Himaul to Tekedan [a 15- to 20-minute walk]. He asked his *koko* to come live with him, and help him with firewood and food. His *koko* came. The old man eventually fell sick and asked his *koko* to take care of his funerary needs. As he lay dying, the old man told his *koko* where to bury him and told him to sit and watch for something where they buried his head. The old man then died, and his *koko* did exactly as the old man had asked. So he died, and was buried.

After a while, a coconut shoot appeared in the cemetery. After the shoot developed the beginnings of leaves, the *koko* made a fence around it and kept close watch over the plant. When the tree was as tall as a man, it put out its first flower. The *koko* wondered whether or not it was food. The tree grew, and the pod grew and broke open. Then a second flower appeared. Then a third and a fourth. Then the second one broke open and the *koko* inferred that the third and fourth would do the same. And they did. And the first one was an immature coconut now. It wasn't red, but blue, with a green skin. And then the first one developed into a drinking coconut, as did the others. Then all four coconuts became dry. And still the old man's *koko* left them alone.

Finally, the first strand broke and the dry coconuts dropped from the tree. The *koko* then lined up all the coconuts along the trunk of the tree. Then the other strands fell, and he arranged them all by the base of the tree. The *koko* began to wonder if these things were food. So he tried one. He wondered how to open it, but figured out a way and got a sharpened stick and shelled it. Then he wondered what to do next, wondering if there was food inside. He got a stone knife, broke the coconut, and drank, and liked the milk inside. Then he used his thumbnail and scraped the meat from around the inside, which came out easily enough. He ate that and liked it even more than the liquid. Then he shelled another, but wasn't able to use his thumbnail; the meat was too strong. So he scraped it [with a shell], and he especially enjoyed that.

He then planted a dry coconut along with its shoot. He cut away the bush and planted many more coconuts with a digging stick. He shelled another one and saw a man's eyes and mouth in the coconut. He said, "Oh, my *koko*'s eyes and mouth!"

So the young man cared for his little plantation. And his trees bore fruit. Other men came and saw his *stesin* [Neo-Melanesian for "station," implying buildings to service the needs of the plantation]. They asked what the coconuts were. The man said he didn't know what they were called, but he did know that they were good. These other men then wanted to buy some coconuts, but the man told them to wait. The young man then made a building. By this time, steel tools had arrived. He made copra, filled the building with two bags, and smoked the copra in the building. When the copra was dried, he cut a coconut leaf and made a big basket, filling it with copra. Then he wondered what he should do with all of this stuff.

That night he had a dream, and the spirit of his old *koko* told him to take care of the copra, because he could get money for it. A white man would come, buy some land, and make a trade store. It came to pass, and the copra was sold to the white man for cash.

The young man could not, of course, have known what money was for. He tried to eat a 10-toea piece. It was no good, so he threw it away. He asked the white man what the money was good for and the white man explained it to him. So he bought some rice and cooked it. Then he bought tinned meat, put it in the rice, and stirred it in. Then the white man told him to try it. He found it to be delicious. He ate it all up.

The white man told him that he had to keep working copra so that he could keep buying food. He bought a large bag of rice, and the white man explained to him that he shouldn't try to eat it all at once, but to use it little by little. So the young man cleared more land, and planted more coconuts, and sold more copra. He made a lot of money in this way. Others saw this and asked for that special tree. The young man told them to buy the trees. They asked with what, since they had no money because they had no coconuts. They finally persuaded the young man to give them the trees with the understanding that he would be paid in cash when these fellows had sold their copra crop. And so they did. Now these people were able to buy food. And now there are coconuts all over the place.

Since the 1920s, people on New Ireland have sold copra for cash, although the trade of green (i.e., undried) copra at very low prices to Chinese traders had been conducted since before World War I. After the war, Patrol Officer J. K. McCarthy reported that a dozen hemispheres of unprocessed coconut meat would be traded for 12 sheets of old newspaper and a stick of tobacco—a total of less than sixpence. The merchants would then dry it and sell it at several times the amount they paid for it. McCarthy describes the plight of the typical New Irelander between the wars. Government regulations requiring a minimum of two miles between trade stores, along with merchant collusion, formed a "small but vicious monopoly of business" (McCarthy 1964:80). Patrol Officer McCarthy distributed the blame in his rather jingoistic analysis of the situation:

While the wily Chinese, who owned most of the trade stores or managed them on some trader's behalf, sat and waited as their exorbitant profits came in the door, the Administration, whose laws had created these efficient petty monopolies, turned a blind eye.

There were several mission stations along the [east] coast [of New Ireland], both Methodist and Catholic, and I was unable to understand why these men, willing to sacrifice everything in life for their calling—except, perhaps, the prize of personal popularity—had not protested against such petty tyranny. (McCarthy 1964:80)

McCarthy goes on to recount a 1932 conversation with a local man that took place in the region of the Patpatar-Sursurunga border:

"Why don't you make your own copra and get a better price for your crop?" I asked. "It is easy to cure the nuts in the sun, or by smoking them by hot air in a kiln."

My question was received with apparent surprise. "Isn't the making of copra by natives forbidden by law?" they asked.

"No, there is no law that says that!" (McCarthy 1964:80–81)

Shortly thereafter, according to McCarthy, copra drying houses appeared up and down the east coast of New Ireland, intensifying what he called the "copra war" (McCarthy 1964:82).

The copra war continued on New Ireland until the Japanese invasion in 1942. During the Japanese Occupation, many coastal New Irelanders fled to the bush. After 1945, the copra war emerged from its latency and resumed with full force. The Sursurunga had a choice: they could work copra at a plantation for wages, or they could cut and process their own copra. The first option was easier and more straightforward, but paid less. The second option required dealing with traders who were committed to squelching any form of local economic initiative, especially where copra was concerned. Patrol officers (known in Neo-Melanesian as *kiap*) who visited the Sursurunga area within the first few years after the departure of the Japanese reported that most people were simply trying to return to normal, as was the case elsewhere in the region (cf. Epstein 1968:32ff.). Having fled the coast for the inland areas, many people had to invest their time and energy in reestablishing gardens and residences along the beach. There was little time for the relative luxury of cutting copra for cash.

In 1949, Patrol Officer F. P. Kaad reported that there were many coconuts lying about, but that most people were reluctant to work for the "meagre payments" offered by the Chinese,[8] namely, 8s. to 10s. [$1.00–$1.25][9] per bag of unprocessed copra or £1 [$2.00] for a bag of dried copra (Territory of Papua New Guinea[10] 1949–50:6–7). This does not mean that there was no commercial activity on the part of Sursurunga speakers. Just a year later, G. P. Taylor reported that "[cash] produces an era of fast moving life. Natives have plenty of money with which to buy food and clothing, . . . amassing quite a collection of possessions and at the same time enjoying themselves immensely" (TPNG 1950–51:x).

Although some of this cash was the result of War Damage Claim payments, the prewar situation with regard to copra sales seems to have been re-established by the early 1950s, although not all parties involved benefited equally: the 1952 local price (i.e., the price paid by local Chinese merchants) for copra, 20s. [$2.50] per bag, represented a 0 percent increase over the 1949 price, whereas the London market price of copra rose 21 percent during that same period (Jackman 1988:234).

By 1954, the colonial administration sought a means of working around the Chinese traders in an attempt to stimulate local economies. To this end, the Sursurunga Native Co-Operative Society (SNCS) was initiated by the Administration when patrol officers collected £2,900 [$5,800] from all but one Sursurunga

---

8. Throughout the historical narrative, I use the term "Chinese" as a synonym for "merchant" or "trader" because the ethnic term renders accurately the emic Sursurunga understandings about the socio-economic world: "Chinese" and "merchant" or "trader" are synonymous; the concept "Chinese trader" would be redundant in Sursurunga.

9. For ease of reading, U.S. dollar equivalents are placed in square brackets.

10. Hereafter abbreviated TPNG.

village[11] for the purpose of purchasing a tractor-trailer combination so that copra might be collected and shipped directly to Rabaul without dealing with Chinese middlemen. The directorate of the SNCS consisted of 10 local leaders under the chairmanship of Kiapsalam of Samo village. The SNCS was a popular endeavor (as evidenced by the ready investment of an average investment of £3 4s. [$6.50] per Sursurunga adult [TPNG 1953–54]), and the level of initial support was high.

The SNCS was in full operation by the middle of 1955. Sursurunga coconut owners were cutting and drying their own copra, and then selling it to the SNCS for a higher price than they could get from Chinese merchants. Patrol Officer Collins noted in late 1955 a "vast improvement" in the "attitude" of the Sursurunga—a change he attributes to the presence of the SNCS (TPNG 1955–56:4). By 1958, however, the SNCS showed signs of faltering, and enthusiasm for the endeavor waned. This was due in part to the fact that Chinese merchants now paid 25 percent more than they had just a few years earlier for undried copra, with the result that the cooperative was undercut. By 1959, the price was 15s. In addition, local private shipping interests, acceding to Chinese pressure, boycotted SNCS business with the result that in 1956, a load of SNCS copra rotted on the wharf at Namatanai. In 1957, the tractor-trailer combination was finally acquired, but the group's clerk used the vehicle and Society funds improperly by paying higher prices to his friends for their copra. The man was jailed in 1958. Also in 1958, the SNCS dropped what it paid for copra from 3–4 pence per pound to 2½ pence (i.e., from about £2 [$4.00] per bag of dried copra to about £1 12s. [$2.50] per bag). Not long thereafter, the tractor ceased functioning, and the Chinese received more and more business.

Patrol Officer Haviland's report for August 1958 states that as a result of these setbacks, SNCS "activities have almost ceased" (TPNG 1958–59a:6). He does not, however, lay all of the responsibility for the demise of the cooperative on the Chinese. Haviland's view was that the local people's "aversion to toil," and, more importantly, the "removal of the Society's clerk after investigations into his activities," coupled with a "failure to replace him" were also to blame. The possibility that some of the money invested in the SNCS lined the pockets of at least one of its officers had a detrimental effect on the Society. By 1959, the assets for the SNCS were a meager £80 19s. [$162]. Still, in spite of everything, the venture had had some success; by 1959, a bag of dried copra would have fetched 15s. [$1.88]. This represents an increase over the 8s.–10s. [$1.00–$1.25] of 1949 even if it is substantially less than the prices offered during the cooperative's robust years of 1955–1958. This prompted Haviland to write in 1959 what amounted to an epitaph for the SNCS: "A small [cooperative] society like Sursurunga can never hope to run successfully unless under constant

---

11. The villages that contributed were Kudukudu, Balai, Hilalon, Poronbus, Himau, Tekedan, Himaul, Nokon, Huris, Likas, Hipagat, Samo, Kápsál, Kembeng, Kabirara, Rukaliklik, and Porbunbun. Inhabitants of Pulpulu village did not participate because there was no bridge over the Dalum River at the time, making it impossible for a tractor to be able to have regular access to them and their copra.

European guidance" (TPNG 1958–59b:1). Haviland's summary statement: "During the period of co-operative activity, the traders threw their energy into the competition with the co-operative. The village people freely admit that they won the race, and appear satisfied at the moment to leave it like that" (1958–59b:16).

The satisfaction with the status quo lasted until 1966, when, again at the instigation of the administration, the Sursurunga Marketing Society (SMS) was formed. Like the SNCS, initial successes were encouraging: "Practically all native copra on the Namatanai East Coast is marketed through the Namatanai and Sursurunga Marketing Societies" (TPNG 1966–67:1), and "The people as a whole are solidly supporting [the SMS]" (TPNG 1966–67:2).

During the first four months in which the SMS was in operation, a monthly average of 14 tons of copra was handled. Four months after that, that figure had expanded to more than 21 tons per month, allowing the SMS to offer, beginning in July 1967, $.04 [2½ cents] per pound for dried copra, up from the $.035 it had been offering. This made the SMS very competitive with the prices offered by the Chinese traders.

A year later, Patrol Officer Liosi reported that the SMS was doing well, but that it was facing stiff competition from the Chinese (TPNG 1968–69a:nno), and the amount of copra handled had leveled off at a range of 15–60 tons per month (TPNG 1968–69b:3). The expected yield for Sursurunga copra in 1969 was 570 tons, or 47.5 tons per month. But there were complications. The vessel M. V. *Ninsa II*, often used to transport SMS copra to Rabaul, had not called for more than two months, and 260 bags of copra were sitting at Hilalon at the time of a March 1969 report, with no likelihood of transport in sight. Speculation that Chinese pressure was being applied was widespread, and the experience of the SMS began to parallel that of the SNCS just a dozen years earlier. Chinese traders began to squeeze the SMS by paying higher prices for copra, and co-op production fell to 12.4 tons per month, half of what the SMS needs to run "economically and efficiently" (TPNG 1970–71b:5).

Patrol Officer Vele wrote in 1970 that

> The Sursurunga Marketing Society is struggling for survival in the face of competition from Chinese merchants. It has been said that should this Society fail, the people will blame the Administration. Of course this theory should be rejected. Should the Society fail the fault will lie only with the people who fail to support it and prefer to go to the Chinese. The time of paternalization has passed. The people have to learn to think and act on their own responsibility and to accept the responsibility thereof. (TPNG 1970–71a:1)

On 15 February 1971 a meeting was held to determine the future of the SMS. At this meeting, the following reasons for low SMS productivity were articulated:

1. Chinese merchants will buy wetter copra, which entails less drying time and effort.
2. SMS tractor pickups are sporadic and cannot be counted on.

3. There are only two shipping points within Sursurunga territory: Samo and Hilalon, and the M.V *Tampi* [sic] *Lass*, owned by the Tong Bros., a major trading firm, was the only vessel to ply regularly the east coast of New Ireland.

4. Too few locally owned copra dryers; Chinese merchants would allow the free use of their dryers on the condition that they purchase the copra.

5. Chinese merchants pay $.045 [2¾ cents] per pound of dried copra; the SMS pays just $.04. Other reasons given for selling to the Chinese include a better short-term return for labor; the Chinese will send their tractors more regularly[12] and will sometimes use them to collect coconuts; and perks: credit at trade stores, assistance in acquiring merchandise from Rabaul, and cheap or free transport. The Chinese also used some of the tactics that had earlier been successful against the SNCS. They refused, for example, to sell burlap copra bags to locals who did not sell their copra; they refused to carry SMS copra on their ships, they refused at times to accept cash, demanding copra for trade store goods, and they refused to allow the SMS tractor to purchase gasoline at their businesses.

By the beginning of 1972, both the Chinese and SMS were offering about $.0275 [1⅓ cents] per pound for dried copra,[13] although at times the Chinese would offer "a little more" (TPNG 1971–72b:3). By 1972, the Chinese were no longer offering more than the SMS price, since price was not the only, nor was it an important, reason for their success against the co-ops; the reasons outlined above were more than enough reason for most people to prefer to trade with the Chinese. The administration would have liked to have seen the marketing group prosper, since it was widely believed that without competition, the Chinese would lower what they paid for copra, which would stifle economic development. Patrol Officer O'Brien believed that the SMS was, in 1972, saddled with "serious difficulties," and that the erosion of the SMS would continue, with the ultimate loss of the initial invested shares. He reports that he tried to point out that the people themselves could make or break the SMS, but he found himself "confronted by a well of apathy" (TPNG 1971–72a:4). He adds that

[t]he future of the Society looks black indeed. . . . They just cannot see that when their Society collapses the price the Chinese offer will be ludicrous, and the only reason for the good price now is competition.

Perhaps the main reason why native trade stores cease to flourish is the fact that all goods are shipped in on the *Pampie* [sic] *Lass* and high freight charges are placed on indigenous cargo. (TPNG 1971a:3, 4)

There are no signs of the SMS today; like the SNCS, it is just a name from the past. But this history informs contemporary attitudes toward Chinese shopkeepers who are in the area: they are seen as an economic necessity, and there is little affection for them. Employees boast of pilfering from them, and loyalty—

---

12. A 1972 Patrol Report notes that Chinese merchants sent their tractors from Namatanai as far south as Balai twice a day to pick up copra (TPNG 1971–72b:2). The SMS, on the other hand, collected copra about once per fortnight, and many people found it difficult to wait *longer* for a *lower* price (TPNG 1971–72b:5).

13. At this time, copra was selling at Rabaul for $95 per ton, or $.0475 per pound.

beyond that which is produced by a concern with the next fortnightly payment of wages—is almost nonexistent.

Today, copra is harvested and sold as the need arises: school fees, taxes, clothing, steel tools, kerosene, batteries, rice, tea, and sugar are some of the items most commonly purchased with copra (and cacao) profits. It is difficult for most people to arrange transport for their copra all the way to Kavieng, or even Namatanai. A load of copra is rightly seen as very hard on a three-quarter ton pickup on unpaved roads, and most vehicle owners are unwilling to carry copra—even their own—the 50 miles to Namatanai.

In the late 1950s, cacao and coffee were introduced as alternatives to copra as commercial crops. Almost immediately, however, cacao fell into disfavor by the colonial administration, and coffee became the administration's cash crop of choice. Coffee was advocated by the colonial administration, which gave the following reasons (taken from TPNG 1958–59b:9):

the soil was not well-suited to cacao
licenses were needed to grow cacao
the costs of cacao fermentation were prohibitive
there was no European available to supervise the care required by cacao trees

On the other hand,

coffee was suited to the soil in the area
coffee can be produced profitably using the labor of family members
coffee allows more trees per hectare
coffee grows to bearing age more quickly (3-4 years, as opposed to 5 years for cacao)
coffee requires no licenses, and can be harvested by old women and children

By 1967, however, the Department of Agriculture was encouraging cacao, and more than 15,000 trees had been planted in the Sursurunga area (TPNG 1966–67:3). A 1969 report indicates that no cacao trees were yet bearing. In the same report, it was noted that 1.5 tons of coffee beans had been produced in 1964, but that the trees had been neglected since then (TPNG 1968–69b:8). By early 1972, a "small amount of cocoa and an insignificant amount of coffee" was being produced (TPNG 1971–72a:3). In 1989–1992, and again in 1998, I saw no coffee trees, and cacao trees abounded as an alternative source of cash.

In comparing copra and cacao, the return on the sale of wet (i.e., not processed in any way—merely taken from the pods with the rind discarded) cacao beans is nearly three times by weight that for copra. The harvesting of cacao requires less brute strength than copra, and smaller children assist in the harvesting of cacao. At the higher price, cacao is seen as more valuable, but in terms of work hours, the payoff is approximately equal. Cacao is seen as more valuable largely because there are fewer cacao than coconut trees, and because there is understood to be the possibility that cacao prices, unlike copra prices,

Table 2.1
Main Type of Economic Activity (Adult Respondents)

	Males	*Females*	*Total*
Worked at Wage Job	4	1	5
Farm/Fish for Food and Money	20	18	38
Farm/Fish Subsistence Only	4	4	8
Student	3	1	4
Desk/House Work	1	0	1
Total	32	24	56

Table 2.2
Items Produced for Food and Money

No. of Households	*Product*	*Use*
16	coconut	cash & own use
15	betel nut	cash & own use
15	fruit	cash & own use
15	bananas	cash & own use
14	vegetables & tubers	cash & own use
14	fishing	own use only
9	cacao	cash & own use
1	betel nut	own use only
1	fruit	own use only
1	bananas	own use only
1	vegetables & tubers	own use only
1	fishing	cash & own use

could return to past high levels.[14] Tables 2.1 and 2.2 summarize current economic practices in Tekedan village. There were 16 (out of 19) households in which at least one adult member indicated that he or she "fished/farmed for food and money."

The government census from which Tables 2.1 and 2.2 are derived did not indicate the amount of income generated by cash crops. My own census conducted 18 months after the government's census showed an average annual household income of K143 from copra, and K57 from cacao. Informants indicated that these were typical figures for the past several years.

---

14. There are two other sources of cash for people in and around Tekedan. The first is outside employment, and the second is royalties paid for timber rights by logging companies.

CONTEXT

Politically, Tekedan is situated within the Sursurunga Census District, located along southern New Ireland's east coast, number 14 of New Ireland Province's 19 census districts. The language known as "Sursurunga" is not quite coterminous with the Census District.[15] The Sursurunga Census District comprises the coastal (or near-coastal) villages of Hibaling (sometimes referred to as Namuh)[16] in the north to Pulpulu in the south, inclusively (see Map 2.2). Sursurunga is also spoken in Kudukudu, in the Rativis Census District to the north, and in five villages on the southern west coast of New Ireland (Hutchisson 1984).

The overlap between the Sursurunga Census District and the villages in which Sursurunga is spoken—the 17 villages between Balai and Pulpulu, inclusive (but not including Namuh/Hibaling, since most people in this village speak Patpatar[17]), and their environs—is what I refer to as the Sursurunga area.

The Sursurunga area can be further parsed along the lines of two other distinctions. The two distinctions—one clan- and the other church-based—are especially relevant to the people of Tekedan and other villages in the Sursurunga area in ways that the Census District demarcation is not.

The first, clan-based distinction, attends to land ownership. As in so many other parts of Papua New Guinea, corporate descent groups have traditionally been land-holding units in the Sursurunga area. Because this is so, a glance at the pattern of traditional clan ownership of land parcels (see Table 2.3) in the area shows that some of the land within the Sursurunga area is owned by people whose only claims are at the extremes of the Sursurunga area—specifically, the Antalis and Pispis clans. (There are members of these clans who reside farther south of the Sursurunga area in the villages of Kombon and Sena.) This pattern of seriation of clan land ownership represents the sociological reality that some of the inhabitants of villages on the fringes of the Sursurunga area have important connections and loyalties outside of the area. In short, Porbunbun and Pulpulu are largely peripheral to most of the other people in the Sursurunga area.

A more important distinction for most people is that based on the administrative units, or Sections,[18] of the United Church. There are three United Church Sections represented along the coast of the Sursurunga area: the Hilalon Section Balai to Poronbus), the Nokon Section (Himau to Huris), and the Samo Section

---

15. The convention of using the name of the language to denote a group of people has an implicit corollary in that cognate languages are found among groups with cognate cultural and social forms. This is the working hypothesis that will recur throughout the comparative sections of the book.

16. Hibaling/Namuh is inhabited largely by speakers of Patpatar, the language spoken to the north of Sursurunga.

17. For a description of the Patpatar language and a summary of cultural and social features, see Condra 1992.

18. About 90 percent of the people in and around Tekedan profess allegiance to the United Church, and church affairs are important in the lives of most individuals.

Map 2.2
The Sursurunga Region

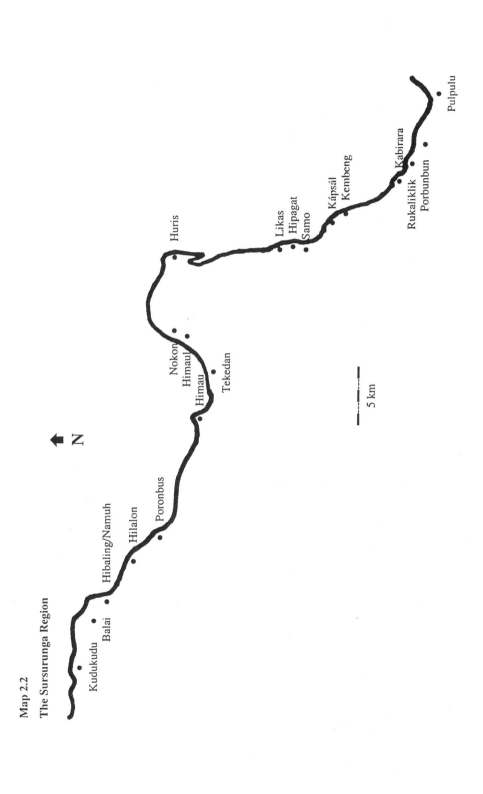

Table 2.3
Land Parcel Ownership by Clan

Clan	1	2	3	4	5	6	7	8	9	10	11	12	13	14	15	16	17	18	TOTAL
Antalis																		3	3
Pispis																	31	12	43
Koris					3			19	3		6	1	24	9		53	4		122
Piklám								10	8	36		3					4		61
Sahwon				1		2				2	3	44	21	22	44				139
Tatau			1						1										2
Piknat						1													1
Tokbol			7			20	12		15				2						56
Irir		1					1												2
Kárpápus		1	3			9		1											14
Rongol	6			21	56	2													85
Seruai			10	1															11
Kurleu			3																3
Káwás		5	1																6
Kurasabau		17																	17
Bulitlimat		7																	7
Anla	3	8																	11
Karbakok	17																		17
TOTAL	26	39	25	23	59	34	13	30	27	38	9	48	47	31	44	53	39	15	600

Key:

1: Balai	2: Namuh	3: Hilalon	4: Poronbus	5: Himau	6: Tekedan
7: Himaul	8: Nokon	9: Huris	10: Likas	11: Hipagat	12: Samo
13: Kápsál	14: Kembeng	15: Kabirara	16: Rukaliklik	17: Porbunbun	18: Pulpulu

(Likas to Kembeng). Local people believe that there are linguistic differences that are coterminous with the Section differences (with the exception that Sursurunga speakers at Likas are usually seen as dialectally more similar to those at Huris than to the inhabitants of Samo), but I do not find these differences to be significant.[19] The grouping that emerges as a sort of "central Sursurunga area" are the five villages of the United Church's Nokon Section (northwest to southeast): Himau, Tekedan, Himaul, Nokon, and Huris. Within the Section, Himau is seen as more closely affiliated with Poronbus (the number of Rongol clan land holdings at both Himau and Poronbus is consistent with this local perception), and Huris is a bit too far away from Himau, Tekedan, Himaul, and Nokon for everyday interaction between people from those places. The result is that Tekedan, Himaul, and Nokon form something of a sociological cluster. To reiterate the point made at the outset of the chapter, what is true for Tekedan is almost always also true for Himaul and Nokon, and a bit less so for the Nokon Section as a whole. Furthermore, a description of Tekedan will be even less germane for what I am calling the Sursurunga area, and within southern New Ireland in general. The same can be said, with appropriate reservations, for the Patpatar-Tolai language sub-group area, to which I now turn.

The Patpatar-Tolai Language Area

The Patpatar-Tolai language sub-group (found in the Gazelle Peninsula of eastern New Britain and southern New Ireland) is a useful starting point for describing some of the similarities (and, also, some differences) between the Sursurunga and their neighbors on New Britain, the Duke of York Islands, and elsewhere on New Ireland. Taxonomically, the Patpatar-Tolai subgroup is part of the Eastern Oceanic group of Austronesian languages. Oceanic grammatical structures are important for later arguments in the book.[20] On the basis of membership in the Patpatar-Tolai subgroup,[21] an ethnographic region with a high degree of commensurability can be circumscribed. The geographical boundaries

---

19. These linguistic differences may have existed in the past, but because there has been a substantial number of marriages across Sections in the past generation, my inclination is to suspect that nowadays the variation is largely a projection of Section differences.

20. This linguistic point needs to be mentioned because it will appear in later analyses. It is the grammatical feature of noun classification found in many Oceanic languages referred to as the alienability of nouns. Part of this structure is that alienable nouns are themselves in two subclasses—subclasses for which an important criterion of membership has to do with consumption. I describe these features in detail in Chapter 6.

21. It is not always easy to determine commensurability in the case of an institution such as matriliny. Nevertheless, the determination of the presence or absence of a rule that states that descent group membership is accorded through the matrifilial link should be free of most epistemological hazards. Linguistics has, of course, a standard—but not fool-proof—method of determining the relative proximity and distance of one language to another: the percentage of cognates in a standard sample of lexical items.

of this area are the northeastern[22] Gazelle Peninsula (including the Duke of York Islands) and southern New Ireland (including offshore islands such as the Tanga and Lihir groups).

Within the Patpatar-Tolai subgroup,[23] Sursurunga has the highest percentages of cognates with Kandas (39 percent), and Tolai, Patpatar, and Siar (38 percent each), according to Beaumont (1976).[24] Chowning (1991) and Pawley and Ross (1993) have discussed Oceanic linguistics historically, and have demonstrated a common origin for these languages (as well as those throughout the region[25]). In thinking about the common linguistic heritage of the area, it must be kept in mind that there is no indication that linguistic commensurability necessarily creates social links between people; the five Sursurunga-speaking villages on the west coast belie that particular notion. Still, these two facts remain: (1) linguistic similarity is not a hindrance to social connections, and (2) there are relationships that transcend language group boundaries in the region—and appear to have done so since before European contact.[26]

Some easy observations can be seen to suggest that there are contemporary, in addition to historical, linkages between the speakers of these languages. The first is that the most renowned storyteller in Tekedan village—the person that local elders said I should go to in order to hear the proper versions—was John (who died in 1996), a middle-aged in-married man from the Kandas area. "The stories are the same," I was told; "John knows them best."

The second datum suggesting that linguistic similarity corresponds with socio-cultural associations is that, as can be seen from Table 2.3 above, clan relationships crosscut linguistic divisions. So, for example, some members of Sor and Antalis clans live north of the Dalum river and speak Sursurunga, whereas others live south and speak Konomala and Tanglamet.

A third bit of evidence is the similarity between the following creation accounts, one the Sursurunga version, and the other the Tolai version provided by G. Brown (1910:354–355):

---

22. That is, roughly the area east of the Karavat River and north of the Warangoi River.

23. The subgroup consists of Barok, Patpatar (also known as Pala), Sursurunga, Konomala, Siar, Kandas (Lambel), Lihir (Lir), Tangga (Anir, Muliama) on New Ireland; and Duke of York (Mioko) and Tolai (Kuanua, Tuna, Raluana) on East New Britain (Beaumont 1976:387).

24. The linguist Malcolm Ross believes these absolute cognate percentages to be far too low, and that the actual mutual intelligibility of these languages is much higher than these figures would indicate (personal communication). He sees no reason, however, to question the *relative* intelligibility between languages as articulated by Beaumont. That is, Sursurunga and Kandas, for example, are still the most closely related languages; but the cognate percentages can be questioned.

25. The one noteworthy exception is the Papuan language Kuot farther north on New Ireland.

26. Furthermore, Sursurunga as a language has been quite stable; contemporary Sursurunga looks remarkably similar to a wordlist taken by the Dutch circumnavigators Schouten and LeMaire in 1616 (Lanyon-Orgill 1960:36–52).

Sursurunga: There were once two brothers who lived with their maternal grandmother.[27] The daily routine was that the brothers worked in the bush while the mother stayed in their village in a cleared area in the bush and cooked for them. She fed the brothers *kumul* [greens] regularly. One day, one of the brothers finally mentioned to the other that he thought the *kumul* tasted terrible. The other agreed, saying that he had also thought so for a long time. They wondered if the *kumul* that their grandmother had been eating tasted bad as well.

One day, they had a chance to sample the grandmother's *kumul* while she wasn't looking, and it tasted quite good. So the brothers decided to find out why the *kumul* they had been eating for so long tasted so terrible. The following day, they told the grandmother that they were going to the bush, and they took off in that direction, but quickly veered off the path and came back to watch the grandmother in the village as she prepared *kumul*.

As the brothers hid, they each cut themselves a small (about four or five feet) length of wood to hide behind. They watched as the grandmother prepared their *kumul*, put some in coconut shells, and then, placing the shells on the ground, proceeded to urinate in the *kumul*. She then placed the coconut shells in a safe place in the house so that the brothers could eat when they got home. Now the brothers knew why their *kumul* tasted so bad. Then, with the remaining *kumul*, the grandmother walked a little way to a large rock which she lifted up and from which sprang up saltwater which she put into her *kumul*. Now the brothers knew why the grandmother's *kumul* tasted so good. Just as the grandmother was about to lower the rock again, the brothers sprang out from their hiding places, and, using their sticks as levers, pushed the rock aside so that saltwater gushed out.

The grandmother was irritated at this, since now the saltwater was going to cover huge patches of bush, and it did. The saltwater kept gushing and gushing until the ocean formed and it is as we see it now.

And the Tolai version:

Tolai: Tabui Kor was a woman, Tilik and Tarai were two men, her sons, whether born or not is not clear. They lived at Kababiai, where the sacred spring is, and from this they made the land (not yet the world). The woman made it and the two men worked it. The men worked whilst the woman cooked the *tuba* or cabbage. The two men, however, found out that their food tasted very nasty, and so one day they agreed that one of them should work with both axes so as to make the woman believe that they were both working, whilst the other went and hid (*ki lalai*) so as to watch the cooking. He went and saw the woman make water (*mimi*) into their cabbage (*tuba*), and put pure sea water into her own *tuba*. He said to himself, *a ru peu mira ba ra ma ut I petpet len ba a mira utna* (alas

---

27. These two brothers are probably the same two who appear in other tales, and whose names are Silui and Kambatari. Their origin is as follows:

There once was a woman who was working in her garden. While working, she inadvertently cut her finger with a knife. As the blood dripped out, she caught it in a taro leaf. She tied up the taro leaf full of her blood and took it home, where she placed it in the rafters of her house. Out of this blood were born the two brothers: Silui and Kambatari.

Many of the features found in this story also appear in a tale explaining the origin of death on nearby Tanga Island (Foster 1990a:434).

indeed for us two if she continues doing that to our food). He went and told his brother, and they agreed upon a certain action which they would take. When they came to dinner they took the woman's *tuba* while she was not looking and substituted theirs instead, which she had mixed with her urine because she was too lazy to go for sea water. They snatched away her food and ate it. She protested, but they ate it still. Then she got angry and went and rolled away the stone which had hitherto kept the sea confined, and the water and sea poured out in a great flood, and this was the origin of the sea. They afterwards took pieces of the earth and sprinkled them on the sea and other islands came up. Then they sprinkled this also on the land and trees, and animals and men grew.

Finally, a somewhat sparse oral history tells of a past of many migrations: the recent (around 1900, by my calculations) arrival, for example, of many members of the Kárpápus clan from the Patpatar-speaking area to the north, or the earlier (perhaps before 1800) arrival of the Tokbol/Kámrai clan from the Muliama and, earlier, Siar area. The degree of relatedness between languages in the area must certainly have helped to make these migrations possible. In sum, there is both a contemporary as well as historical basis for the sense of integration that exists in the region.

In addition to linguistic similarities, the importance of matrilineal descent[28]—as ideology and as actual (that is, what *act*ors do) social relations—is also a common feature throughout the region, and since matriliny plays a large part in the argument of the book, I turn now to how this principle of social organization is manifested in the region.

Matrilineal Descent in the Region

Two specific aspects of matrilineal descent group theory show the similarities between Sursurunga matriliny and that of other nearby groups.[29] The first is that the forms and uses of descent principles can vary. The second is that the link of complementary filiation, being an intrahousehold connection, can be expected to be rather strong. Even within the Gazelle-Duke of Yorks-southern New Ireland region, there are differences along just these lines.

We find within the region, for example, that there is some variation in the ways in which descent groups are configured. Although conventional matrilineal understandings can be found throughout the region (namely, a person is accorded membership in the descent group of her or his mother at birth), the uses to which these matrilineal understandings are put are not identical. A. Epstein (1969:123) notes that for the Tolai of East New Britain, unlike the Sursurunga, clans are not named, and that the most prominent social unit on Matupit, as on the neighboring Duke of Yorks is the clan section, or *a apik* (cf. on the Duke of Yorks, *apik*; Errington 1974:*passim*, Davies and Fritzell n.d.:*passim*). Filer and Jackson's description of Lihir is consistent with Sursurunga descent constructs:

---

28. The use of social features as ethnographic boundary markers is not uncommon. There is, for example, the "matrilineal belt" in Africa; and linguistic labels are used widely as higher-level descriptors: Austronesian, Bantu, Caddoan, and so on.

29. Both of these aspects apply to either form of unilineal descent.

named matrimoieties, named matriclans, and unnamed matrilineages (Filer and Jackson 1989:49). Foster reports that on Tanga, clans are also named, but they do not function as corporate groups (1988:80). This is similar to the situation among the Sursurunga, where the occasional attention to lineage and moiety membership is more salient even in daily life than clan membership. Albert, on the other hand, notes that, unlike the rest of the region, "Lak mortuary rites do not accent moiety relations" (1987:108). With regard to the functions of matrilineal descent groups, mortuary feast sponsorship has important matrilineal ramifications throughout the area (cf., for example, Albert 1987:*passim*; A. Epstein 1969:257–258;[30] Foster 1988:87–88).

Another institution related to matrilineal descent groups in the region is male secret societies, in which matrilineal social organization is said to generate the need for some sort of political association that extends beyond and across matrilineal descent groups within the society (Allen 1981). The argument is that lineage solidarity is often weak, because of men's competing ties to their nuclear families. Allen argues, then, that the need for non-kin-based political associations of males is thereby generated by this weakness. The need is met by secret societies, and the supra-kin-based men's secret societies throughout much of matrilineal Vanuatu (and, by extension, matrilineal Melanesia in general) are assumed to be indices of that need (Allen 1981:16–19). Although secret societies do not seem to be as prominent today as in the past among the Sursurunga,[31] other groups in the region have vigorous secret societies (A. Epstein 1969, 1992; Salisbury 1970; Neumann 1992a; Errington 1974; Errington and Gewertz 1995; Foster 1988; Albert 1987).

Other applications of the matrilineal descent principle in the region center on land use and ownership. In a court case on Matupit, A. Epstein (1969:155ff.) reports that proximity at burial is understood to be commensurate with genealogical proximity. Salisbury's (1970:67–74) description shows that control over land is based on clan membership.

The link of complementary filiation—the patrifilial connection—is strong throughout the region, and there is some evidence that this has been the case since before European contact. Epstein (1969:107–108), for example, argues for the presence of precontact patrivirilocal residence. And among the Sursurunga,

---

30. A. L. Epstein uses a negative instance among the Tolai—in which a man fails to conform to mortuary feasting protocol—as a diagnostic case to show just how important mortuary feasting obligations are (1969:151). In Chapter 8, I employ a similar strategy by using a case from the Sursurunga in 1991 to make a related point.

31. Bell (1934:314) mentions an active *tambaran* society around Nokon. Also, older informants state that dancing was formerly a part of mortuary activities, just as other recent scholars have described as modern behavior elsewhere in the region (Albert 1987, Foster 1988, Neumann 1992b). Jackson (1995:306–331) notes that he has witnessed *tambaran* activity at two Sursurunga funerals. My own observations of *tambaran* activity were not in the context of funerals. The best conclusion is that Sursurunga *tambaran* activity is sporadic compared with other societies within the region. There is also no evidence of the *buai* cult found in other parts of New Ireland (Eves 1995).

the transfer of land from father to son for a token payment is mentioned as always having occurred, as it does today (cf. also Epstein 1969:133). On Tanga, the paternal link is also important (Foster 1988:72–73), even to the point of an exceptional kinterm pattern, in which the term for FB (*tuaklik*) is the same as the term for a man's B (Foster 1988:94). The same-sex sibling relationship—the locus of Fortes's "axiom of amity"—is expected to be a close, caring link throughout the region, and to call someone by a sibling term connotes goodwill. The standardized term on Tanga suggests a norm of congenial patrilateral relations. This kinterm pattern does not exist anywhere else within the region, although the importance of patrilateral kin, especially fathers, is marked throughout the region.

Finally, there is the question of why the region includes, along with the Gazelle and Duke of Yorks, only *southern* New Ireland; more pointedly, the issue is the criteria for including Barok but excluding Mandak. Northern New Ireland (which I take to be the area north of the Barok), does have much in common with southern New Ireland and the Gazelle, but the societies in that area also show some differences, such as the absence of moieties in the Tabar Islands and in the Kavieng area. The most significant variable, however, is the presence of the *malanggan* carving complex, which is not found in the south. The Mandak (Clay 1986:*passim*) use them, but the matter is not entirely clear with regard to the Barok. According to Wagner, the Barok "seem never to have been involved" with *malanggans*, although they "may have flirted" with them in the past (1986:27). Another indication of Barok liminality is that Capell (1971) excludes Barok from the Patpatar-Tolai linguistic subgroup, whereas Beaumont (1972) includes them in the same classification. As a result of Wagner's description of the contemporary absence of *malanggans* among the Barok, coupled with Beaumont's more recent (cf. also Beaumont 1976) linguistic grouping, I have chosen to include Barok in the same ethnographic region as the Sursurunga.[32]

Local Ideas About the Integrity of the Region

A common linguistic heritage and similar descent rules establish the region's identity. I have also indicated, with the anecdote about Kandas stories being Sursurunga stories, that people within the region consider themselves to be connected. There are other indications that the Sursurunga consider themselves linked to other groups within the region. No one, for example, questioned the presence of a contingent of Duke of York Islanders at a United Church celebration at Kudukudu, or of Lihir dancers at a church opening at Nokon. It was thought natural that I should want to go to witness the ceremony surrounding a

---

32. I do not include the Nissan Group, even with its historical connections to the Tanga Group. Nachman (1978:7–13) makes it clear that Nissan is much more closely related in a number of ways to Buka than to New Ireland. Back on the Gazelle, Chowning (1969) shows that Tolai is distinct from other languages on New Britain, and this difference serves as a basis for delineation.

church opening south of Sena. The segmentary structure of the dominant United Church (Sections comprise Circuits, which comprise Regions) offers people a means of connecting themselves with others—a means that is (naturally enough, perhaps) sometimes articulated in the idiom of descent ideology.

There is little doubt that the ancestors of those who today call themselves Tolai originated from New Ireland.[33] This idea can be found in stories among the Tolai (e.g., Neumann 1992a:51–55), as well as in commonly accepted understandings on New Ireland. Salisbury's evidence (1970:286) for a Tolai emigration from southern New Ireland leaves little room for doubt, but the date(s) of the migration are not clear. This view provides another strand to the connections that people within the region understand themselves to have with each other. A common source can be inferred from the similarity in the Tolai and Sursurunga versions of the myths found above. The similarity between these two stories strongly suggests the similarities across time and space.

Finally, a southern New Ireland-Duke of Yorks-Gazelle region is marked by the fact that Rabaul has been the major commercial center of—and beyond—the region.[34] Rabaul has served as a magnet along with Kavieng in extreme northern New Ireland and with Hoskins and Talasea farther west on New Britain. Most people in Tekedan, for example, listen to radio broadcasts from Rabaul at least as often as from Kavieng. Indeed, were it not for the fact that Radio New Ireland (from Kavieng) broadcasts announcements of interest to southern New Irelanders, I believe that Radio New Ireland would have even fewer listeners in the region. Rabaul, then, serves as a hub for the region, reinforcing traditional connections such as language and history, and providing an economic and political[35] central place for the region.

SUMMARY

The Sursurunga are more or less centrally located in a region in which they share with other groups, importantly, matriliny, an emphasis on mortuary feasting, closely related languages, and perhaps of most relevance, an awareness of these similarities. The United Church informs much of social life, including aspects of "traditional" life. But for most people, the distinction between "traditional" and "introduced" is not relevant; Christianity constitutes part of the logic of actors' social situations in the same way that mortuary ritual and matriliny do.

---

33. Salisbury (1970:286) argues that the Tolai arrived on New Britain much earlier than the commonly accepted date of ca. 1750.

34. Rabaul's long-term role in the region will certainly be altered by the volcanic eruptions of September 1994. The building of a new airport at nearby Tokua, and the nostalgia that Rabaul engenders (Neumann 1997), however, suggest that the Rabaul vicinity will continue to retain its importance.

35. For example, the People's Progress Party of former Prime Minister Sir Julius Chan (whose Sursurunga mother is from Nokon village) has an office in Rabaul, but none on New Ireland.

These features play an important role in many aspects of social life in the region and, more immediately, in the analysis presented here.

In this chapter, I showed that matrilineal descent is an important feature of the sociological landscape throughout the region. Anthropologists have long been concerned with matriliny, and so for the next two chapters, I look at what anthropologists have thought about the theoretical issues generated by matriliny, all with an eye to the Sursurunga data.

Chapter 3

Land and Matriliny

In this chapter, I use Sursurunga land use and acquisition as a basis for addressing the traditional anthropological idea that descent understandings are related primarily to certain social relations—usually, those relations that involve the transmission of rights to land. The purposes of this chapter are (1) to describe Sursurunga uses of, attitudes toward, and patterns of the transfer of land; and (2) to show that a thorough understanding of a matrilineal descent system need not be tied to social relations that involve the issue of land tenure.

LAND USE AND LAND TENURE

In general, the Sursurunga distinguish between three different kinds of land: residential land, garden land, and the "bush." The bush is tropical forest and is qualitatively different from gardens and residences in that it is largely devoid of human activity. Outside of hunting purposes, the bush is considered to be nothing but potential garden (and, less often, potential residential) land. Since the bush is beyond the concerns of our interests here, I will attend only to residence land and garden land—that is, those land parcels that are especially relevant in the Sursurunga behavioral environment.

Residential Land and Residences

Tekedan village is divided into smaller residential units known as *kuranu*. These units are owned by matrilineal groups and have quite definite borders, which are normally sections of the road, the river, or cordyline shrubbery.[1] Patrivirilocal residence (that is, a nuclear family that is coresident with the husband's father), one result of the migration of "bush clans" to the coast, has altered the dynamics of residential land use and acquisition. It is not uncommon for residential land to change hands across matrilineages each generation. The following case illustrates two important features of residential dynamics at Tekedan village. The first is the ease with which residential land is transferred; the second is the difference between the ways in which residential land and garden land are perceived.

The Tekedan *kuranu* known as Mátánkám is located on the beach at the southern end of Tekedan village and borders the northernmost *kuranu* of Himaul village, Mátánkanih. Mátánkám was traditionally Tokbol clan land and has only recently (i.e., within the last 17 to 20 years) come into the hands of the Kárpápus clan. The previous owner and occupant, himself named Tokbol, sold the land to his Kárpápus wife, Vini, and their children so that they might have a place to live after his death (which took place about ten years ago). The oldest son of Tokbol and Vini, Mosili, was about 18 years old at the time of his father's death.

Mosili and Vini say that arrangements had been made between Tokbol, Tokbol's enates, and themselves that would have allowed the transfer of some of Tokbol's garden lands to them as a supplement to the purchase of Mátánkám in 1970 for K4.00. This was especially important, since Vini's Kárpápus enates originally came from the Patpatar region to the north. All Kárpápus land in the Tekedan region has therefore had to be purchased. Tokbol's sudden death occurred before any other transactions were finalized, however, and Tokbol's enates were not obligated to surrender any land. Tokbol's enates remained adamantly opposed to the alienation of land that would be used for gardens. This is due partly to the fact that Tokbol, as a local big man, had already sold off quite a bit of land; 24 other recorded sales of land parcels were engineered by Tokbol at an average price of just over K13.00.

Vini's purchase of Mátánkám around 1980 is typical. The dilemma posed by the combination of matrilineal inheritance of land and patrivirilocal residence is most commonly solved by the same sort of token purchase described here. Mátánkám is now Kárpápus property and will remain so until Mosili and his brother Tovut—the only other permanent resident of Mátánkám—marry and have children. Mosili has said that he will sell Mátánkám to his children when the time comes.

It is possible that Tokbol's surviving enates were unwilling to surrender garden land because Tokbol had already alienated so much land through sales. I am unable to confirm that proposition one way or another from interview material. It is the case, however, that garden land is much less frequently transferred between clans (compared with *kuranu* land), and the unwillingness to allow Vini and Mosili to acquire more Tokbol land is better explained by the fact that garden land is understood to be a more permanent and more valuable (Jackson

---

1. Jackson (1995:72) notes that the Sursurunga are "fascinated" with boundaries. I cannot disagree.

1995:108) holding. A residential *kuranu*, then, is the most frequently transferred kind of land.

The three components of a *kuranu* are (1) the land upon which the household physically sits, (2) the buildings upon the land that house the household, and (3) the individuals who view themselves as part of the household.

Land. It is not an overstatement to say that for the Sursurunga, a parcel of land—especially a *kuranu*—is an extension of its owner. In response to a typical Sursurunga greeting, *"U han urei?"* ("Where are you going?") it would be appropriate to say either *"Ina han uri Barbar,"* ("I'm going to [the *kuranu* known as] Barbar") or *"Ina han uri Tovina,"* ("I'm going to [the *kuranu* owned by] Tovina"). In this case, the name of the parcel of land and its owner are grammatically interchangeable. This interchangeability, I suggest, is an index of the way in which Sursurunga conceptually link a person with land.

The appearance of a *kuranu* is a reflection of the moral aspect of its inhabitants. Weeds, debris, animal feces, and cooking detritus are considered to be quite unsightly and are normally disposed of in quick order. Informants often privately disparaged others with whom they were not on the best of terms by saying how they failed to maintain the orderly appearance of their *kuranu*. To Sursurunga, bad people fail to keep a tidy *kuranu*, and a person who does not provide proper upkeep on her or his *kuranu* is a bad person.

The onus of *kuranu* maintenance falls to women, and it is women who bear the majority of the moral load of the appearance of the *kuranu*. Although a man might be quietly gossiped about because the *kuranu* in which he lives is unkempt, it would be the woman or women of that *kuranu* who would be liable to public censure at a weekly community meeting. Men are not entirely exempt, however; in one case, a man was threatened with legal action by his wife's enates for failing to do any work at all around the *kuranu*. This is in part because a woman (usually, but not always, the wife of the *kuranu* owner) has a stake in a *kuranu* that goes beyond her ability to keep the place clean. Often, the land will eventually belong to *her* lineage (as in Vini's case above), and there is a sense in which a woman maintains a *kuranu* not as a wife, but as an overseer of property that will be turned over to her children—her lineage—in good condition.

In short, a *kuranu* is the locus for a household, and is almost always owned by a married man, to whom it is seen as explicitly connected. Women—especially as a wife or daughter of the owner—also have a significant interest in the *kuranu* in which they reside since (1) the appearance of that *kuranu* is an important index of their status as moral persons in the community, and (2) they are the custodians of land that will eventually, in most cases, belong to their enatic group.

Buildings. Each *kuranu* in Tekedan is different, but each has the following components: (1) a men's house, or *bang*; (2) a cooking area/kitchen, or *pal*; and (3) a house, or *rum*.

(1) *Bang*s are sleeping venues for adolescent boys, older bachelors, and the occasional husband. Men's houses at Tekedan fall into two categories: those associated with a cemetery and those not. Those that are not adjacent to a

cemetery are little more than shady places to sit and visit. *Bangs* that are connected to a cemetery are places in which women feel less comfortable visiting; they are more incontestably *men's* houses, and by virtue of their proximity to a cemetery, the pig mandibles in the rafters, and the orientation of the door, signal that they are monuments of matrilineal descent groups.

Older informants report that in days past, the dead were buried under the floor of the *bang*. Nowadays, a corpse is laid in a *bang* prior to burial, and it is in and around the *bang* that mourning takes place most intensely. The mandibles of pigs killed for mortuary purposes in the name of a descent group's deceased members are arrayed in the rafters of the *bang*. I recall the poignancy with which Tobung, an elderly Piknat clan member, pointed to the rows of mandibles in his *bang*, saying, "That is my mother; over there is my mother's brother; here is my brother." A *bang* thus serves as the indoor part of a cemetery, and a cemetery serves much as an outdoor *bang*. *Bangs* are constructed as somewhat simple rectangular buildings. *Bangs* of the Kongkong matrimoiety have their single door on one of the short sides, and those of the Malai matrimoiety have theirs on one of the long sides. Simply by looking at a *bang*, one knows whether he enters as a "guest" or a "host." Sursurunga *bangs*, then, are monuments to the distinctiveness of the matrimoieties, as well as being repositories of the past (the cemetery) and present (the stories for which the pig mandibles serve as mnemonics) of a matriclan.

Men's houses do not change hands when *kuranu* do. In the case from Mátánkám *kuranu* described above, the (now dilapidated) Tokbol clan *bang* is next to the Tokbol cemetery; together they constitute an island of Tokbol territory within Kárpápus land, not unlike the position of West Berlin in the former East Germany. When the dilapidated *bang* is torn down, the land upon which it rests will become Kárpápus land. Only the cemetery is understood—in principle, at least—to remain Tokbol land in perpetuity.

As is true elsewhere on New Ireland (see, for example, Foster 1995), a Sursurunga men's house is an important symbol of a matrilineage's ritual activities (Jackson 1995:180ff.). In Chapter 5, I will discuss in more detail the men's house and its place in the performance of Sursurunga ritual. It is enough to say here that the Sursurunga *bang* is viewed as a representation or embodiment of a lineage rather than of an individual, something that is not true of the other two types of buildings found at a *kuranu*, the *pal* and the *rum*.

(2) Each *kuranu* will have at least one cooking area, or *pal*. This is often little more than a three- or four-walled shelter and is normally used only for cooking. Some *pals* are more elaborate and double as food storage areas. One elderly woman at Tekedan prefers to sleep in her elaborate *pal*. Due to the nature of the kinds of activities that transpire in and around it, a *pal* will normally generate a disproportionate amount of rubbish, and the appearance of a *kuranu* is dependent on the appearance of the *pal*. This is one reason a disproportionate amount of responsibility for the appearance of a *kuranu* falls to women: women are normally the food preparers and cookers, activities that take place in the *pal* and that generate trash.

The *pal*—or, if the weather is pleasant, just outside the *pal*—is where couples, families, and friends sit in the evening and chat after the day's activities. In the morning, the fire of the *pal* takes away the chill, especially if there is rain. The North American notion of "hearth" is not incommensurate with the Sursurunga *pal*. It is the source of good things: food for the belly, warmth for the skin, and camaraderie with others, usually one's kin.

(3) A *rum* is the edifice in which, minimally, a woman and her children sleep. Almost always nowadays the woman's husband also sleeps in the same building, although this was not the case in the past. Like *pals*, but unlike *bangs*, a *kuranu* will often, but not always, contain more than one *rum*. Most houses in Tekedan are built on stilts and are normally constructed of splintered bamboo walls and grass roofs. A *pal* looks hastily thrown together, but a *rum* entails much more work, more even than for a *bang* since *bangs* are usually smaller and less elaborate, and because *bangs* are built on the ground.

House-building normally involves a group of at least a half-dozen adolescent boys and men, and the atmosphere is jocular. It is not at all uncommon for members of a work crew to shout good-natured epithets at each other for bending nails, dropping hammers, or doing something improperly. Machetes are used to "goose" those on ladders, personal baskets are ransacked for cigarettes, tobacco, or betel nut when their owners are carrying loads, and ridicule is heaped upon the one who hits a thumb with a hammer, cuts himself on bamboo, or trips over the ubiquitous rubble of the construction site.

Those who participate in a house-building work crew are said to provide help, *artangan*.[2] Those members of the work crew who are not part of the core of the house-building household will normally receive a meal from the household's woman or women later in the day. This is not viewed as payment, but rather as reciprocal *artangan*.

The completion of a house is sometimes marked by a small feast known as *mansin rum*. (*Mansin* is the verb "to compensate for" but it also is a noun for "core," or "heart." *Mansin rum* is therefore literally "compensating for the house" but it is also idiomatically "the house is now a real, to-the-bone completed house.") In terms of formal protocol, this feast is only for the opposite-moiety members of the work crews who helped, since same-moiety work crew members have an obligation to provide *artangan* without expectation of reward. In fact, however, anyone who assisted is welcome to consume pork and tubers at the *mansin rum* feast.

Once completed and occupied, a house represents, for those who live in it, a place of privacy. Personal possessions are kept in houses and are expected to be sacrosanct. Tobacco, for example, that is found in a men's house may be smoked by anyone who finds it (including women) since it is assumed that the tobacco is a sign of the hospitality, magnanimity, and prosperity of the owners of

---

2. Jackson (1995:*passim*) views *artangan* as the central concept in Sursurunga social life.

the men's house. A tobacco supply in one's house, however, is another matter, and taking from a *rum* rather than a *bang* is theft, and makes one liable for a fine.

Activities that take place inside the household are also considered to be private. Postpubescent brothers and sisters should not, for example, be found in the same house alone. Local notions of epistemology assume that since what happens inside a house cannot be known, then it cannot be known with certainty that the two did *not* engage in incestuous sexual relations.[3]

A corollary of the idea of a house's privacy is that what happens inside a house is considered nobody's business but the occupants'. Naturally, one of the occupants can opt to make public what happens inside, but until then, speculation is kept at a minimum. Once, at Tekedan, a husband and wife could be heard arguing over alleged infidelities on the part of the husband. Although the voices were very clear, no one outside (publicly) commented on the event. Even later, only general comments were made on the volume of the exchange and the relative frequency of this particular couple's similar exchanges. Opinions about the truth of the allegations were not to be heard. When I pressed, people responded that it was the business of the couple, and who could know anything about their business?

This case also suggests another important aspect of a *rum*: marriage. A *rum* normally houses a marriage, and in the case above, the epistemology of not being able to know about what transpires inside a house extends to not knowing much about what transpires between a married couple—inside or outside the actual house. The *rum*/marriage equivalency is demonstrated by bachelor living situations: of the five adult bachelors in Tekedan, four do not have their own houses. The fifth has a house about 30 minutes away from the village, but when he sleeps at Tekedan, he sleeps in a *bang*.

The equivalence of marriage and house is exemplified by the comments of Tomaibi, a United Church leader from nearby Huris village. The local United Church bureaucracy has quarterly meetings during which leaders attend to a number of organizational matters. One of these matters is the status of the marriages of church workers such as deacons. When the issue came up, Tomaibi argued that although it might be possible for a married couple to hide marital difficulties in public by being kind to each other, they might still have a problem that one would know about only from being inside their house. This comment exemplifies both of the Sursurunga understandings about houses that I have been discussing, namely, that a house is an epistemological uncertainty, and that a house is the physical token or manifestation of a marriage.

A Sursurunga *rum*, then, is a place of privacy, and normally houses a marriage. If a *kuranu* can be the locus of more than one household, then the *rum* is the symbolic representation of each household. Those outside the household identified by the *rum* do not expect to know about the insides of the houses of others—in either concrete ways (e.g., where people cache their valuables) or in

---

3. Foster (1995:175) follows Wagner (1986) in arguing for a New Ireland epistemology that is grounded in visual, rather than auditory, input.

abstract ways (e.g., the nature of the relationship between a pair of spouses). It is important here to note that a *rum*/marriage alters the social statuses of the individuals who dwell within it. Specifically, it is significant that within the *rum* context, a woman's "wife" status is—or should be—most salient, and a man's "husband" status is—or should be—most salient.

Inhabitants. Most *kuranu* are occupied by multiple households, each of which has at least one member with a matrilineal connection to the other households. By "household" here, I mean an English gloss of the Neo-Melanesian term *wanpela sospan,* literally "one saucepan," or "one kettle."[4] In other words, these are units that provide, prepare, and consume food together. Households are sometimes coterminous with a *kuranu* (see Table 3.1), and sometimes coterminous with the different *rum*s within a *kuranu*. Sometimes the *wanpela sospan* group includes more than one nuclear family unit; in other cases, a nuclear family and a *wanpela sospan* group are coterminous. The family, then, is the smallest social unit in Tekedan. There are three types of family groups at Tekedan: nuclear (including divorced or widowed adults and their children), extended (a nuclear unit plus an additional generation of lineal kin), and joint (nuclear units connected by a sibling tie). The distribution of family types, *wanpela sospan* units, and *kuranu* at Tekedan village are shown in Table 3.1.

Of the 23 families at Tekedan, the residential arrangements are as follows:

Virilocal: 13
Uxorilocal: 4
Patrivirilocal: 3
Patriuxorilocal: 3

Virilocality and its reiteration in the ensuing generation, patrivirilocality, together describe more than two-thirds of the residential reality at Tekedan.[5] In general, there are four types of individuals who make up a household: married adult men, married adult women, unmarried adult men, and children. Children rarely have any choices about where they live. When a child does not live with her or his genetrix and her husband (usually also a child's genitor), she or he lives where the parents decide. In one case, a childless widow acquired three girls from different families; she is now the girls' mater. In another case, a childless woman is mater for two of her sister's children. In no cases at Tekedan (nor, to my knowledge, in other villages) do children's "adoptions" entail a matrimoiety switch; in other words, the genetrix/ex-mater is always of the same moiety as the current mater.

---

4. *Wanpela sospan* is the particular term used by the national government for census purposes. The nearest cognate vernacular expressions for this unit were either *rum* ("house") or *ring támán* ("those who are of the same father") in response to my queries.

5. Less detailed figures from the neighboring villages of Himaul and Nokon suggest that the Tekedan data are typical. Unless otherwise stipulated, "virilocality" includes "patrivirilocality" in this description.

Table 3.1
***Kuranu*, *Wanpela Sospan* Units, and Family Types at Tekedan**

Kuranu *(Pop.)*	Households	Family Type	Residence*
Porsiul (6)	1	Nuclear	Virilocal
	2	Extended	*Virilocal*
Kankapgam (11)	1	Nuclear	*Uxorilocal*
	2	Nuclear	Virilocal
Bangun (10)	1	Nclr, Extnd	Patriuxorlocal, *Virilocal*
Kabintalis (5)	1	Extended	*Virilocal*
Lalimbihi (4)	1	Nclr, Nclr	*Virilocal*, Patriuxorlocal
Poronyar (4)	1	Nuclear	*(Uxorilocal)*
Barbar (14)	1	Nuclear	Patrivirilocal
	2	Extended	*Virilocal*
Tekedan (26)	1	Nuclear	Patrivirilocal
	2	Nuclear	Patrivirilocal
	3	Nuclear	Patriuxorilocal
	4	Nclr, Extnd	*Virilocal*, Virilocal
Gavman (7)	1	Nuclear	(Virilocal)†
	2	Extended	*(Virilocal)†*
Moro (15)	1	Extended	*Virilocal*
Kabinkatit (7)	1	Joint	*Virilocal*
Kamburam (7)	1	Nuclear	*Uxorilocal*
Mátánkám (3)	1	Nuclear	*Uxorilocal*

Notes:
*This is the relationship of the owner of the land to a member of the marriage, which constitutes the core of the family unit. Italicization shows that the *actual* owner of the *kuranu* is resident.
†There is no *de jure* owner of this *kuranu*, but the *de facto* owner is a classificatory moiety mate of the husband in the other family.

I have mentioned bachelors above as men who do not have village houses. These men attach themselves to a household and its *rum* and sleep in the *bang* at that *kuranu*. These men are all, by my estimation, at least 40 years old. There are, of course, younger bachelors, but these five men have been unmarried longer than they have been married (if they ever married at all) in their adult lives. Younger men—adolescents—are referred to *kalilik* (see Bolyanatz 1994b:58–59). *Kalilik*, as adults-in-process, move around. A few nights in the bush as part of a hunting party, another night in the *bang* of a friend, and two nights at another *bang* before returning to one's own place is not atypical, especially for older (20 years and beyond) *kalilik*. The study of the residential choices of *kalilik* would attend to convenience, sexual opportunities, comradeship, and the obtaining of food. Children are dependents of their parents, but *kalilik* are dependent upon (as they would wish it) no one, and have (as they would wish it) no one dependent upon them.

Garden Land and Gardens

Garden land is a conceptually different kind of land, and this is reflected in the relative abundance of terms that are used to describe these particular parcels of land. A garden just beginning to be transformed from bush to agricultural site is a *rákrák*. A plot that is bearing is known as a *num*,[6] and an old, no longer bearing garden is a *moksu*.

Gardens are usually planted three times, and there is a noticeable decrease in the size of the produce by the third planting. The garden with which I was most familiar provided taro which averaged better than the size of a softball during the first planting. By the third planting, most of the taro produced was smaller than a baseball. The first planting produces "feast quality" taro—that is, taro that is cut into four-to-six-inch disks and made into a *páhyum*, or food packet. Only large taro is used for feasting, which means that the construction and maintenance of gardens is at least partly regulated by feasting needs, as I discuss in Chapter 7.

Typically, gardens take shape in the following manner: Once the dry season begins (May or June, by which time the prevailing winds are from the southeast), the undergrowth is cut down. Men (normally) then cut both small and large trees and let them dry where they fall. The leaves are burned off, and the trees or branches are cut into short lengths to be used as fencing. This is done over a period of several weeks so that the vegetation that has been cut down has ample time to dry in the sun. The onset of the rainy season occurs in October, and the burning must take place as close to the end of the dry season as possible. At this time, the detritus is heaped at the bases of the large tree stumps and ignited.

Gardens require protection from pigs—both feral and domesticated. The boundaries of the fence are marked, and holes are dug for the fence posts, which are made of either bamboo or the branches accumulated during the process of preparing the garden. Vines are then prepared to hold the fence together, and the typical fence is built with pairs of upright posts holding a stack of horizontal bamboo poles between them.

After the plot has been burned, sections are laid out inside the plot by using long saplings that were felled during the clearing stage. These sections, known as *dáu*, represent parts of a parcel that are to be gardened by different people, and/or constitute different areas of a garden, so that one *dáu* might be dominated by taro, another *dáu* by bananas, and so on. Planting takes place in October or November (the beginning of the wet season) and gardens normally bear (depending on the age of the garden) from March until August.

In general, then, the wet season (November-February) is characterized by planting and weeding. Between the height of the wet and the beginning of the dry season (March-May), less time is needed for weeding, and most garden activity consists of harvesting. This is the time of year when other projects are attended to, such as building new houses. During the peak of the dry season

---

6. *Pokon* is an archaic term for a garden, elicited in interviews, but never heard in conversation, except when used as a term meaning "grove."

(June-August) new gardens are begun. Other gardens are also sometimes begun at other times, and most families have a smaller garden that is planted so that it can be harvested when the main garden is not producing (i.e., October-January).

Acquiring Land

A Sursurunga individual can acquire land by three methods. The first is traditional inheritance within the matrilineage; the second, which has become more prominent recently and is exemplified by the case at the outset of the chapter, is the patrifilial transmission of land, a transaction that normally takes the form of a purchase for a small price. The third is the purchase of land from a person outside of ego's matrilineage or nuclear family.

Inheritance within the matrilineage is a quick and easy process under normal circumstances. Individuals—women or men—who wish to make a new garden on matrilineage land have only to make sure that no other lineage mates wish to use the same parcel. I know of no instances of conflicting wishes, but informants say that seniority would be the basis for determining priority. In the case of *kuranu* land, matrilineal inheritance rarely obtains, since *kuranu* are usually passed from a man to his children for a small price.

The token (i.e., normally between two and five kina) purchase from one's father or husband is the normal means of acquiring *kuranu* land. Garden and bush land may also be acquired by means of a token purchase, although with the advent of written land records, patrifilial inheritance has become a more frequent method, as many people have been recorded as heirs of particular parcels upon their father's demise. Table 3.2 reflects this trend in Sursurunga land inheritance patterns.[7] For most of these transactions, the buyer and seller are named, as well as the amount paid, usually in cash, but sometimes also in the form of pigs and/or strands of shells known as *reu*. In addition, many of the recorded transactions note an heir designated by the claimant in the event of his or her death.

The third way of obtaining land is outright purchase and is uncommon. This entails an alienation of clan lands from the clan and requires consensus on the part of the clan's adults. I was told of one particularly powerful leader in the 1960s who profited from the sale of his clan's land without their permission, but such cases are rare, it seems.

---

7. The information for these tables was taken from records of the Land Titles Commission (LTC). The purpose of this committee, consisting of province (then district) administrators and local leaders in 1968, was to record extant landowners and to formalize land transactions. The result is that when the committee began visiting villages in the Sursurunga area in early 1969, people rushed to record land titles and transactions. The pace slowed considerably after 1971, and after 1978, people were required to travel to Namatanai to record their land transactions, with the result that most people did not bother. See Foster 1995:57–59 for an account of analogous activity on Tanga.

Table 3.2
Heirs Designated by Male and Female Landowners

	Men	Women	Total
Who Named Enatic Heirs	308	157	465
Who Named Non-Enatic Heirs	162	3	165
Total	470	160	630

Note: $\chi^2 = 65.6$ $p < .01$

The Demise of Avunculocality

There has been a shift away from primarily matrilineal inheritance of land—as reported by older informants—to a pattern that is increasingly patrifilial, as shown by the figures in Table 3.2. These figures are consistent with an unsolicited comment from a middle-aged man, who said, "Our custom[ary means of transferring land] changed between 1960 and 1970." This change can be attributed to early colonial policies and their effects upon traditional avunculocal residence patterns.

Patrivirilocal residence among the Sursurunga has been largely the result of the migration of "bush clans" to the coast after World War I, and has since set in motion or exacerbated a number of social changes, including, importantly, the economic primacy of the household (as it has on Tanga; see Foster 1995:57–61). The shift to patrivirilocality from avunculocality began after the German Administration established the Namatanai outpost in 1904. German hegemony was not widespread south of the Namatanai area, but to the degree that the administration was able to impose its wishes on local people—usually in the form of a head tax—there was pressure on the local population to congregate in places where they might be more easily accounted for. This process was accelerated by the Australians, who took over in 1914 with the outbreak of war in Europe, and who maintained control when Germany was forced to surrender its overseas colonies as stipulated by the Treaty of Versailles.

The Australian administration's resettlement mandate (*ca.* 1920) made it clear to most people along the southern east coast of New Ireland that sooner or later, bush groups would have to relocate. The Administration urged those people who lived away from the beach to resettle along the coast, the result of which was the formation of *kems* (Neo-Melanesian, from the English "camp") along the coast. A *kem* thus became a conglomerated village—a collection of adjacent *kuranu*, including people from descent groups who traditionally occupied the coast (Koris, Antalis, Bulitlimat, Kimri, Tokbol, Kárpápus, and Irir clans) as well as those who traditionally lived up in the bush (Piknat, Sahwon, Karbakok, Sor, Silbat, and Suabu clans).[8]

Upon this resettlement, residential blocks along the coast became more crowded, and groups of people who had been dispersed previously found themselves living adjacent to each other along the beach. The resulting *kem* consisted of multiple *kuranu* and multiple *bangs* (men's houses), with each *bang* representing and being the focus of a separate lineage.

Prior to resettlement, according to older informants, each lineage had its *bang* more or less in the center of the territory that it controlled, and residential land was nestled within garden lands. With the migration to the coast, garden land and residential land became separated: beach clans lost garden land to incoming bush clans, and bush clans left garden lands behind when they took up coastal residence. The colonial government eventually bought a parcel of land named Tekedan (from *teken*, "dregs"/"refuse"/"waste" and *dan*, "water") along a river so that bush people would not be able to plead poverty as an excuse for not settling along the coast. The crowding of the beach was not necessarily a hostile invasion. An older informant assured me that the following resettlement account was typical of the early Australian era. I estimate the events in this story to have taken place about 1925.

The *kuranu* known as Moro [in what is now "central" Tekedan] was purchased by Dunghat, a Sahwon [clan] big-man. He was from the bush and came down to the beach before the Japanese came. The Australians tried to get people to come out of the bush and live down near the beach. Dunghat was one of those who was told to come down. Sometimes the Australians burned bush houses[9] so that people had to leave the bush. Dunghat made friends with a [man of the] Tokbol [clan] at Himaul [village, about a 20-minute walk northeast from modern Tekedan]. There was no Tekedan [village] at the time. Moro was the first place settled. Then, [the *kuranu* known as] Gavman [the site purchased by the government] was opened up.

At the base of the big casuarina tree at Moro there was nothing but mud. So Dunghat got some help, including some people from Himaul and brought stones up from the reef and put them in the mud. This dried up the area and it became the site of the first Moro *bang*. They made two parallel walls about a meter high of stones and put a *bang* in the middle. Dunghat bought three huge pigs with strands of *reu*. He invited all of Himaul to come and they ate pork together. One large pig was cut in half and its head was put aside. The women ate one pig, while the men all ate one and a half. The uneaten pig's head was the purchase [price] of the ground. It was then carried to Himaul, where the Himaul [villager]s ate it. Purchase complete. Then Himaul [villagers] marked from what is now [the *kuranu* of] Gavman to [the *kuranu* of] Kabinkatit as Dunghat's place.

Then the Piknat [clan] arrived. As was the case in the bush, Piknats and Sahwons intermarried and cooperated. But the Piknats had no pigs or money to buy land when they left the bush. By this time, the government had bought Gavman as a public place so that anyone could settle there. So the Piknats did. Now they think it is theirs, but it is

---

8. Informants report that some clans traditionally occupied both coastal and bush lands: Rongol, Piklám, Builbuil, and Korohi.

9. This is the only reference to Australians doing this. I believe that my informant misremembered, and was in fact thinking about the earlier German occupation.

not, because they didn't buy it as Dunghat had bought his land. Dunghat died during the Japanese Occupation. He was then buried at Moro, at the site of the *bang*. Eventually, the *bang* was destroyed during the war, so all that remains is the cemetery.

But Dunghat was not the first Sahwon to be buried at Moro. That would have been Kiaprou, Dunghat's brother. He was a *luluai* in the bush under the Germans, at a place called Bimioh. Kiaprou came down with Dunghat, but died shortly after they settled in Moro. He became the first person to be buried in what is now a full cemetery.

The result of this and other such movements of people was experienced as a scarcity of garden land: although the actual amount of land was not reduced, the amount of readily accessible land dropped. This is one reason for the contemporary assessment of garden land as more valuable than residential land. Garden land is still inherited along lineage lines and tends to exist in blocks—contiguous named clusters of parcels owned by the same descent group, but ownership of *kuranu* residential land along the coast is not in blocks.

The clustering of residences along the beach, coupled with the cessation of warfare and cannibalism (and the concomitant need of the lineage as a defensive/offensive military unit), served to reduce the need for a young man, upon reaching puberty, to leave his natal household to go live with enates as in traditional avunculocal residence practices. In many cases after relocation, a young man's *koko* (MB) lived within the same *kem*, so he was *already* coresident with his MB. It was simply easiest to remain living in and associated with the *bang* that he grew up in as a child: his father's *bang*. At the time, of course, no one recognized this as the beginning of the end of avunculocality; men still had younger enates around who could be conscripted for labor. It was assumed to be of little substantial difference where a young man slept (recall that the residential patterns of adolescent males—*kalilik*—are and were extremely fluid), as long as his diurnal activities were under enatic auspices. But when those young men grew up to become fathers, and *their* children lived with them, it was their fathers' residences—that is, their *kuranu* parcels—that the younger generation acquired and lived on. This pattern, hobbled by the devastating interruption of World War II and Japanese occupation, effloresced during the 1950s, the same period in which the Australian government encouraged the development of copra cooperatives, described in Chapter 2.

The shift in inheritance patterns among the Sursurunga has resulted in the tendency for men (but not women) to alienate all types of land from their enatic groups by naming their children as heirs to parcels of land that they owned. This shift toward patrifilial inheritance among the Sursurunga is important because it represents what might easily—but mistakenly—be taken to be the disintegration of matriliny among the Sursurunga. Anthropological descriptions of matrilineal descent that would evince the disintegration of matriliny among the Sursurunga fail to take into consideration the realities of Sursurunga matriliny.

MATRILINEAL DESCENT GROUP FUNCTIONS AND THE SURSUR-UNGA CASE

I have elsewhere (Bolyanatz 1995, 1996) addressed the history of the anthropological interest in matrilineal descent. The substance of my argument is that there is no intrinsic connection between land tenure and descent; that is, there is no reason that the primary function of a descent group has to be the transfer of land across generations. Conflating a rule of descent and a pattern of inheritance is a notion that has been around since Malinowski, who, in describing the Trobrianders, defined "matrilineal" as "in tracing descent *and settling inheritance*, . . . follow[ing] the maternal line" (1961:55; italics added). This way of seeing matriliny (and probably patriliny, for that matter) conflates two very distinct things. The tracing of descent is an abstraction, a way of seeing connections in the social world. The settlement of inheritance issues is an outcome or effect of that abstraction. Lumping together an effect with its cause leads nowhere, but because so many unilineal descent systems examined by anthropologists earlier in this century did function as land-transmitting groups (such as the Trobriand Islanders), it is easy to see how the mistake was made.

Understandings that guide descent group composition—cultural ideologies about who is a member and, importantly, understandings about the salience of group membership—are one thing. The conspicuous behavior of human beings conducted *qua* members of a group is another. The salience of beliefs is not the same thing as behavior, although as I discussed in Chapter 1, salience can be both cause and effect of behavior. Descent group functions—the conspicuous behaviors of individuals who, together, constitute an activated group—can be and often are the transfer of land rights. But they can also be, and often are, rituals such as mortuary feasting that are only indirectly, if at all, related to land rights. This means that the matrilineal transmission of land can disappear without the concomitant disappearance of the salience of matrilineal descent understandings. Matrilineal descent, then, can be an integral component of a social system by being related to other functions, such as the activated group behavior found in the social relations that are involved in mortuary feasting.

Of course, land is not the only form of wealth that might be transferred according to a principle of matrilineal descent. When men have access to forms of wealth that are partible and not easily identifiable, and that can be employed without others' scrutiny, then the possibility exists that a man might pass some of his wealth to his own children, rather than to his sister's children—a pressure that has been dubbed the "matrilineal puzzle." Problems occur when a man gives a disproportionate amount of wealth to his own children, leaving an insufficient amount for him to pass to members of his own lineage. Malinowski describes this phenomenon for Trobriand matrilineal descent groups, noting that a father "always tries to give as much as he can to his own sons at the expense of those [sons] of his sister, who are his legal heirs. His *natural inclinations* are seconded by customary usage which almost defies and certainly circumvents the *rigid matrilineal law*, by giving the father a number of opportunities to favor his sons and to curtail the rights of his matrilineal nephews" (1935:205; italics added).

By contrasting "natural inclinations" and "rigid matrilineal law," Malinowski makes clear that a man is required, within a social context, to do *something* with his wealth, and his two most likely choices are his son and his sister's son. The ethnographic evidence on this point is quite clear: when wealth is available in the form of cash, men *do* sometimes provide their own offspring with much of their profit—especially if a man perceives his own children to have contributed to the acquisition of that wealth (e.g., T. S. Epstein 1968). Indeed, this happens often enough that capitalism has been perceived to be the single greatest enemy of matrilineal inheritance ideology (cf. Gough 1961). Furthermore, in the case of a local high-intensity capitalist enterprise, such as a plantation or a mine, any tension between matrilineal jural rules and patterns of largess rooted in complementary filiation are sure to be exacerbated. What makes this scenario even more likely to occur is that, *ceteris paribus*, men with relatively little authority within their own matrilineage are more likely to be employed in wage labor, since the earnings from wage labor are usually not likely to motivate a man of high standing (and concomitant access to wealth) in the lineage to undergo the often miserable conditions of mine or plantation work. Wage earners are thus men who are already likely to be established in a pattern of non- or little involvement in the activities of the lineage and who are therefore less likely to adhere to the jural norms of matrilineal inheritance. In other words, those most likely to seek wage labor are among those least likely to pass on their cash matrilineally: the erosive effects of a cash-based system on matrilineal inheritance patterns, but not necessarily the salience of matriliny, can be, therefore, doubly erosive.

In a more recent analysis of how matrilineal descent operates, Oliver (1993) also assumes that the matrilineal descent group is paradigmatically a land-transmitting group. In describing father-to-son land transfers among the Siwai of Bougainville Island, Oliver notes that such a transfer represents the "founding [of] an incipient patrilineage" (1993:30). But there is no indication given that patrilineal descent understandings are emerging—let alone are salient—among the Siwai. Father-to-son land transfer conflates patrifiliation with patriliny when the descent group is seen as primarily or exclusively a land-transmitting group.

Some, but not all, matrilineages function primarily as property-owning and -transmitting corporate groups. The problem comes in seeing this function as inherent of descent groups wherever they are found. Where a primary function of matrilineal descent groups is similar to that of Trobriand matrilineages, then the threat of cash to the integrity of the group is realistic. On the other hand, if the matrigroup is not intricately linked to the transmission of wealth across generations, then cash-cropping, patrifilial inheritance, and matrilineal descent can quite easily coexist, as among the Sursurunga and other groups.

In a wealth- or land-based theory of matriliny, the benchmark for establishing the demise of matriliny is when the inheritance of goods, cash, and/or land ceases to pass exclusively or primarily through the matriline. In an analogous argument, Allen takes "political functions," rather than inheritance to be the essence of a descent group (1981:14). He notes that since membership in a matrilineage is relatively inflexible (that is, matrifiliation is not nearly as negotiable as patrifiliation), other kinds of more flexible groups are required for political action. Allen uses this assumption to argue for the genesis of male secret societies in Melanesia on the grounds that "in pre-state societies matriliny, because of genuine internal problems . . . is much more likely to stimulate [political] evolutionary development than is patriliny" (1981:13).

The choices facing a father/uncle are not, after all, nearly as stark as the quotation from Malinowski would suggest. Fortes, foreshadowing his later (1969), richer treatment of the subject, noted that Malinowski had failed to distinguish between (patri)filiation and (matrilineal) descent, and the ways those relationships are used. Malinowski missed the significance of complementary filiation by failing to see that a man's contribution to his son "arises quite normally out of the father's duty to rear his children to adulthood" (Fortes 1957:184). In other words, "traditional" matrilineal understandings can exist where there are not "traditional" matrilineal descent group functions.[10]

Individuals who perceive themselves to be linked by a principle of matrilineal descent do not necessarily have to conform only to the traditional sorts of functions such as inheritance and succession to function as a group or to retain the relevance of the principle of matriliny. One of the reasons that changes in inheritance and succession cannot by themselves eliminate the importance of matrilineal descent is that matrilineal understandings have their roots in human physiology in ways that patrilineal understandings do not. Although this is not the only reason for the perseverance of matrilineal understandings, I suggest that, *qua* understandings, matriliny will retain its salience in some contexts even if a matrilineal descent group finds itself with only few or relatively insignificant sociological functions. In this vein, Allen argued that matrilineal principles are less "flexible" than their patrilineal counterparts (1984:27ff.), since agnation is less demonstrable—and therefore more open to negotiation and interpretation—than enation. Part of this "inflexibility," I am arguing, is a perceptual-cognitive resistance to change in descent understandings: women give birth; the idea that people are no longer to be considered part of their mother's group is experienced by them as counterintuitive (Allen 1981:11–12).

To argue that the loss of matrilineal inheritance of land is an index of the disintegration of the matrilineal descent group is tautological, and rests on the

---

10. Nash (1974), for example, showed that matrilineal descent among the Nagovisi did not "disintegrate" in the face of cash capitalism on Bougainville Island. Similarly, A. Weiner shows that matrilineal descent in the Trobriands is intact and even co-occurs with the institution of *pokala*, a conventional means of transferring rights to land patrifilially (1976:137–167). Beyond Papua New Guinea, Petersen (1982) provides evidence demonstrating that matrilineal descent ideology does not necessarily have to be expressed in terms of matrilineal inheritance of land. His Ponapean case shows that matrilineal understandings are not dependent upon a functioning system of matrilineal land tenure or a residence pattern more commonly associated with matriliny.

notion that the matrilineal descent group—or any unilineal descent group, for that matter—is centrally defined by its ability to pass on important resources to its next generation. Although it may be the case that this has been and is an important function of some unilineal descent groups, it is not clear that this feature need be a defining characteristic of unilineal descent groups. The issue is: does attention to inheritance—as a central part of the definition of unilineal descent groups—promote our understanding of these groups? It seems that it does not.[11]

Among the Sursurunga, descent group understandings are not rooted in the transfer of lineage land through generations. Rather, descent group understandings are most clearly instantiated in and seen to have on-going utility as important guides to life through moiety exogamy and the mortuary feasting complex.[12]

As described above, a shift has taken place in the way land has been transferred among the Sursurunga. But this shift has not been accompanied by the disintegration of matrilineal descent groups. The regard in which the matrilineal descent principle is still held among the Sursurunga is evidenced by the fact that prescribed matrimoiety exogamy is still in force, and still followed in more than 90 percent of all marriages. Furthermore, as I show later, the mortuary feasting complex makes salient social statuses that are informed by the matrilineal principle, as many behaviors and aspects of comportment within the feasting complex are derived from matrilineage, matriclan, and matrimoiety membership.

SUMMARY

In this chapter, I have shown that there has been a tendency to view the matrilineal principle as a feature of what Errington and Gewertz call "inflexible tradition" (1995:5ff.). In other words, there is a predilection to view people's behavior in terms of (often, exotic) differences between "them" and "us"—in this case, matrilineal descent. This is wrong, because nowhere in the world is there an account of a group of people whose behavior is overwhelmingly influenced by one concept—such reductionism is misplaced. Any particular behavior in the life of an actor is likely to be overdetermined; even in those instances in which matrilineal group membership is a cause of behavior, it is unlikely to be the *only* reason.

---

11. The Mae Enga in the Highlands of New Guinea (Meggitt 1965) are a case in point. During periods of population pressure on the supply of land, patrilineal understandings "tightened up," and only "true" agnates had full land rights. When the land supply was less a problem, agnatic group membership was extended to men who were not demonstrably agnates. Thus, the relationship between control over land tenure and descent group understandings is variable, and it is easy to imagine that in an area with little or no pressure on land supply, the connection between land tenure and the unilineal descent group might be extremely loose.

12. I do not mean to suggest that the matrilineage has nothing to do with the transfer of land. Traditionally, most land was passed through the matrilineage. But apparently, land was also at times acquired through other means—namely, from the father's side—without the "disintegration" of the matrilineage or of matrilineal understandings.

Chapter 4

Rethinking the
Logic of Matriliny

The previous chapter showed that there has been some question about the function of matrilineal descent groups; that is, what is it that such groups do? There has also been in anthropology some discussion about the structure of such groups; that is, how are matrilineal groups formed? In this chapter, I review anthropological analyses of the ways in which matrilineal descent groups are made, looking especially at the phenomenon known as the "matrilineal puzzle."

Not long after Malinowski's Trobriand work, Radcliffe-Brown (1924) noted the differing implications of matrilineal descent for patrilateral and matrilateral kinship relationships in Africa, and thereby generated a tradition of cross-cultural comparative analyses of systems of matrilineal descent. After World War II, Richards initiated a renewed anthropological interest in matriliny, conducting a systematic comparison of societies labeled "matrilineal" among Central Bantu groups (1950). Richards's work included a coherent treatment of what was known about both the structures and functions unique to matrilineal descent groups, including, perhaps most importantly, identifying the "matrilineal puzzle" (1950:246). The "puzzle" centers on tension/conflict inherent in certain social relations resulting from the fact that whereas descent group jural authority resides with ego's MB, domestic/household jural authority resides with ego's F (see Diagram 4.1). Richards, for example, referring to the conflicting pattern of rights and obligations that crosscut the household and the descent group, points out that "the balance of interest between the two sides of the family is bound to be an uneasy one in the case of matrilineal communities" (1950:211). The uneasiness exists in more two places: not only are men expected to provide both for the younger members of their descent group as well as the younger members of their own households, as we saw in Malinowski's description in the preceding chapter ("natural inclinations" opposed to "rigid matrilineal law"), but children are required to recognize the authority of both father and mother's brother.

Diagram 4.1
The Matrilineal Puzzle

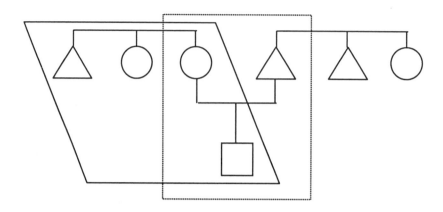

Matrilineal Descent

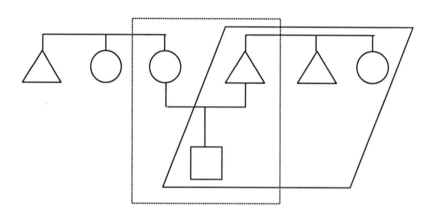

Patrilineal Descent

Unilineal Descent Group

Domestic/Household Group

Note that this way of thinking about the "matrilineal puzzle" does not really address the issue of the "puzzle's" psychological reality: that is, it is not clear whether a peculiarly "matriliny-genic" tension is claimed to exist in the minds of members of matrilineal descent groups, or whether it is merely something perceived by anthropologists. The following case illustrates the uncertainty:

At a *tambaran* rite at Himaul, I spoke with Maro, from the offshore Tanga group. We began by talking about whether he knew the anthropologist Bob Foster and his ethnographic work on Tanga. Being an administrator from Namatanai High School (and quite articulate in English), Maro replied that his work kept him from Tanga except for the occasional holiday or mortuary feast, and that he knew Foster only by reputation.

I asked about Foster's references to young men walking on the roofs of men's houses (1990a:443) and Maro then animatedly told me the story of when, in the early 1970s, he walked on the roof of the men's house of his matriclan, Ku. At that time, he heard the clan narrative telling him that the Ku group was not originally from Tanga, but from a distant place called Himaul. He eventually discovered Himaul, and upon visiting the place, looked up an old woman who told him that a long time ago, some members of the Tokbol clan had headed to Tanga, and that the Tokbols were the source of the Ku.

Maro has since spent some time at Himaul, building a house there, and has provided things for what he takes to be his younger enates, such as buying a bicycle for Tovevel for K150. His presence at a ceremonial event at Himaul, therefore, is easily understood.

Maro told the story of how he had also contributed K100 for a pig for that day's event and how, that very morning, he and his wife had had an argument as they drove the two hours down from Namatanai. It turns out that on their way out of town, they had stopped to purchase some diapers for their baby daughter. Maro asked his wife for some money as he got out of the car, and she responded angrily, "What? You can pay K100 for a pig but you can't pay K2 for your own daughter?" As he had no money with him at all, she reluctantly gave him the money for the diapers, and they drove the two hours to Himaul in silence.

When I first heard this story, I had a "Eureka!" sort of moment: the "matrilineal puzzle" existed! But after reflecting on Maro's story, I realized that I had had similar quarrels with *my* spouse. So it could not be said that arguments over how money is spent—on one's consanguines versus one's children—are due to matrilineal descent. Furthermore, I could not determine that Maro experienced the tension in a way that was profoundly or qualitatively different than I or anybody else would. In other words, just what is so matrilineal about Maro's case? This is the point where I began to see the "matrilineal puzzle" as a chimera.

For the most part, the psychological reality of the "matrilineal puzzle" has gone unexamined, and has been seen as a concern of anthropologists (and others) who cannot quite seem to understand how such a system could have much—or any—stability at all. These days, the idea of a "matrilineal puzzle" is under attack. One argument is that the "matrilineal puzzle" is nothing but the result of male ethnographers whose Western European "androcentric" assumptions kept them from seeing a "woman-centered" system as anything but puzzling (Watson-Franke 1992). I also think the "matrilineal puzzle" may have outlived its usefulness as an analytic concept, but for other reasons, which I articulate in Chapter 8.

The late David M. Schneider took the development of matrilineal theory a step forward by condensing what was known about matriliny in his well-known Introduction to *Matrilineal Kinship* (1961). Schneider's essay is perhaps the best-known piece of scholarship on the dynamics of matrilineal descent groups. It is not difficult to find an introductory textbook in anthropology that refers to Schneider's essay. (Of course, some authors refer to the essay as a foil or starting point of a discussion of matrilineal descent groups, as I do here.) Schneider sought to provide a description of the "nature" (1961:2) of matrilineal descent groups. This description foreshadows his later work in that it is an anthropological study of kinship that eschews the "impediment" of "analytic categories" such as "'parents,' 'mother,' and 'father'" (1961:2; f.n. 2).

In his analysis, Schneider articulates features of matrilineal descent groups that are explicitly contrasted with patrilineal descent groups, and although he refers to it only once (1961:22), much of his essay is an explication of the implications of the "matrilineal puzzle." Schneider acknowledges that the features listed may not reflect the realities of actual matrilineal descent groups; but on-the-ground reality is not at issue for Schneider. He is, rather, primarily concerned with the "logical" (six times in the first three paragraphs, Schneider uses "rationale," "logic," "logically," or "logical") entailments of matrilineal descent. He constructs a model—an idealized world—so that his readers might see the systemic dynamics of matriliny without the "noise" of socio-cultural variation. Schneider defends himself against empirical data by saying he is interested only in the "logic of the system." But the consistency of the logic of his analysis is a problem. In the following section, I show that on both logical and empirical grounds, the Schneiderian approach to Sursurunga matriliny is not without shortcomings. Schneider's analysis generates two questions. The first has to do with how well he did what he claimed to have done, and the second has to do with whether—or to what degree—such an approach is valuable in anthropology. I address these two questions in detail at the end of the book. Here, I take Schneider's exposition of the unique features of matriliny as the earliest example of what one author (Marshall 1983:2) has called the "cultural category" approach to the study of kinship and descent, and what another has derisively called the "antikinship school" (Scheffler 1991:361). This is an approach of which Schneider can claim to be a progenitor, and which has largely been charted in his book *A Critique of the Study of Kinship* (1984). But I am getting ahead of myself. The rest of this chapter concerns itself with Schneider's "antikinship" claims about matrilineal descent and brings Sursurunga data to bear on those claims.

MATRILINEAL DESCENT GROUP STRUCTURE AND THE SURSUR-UNGA CASE

Schneider bases his analysis of matrilineal descent groups on three explicit assumptions. The first assumption is that women care for children. The second is that men have authority over women, in both the domestic *and* descent contexts. (See Fox [1983:5–6, 31–33] for a discussion of this assumption.) Finally, it is assumed that descent group exogamy is required. Note that he does not assume that these things are everywhere always true. Rather, what he says about matrilineal descent groups are true only if these three things are also the case. Before proceeding, it is worth noting the first two assumptions in more detail.

With regard to the first, namely, that women care for children, "care," as Schneider uses it, does not refer to women's affection, comforting, or even concern about their children, but refers, rather, to the responsibilities of feeding, washing, and protecting a child from harm. This is either because women are assumed to have no affect-laden connections to their children worthy of mention, or because "natural" maternal instincts are assumed—an assumption that seems unlikely in Schneider's kind of analysis. The point is noteworthy because, as we shall see later, Schneider's handling of the issue of emotion, as in the "strong, positive affect" between fathers and children (1961:22) leads to a misunderstanding of the affective dynamics within the household.

The second assumption is that men have authority over women. At times, Schneider uses "authority" as a shorthand for the unquestioned jural advantage in group decision making (e.g., 1961:6–7). At other times, "authority" is used as the capacity to command personal loyalties (e.g., 1961:19). The latter, it seems, could be any of a number of things, depending on one's disciplinary predilections: "power," "charisma," or even "projective identification." But whatever it is called, it is not quite the same thing as jural authority, and the two do get conflated at times.

Siblings and the "Matrilineal Puzzle"

Schneider begins his analysis by noting a fundamental difference between patrilineal systems and matrilineal systems: authority in the descent group and in the domestic group coincides in the status of father/husband in patriliny, but not in matriliny. This means that matrilineal groups must retain control over *both* female and male group members, since women provide the requisite descent link whereas men provide leadership. In patriliny, both of these functions can be performed by one man. Baldly put, a patrilineage does not require its women for social or biological reproduction, but it does need its men. On the other hand, a matrilineage needs its women as descent links, but, given the assumption about male authority, a matrilineage also requires its men in order to continue.

To say that matrilineal descent groups need to retain control over both male and female members for their continuity and operation (Schneider 1961:8) is to say that matrilineages need men in ways that patrilineages do not need women. But Schneider also claims that there is potential strain within a matrilineal descent group in that although the sister is a proscribed sexual object for her brother, her sexual and reproductive activities are necessarily a matter of interest to him since she provides the next generation of his descent group members (1961:13). So, although both men and women are logically required for the maintenance of the matrilineal segment, the paradox is that relations between them are burdened with a dynamic—simultaneous "need" and "strain"—not found in their patrilineal counterparts. The combination of these two aspects provides something of a problem in this "logical" treatment of matriliny in that "need" and "strain" are simultaneously part of a "coherent" system. Of course, such ambivalences pervade the relationships of actual brothers and sisters; the difficulty, however, lies in positing as elements of a functioning system two characteristics that are at cross-purposes with each other when articulating the "coherence or logic" (1961:2) of a descent system. Sursurunga data reveal that this "logical" problem need not be difficult to live with in reality.

There is very strong brother-sister avoidance among the Sursurunga, and it extends to classificatory siblings at the moiety level (though with less moral force). A concomitant of shared origin among the Sursurunga, as well as in many other parts of Papua New Guinea, is the restriction placed on intimacy between opposite-sex siblings. *Rumrum*, or "shame," is the outcome of even inadvertent interaction between brothers and sisters, and the reason given for this moral anxiety is the possibility of brother-sister sexual relations. The Sursurunga view brother-sister incest as heinous, but also altogether too possible; hence the need to carefully guard against even the opportunity. Even to know of one's sibling's sexuality is proscribed and is the cause of great distress. Although I never saw it happen, I was told that to discuss a man's sister's sexual behavior in his hearing makes one liable for a pig for the shame that results.

In one case, a married woman was involved in a sexual relationship with another man. She wished to leave her husband and marry the man with whom she was involved. The husband was quite willing for this to happen, demanding only that the bridewealth payment he had made be restored to him. Three of the woman's brothers were on hand for a late evening meeting to resolve the conflict. Everyone appeared to be angry, and on two occasions the brothers were verbally restrained from attacking their sister by Sam, who was serving as adjudicator of the dispute. Their anger was not at the loss of the bridewealth—the new husband-to-be was quite willing to make that payment. Rather, their anger was aimed at the "play" of their sister, whose sexual activity had become a matter of public conversation. With the village discussions about what to do about this woman and her marriage(s) in the preceding days, the brothers were continually being assailed by knowledge of their sister's sexuality—but with no one to blame except, as they saw it, her. In sum, Sursurunga descent understandings constitute a conceptual connection between people who have matrifilial links, but they also conceptually differentiate people within the descent group who are opposite-sexed.

Brother-sister avoidance can be viewed as either an expression of Schneider's "strain," or as a kind of mitigation of "strain." Brother-sister avoidance is taught to Sursurunga children through corporal punishment as they approach puberty. Parents—including, importantly, fathers—who try to reinforce brother-sister avoidance say that they are only helping their children learn the proper ways to behave. If brother-sister avoidance naturally emerged from an inchoate sibling "strain" created by the acquisition of matrilineal descent understandings,

Diagram 4.2
Prikila and Tinamel

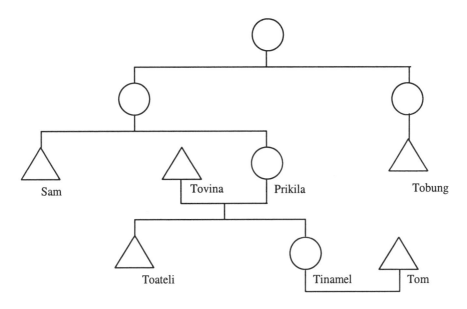

there would be no need for parents to strive to effect the avoidance patterns. Clearly, whatever the ultimate cause of B-Z avoidance might be, one of the proximate causes is the inculcation of avoidant behavior patterns by parents.

Sursurunga brother-sister avoidance actually serves to lessen any "strain" by keeping brothers and sisters away from each other. The taboos on brother-sister interaction among the Sursurunga, if taken as an instantiation of the "strain" to which Schneider refers, resolve the "need"/"strain" paradox by making the relationship one dominated by a minimum of interaction: the avoidance is so strong that there are no social settings in which opposite-sexed siblings "need" each other.

Recall that this "need" is a politico-economic phenomenon: a matrilineage requires, according to Schneider, both reproducers and leaders. But in one case in which a new matrilineal segment was formed among the Sursurunga, a man was not needed at all. Here is that case:

In 1990, Tinamel's stillborn child was not buried in the lineage cemetery at Bangun *kuranu*—much to the displeasure of Tobung, a locally renowned big man of the Piknat clan (Tinamel's MMZS) and some other lineage members (see Diagram 4.2). They buried the infant at Barbar *kuranu*, where Tinamel lives patriuxorilocally with her parents and her husband, Tom, who is from the southern end of New Ireland. Barbar is Sahwon clan land; but Barbar is expected to become Piknat land. This is because Tovina, Tinamel's F, has designated Toateli, Tinamel's B, as the heir to Barbar.[1] Toateli had little to say about the episode, but Prikila, Tinamel's M and Tobung's classificatory B, was adamant that the infant be buried at Barbar. This constituted the inauguration of a Piknat cemetery at Barbar, and was expected by all to be the site of future burials of people descended from Prikila. In 1994, Sam, Prikila's uterine brother, died and was buried at Barbar. In the letter informing me of this fact, no details were given about any disagreement concerning this decision, but it is important to note that the burial site was thought to be the only detail worthy of mention in the letter.

Given the local understandings about the relationship between a cemetery and a descent unit described in the previous chapter, the burial of the infant away from Bangun and the initiation of a Piknat cemetery at Barbar was the tangible display of the genesis of a new matrilineage. The point of the case is that Toateli was not needed in the establishment of the new matrilineal group segment; Prikila and Tinamel—two women—were the individuals responsible for the establishment of the new lineage.

A second logical problem also obtains in the "need"/"strain" paradox: there is no reason to assume that an absence of authority in the group leads to indifference about the group. Think of it this way: What about women who are members of patrilineal descent groups; how do they feel about their brothers' "sexual and reproductive activities"? Schneider does not discuss the matter, and a telling omission it is, since it implies that the genesis of this strain is the existence of descent understandings rather than, say, psychodynamic processes. Schneider's apparent view is that women do not have interests in their brothers' reproductive capacities in patrilineal groups since, not normally retaining positions of authority, they are uninterested in the future of their descent group. If the logic of the argument is based on the idea that an absence of authority necessarily translates into apathy about the descent group's future (with its concomitant lack of interest in brothers' reproduction in the patrilineal case), then the argument is fallacious. There is no association I know of that requires that an absence of legitimate power or authority leads to indifference. If anything, it could be argued that the absence of authority should lead (logically) to an *increased* concern with redressing that absence.

The case of Tinamel's stillborn baby shows clearly that an absence of authority in the group does not necessarily lead to indifference about the group. Prikila was, in fact, opposed to her classificatory brother's wishes in the matter; she neither needed Tobung, nor was she indifferent to the affairs of her matrilineage. So, "need" does not necessarily describe a Sursurunga woman's relationship with her brother. As for "strain," yes; but not all strain is related to fears of incest and/or brother-sister avoidance, since Prikila and Tobung were in conflict over the issue of where to bury Tinamel's child and, later, Sam. Indeed, the "strain" between Prikila and Tobung seems to have less to do with matrilineal descent and more to do with a concern over *location*—as might be found in

---

1. Recall from the previous chapter that this alienation of residential parcels of land is only rarely contested by members of the land-losing lineage.

any unilineal descent group context. Residence patterns are related to segmentary fission within unilineal descent groups. For example, when an exogamous patrilineal descent group becomes quite large, intra-group marriages begin to occur because the two parties are *residentially separate* (A. Strathern 1969:41–57). In time, the group splits and each sub-unit becomes a separate exogamous descent group itself. Residential separation thus contributes to the fission of any unilineal group, as the case shows. In Chapter 8 I show that, at least in Melanesia, interment in matrilineal systems is functionally analogous to marriage in patrilineal systems. Segmentary fission and concomitant "strain," then, is a consequence of *uni*lineal descent plus physical separation, not a result of matrilineal descent.

Spouses and the "Matrilineal Puzzle"

Another putative implication of the "matrilineal puzzle" is that the sex role of the in-marrying affine is different. This means that in a matrilineal system, a man who marries forms the basis of a household in which his rights and obligations are not the exact duplicate of a woman who marries in a patrilineal system. In other words, a woman marrying into a household in which the (patrilineal) descent group overlaps with the domestic group finds herself cohabiting with a man who has legitimate authority over her and her children *qua* household head and *qua* patrilineage segment head. In the case of matriliny, a man is expected to have domestic authority, but not descent-group authority, over those with whom he lives.

Naturally enough, perhaps, we then have the assertion that matrilineal descent groups do not require the statuses of father and husband (Schneider 1961:14); matriliny is therefore seen to be incompatible with strong conjugal ties (Schneider 1961:16–19). This is another manifestation of the "matrilineal puzzle": the pull of the conjugal family on the one hand, and that of lineage on the other. Of course, both patriliny and matriliny include structurally-induced tensions involving consanguines and affines: marriage is at odds with lineages everywhere. My point here is merely that in matrilineal systems, this tension receives more attention because of its being attributed a greater role in sociostructural stresses. The assumption of conflict between household interests and descent group interests is tied to the—in my view, mistaken—assumption that commensurate matrilineal descent principles generate commensurate matrilineal descent group functions, as discussed in the previous chapter.

Schneider's view rests on the notion that a matrilineal segment needs only semen to maintain itself.[2] In other words, it is required only that a matrilineage's women become impregnated (marriage—a *husband*—is not "logically" necessary) and that the children are somehow succored and nurtured (specifically paternal care—a *father*—is also not "logically" necessary). But patrilineal groups

---

2. Indeed, *men* are not needed at all; *one* male would be adequate to provide the requisite reproductive services for entire lineages.

could also simply import their required biological services. It is true that the biological services (such as childbirth and nursing) that would need to be imported would be more burdensome in the patrilineal case, but there is no *logical* basis for this not to be possible. Of course, nowhere in the world do humans engage in such minimalist reproductive strategies. Part of the reason for this is that, given the sexual division of labor, most people in most societies find the status of "father" (irrespective of whether such a person is also the genitor) to be a convenient source of the adult male labor, energy, and care needed by the younger members of a household.

Schneider assumes that these aspects of a child's care and upbringing could be attended to by the child's mother's brother (1961:14–15). But this cannot be part of a logical analysis for two reasons. The first reason has to do with the coherence of the analysis: if there is "strain" between a woman and her brother, and if that "strain" is related to his interest in her reproductive activities, then it would be expected that a man would make every effort *to remain clear of*, rather than provide succor for, the indisputable evidence of his sister's sexual activity: her offspring.

The second reason is that a child's mother's brother will not be near at hand. Every residential pattern separates adult opposite-sex siblings, so children's most prominent adult male caretaker cannot be their mother's brother, since he will not normally be coresident with them.[3] In sum, the statuses of father and husband *are* logically necessary since mothers' brothers may wish to avoid their sisters' progeny and therefore be unavailable in caring for their sisters' progeny. Furthermore, residence patterns are such that men are not likely to be coresident with their adult sisters and are therefore unavailable to care for their sisters' progeny.

Even if it is conceded that "father" and "husband" are marginal statuses—that is, "marginal" vis-à-vis their counterparts in patrilineal systems—it does not necessarily follow that "the institutionalization of very strong, lasting, or intense solidarities between husband and wife is not compatible with the maintenance of matrilineal descent groups" (Schneider 1961:16). The argument here is grounded on the notion of "authority." For her part, a woman is expected to conform to the wishes of either her husband or her brother, and it is assumed that these will sometimes (often?) conflict: marital solidarity comes with a high cost to descent group solidarity. Likewise, a man may be uninterested in his conjugal (domestic) group—and by extension, his marriage—and attend to descent group concerns where his authority is less ambiguous and, presumably, less diluted.

Fathers and the "Matrilineal Puzzle"

Among the Sursurunga, the statuses of husband and father are often salient and seem to be logically required. The Sursurunga, like other New Irelanders

---

3. Recall that no particular residential pattern—including avunculocality—was assumed by Schneider.

(see, for example, Clay 1975, Jackson 1995, and Foster 1995), acknowledge the importance of paternal nurture in a number of ways.

Three Sursurunga words can be glossed as "father." The first is *kakang*. This term refers specifically to a person's father, step-father/mother's husband, or father's brother. *Kakang* is a referential term, and I never heard it other than when I was investigating kin terms and their usage. By far the more commonly-used term is the vocative form, *tata*, which I gloss as "dad." *"Tata"* is used for any man who would be referred to as *kakang*, as well as an honorific for any opposite-moiety big man—an aspect of the use of *tata* to which I shall return shortly.

The third type of "father" is *kámlang*—a term used both as a referential and a vocative form. *Kámlang* is the default term that men use for any male in the opposite moiety, and is to be used unless *tata* is appropriate. *Kámlang*, on the other hand, has little in the way of connotations of unilateral indebtedness. To the degree that such connotations exist, they are balanced by the fact that *kámlang* is a reciprocal term. [4] *Kámlang* is a relationship of equality, whereas a *tata* is anything but equal. (Women normally refer to opposite-moiety men—that is, men in the marriageable moiety—as *tau*. *Tau*, however, was never glossed as "father," but implies either an affinal connection—"a man who has married my *enate*"—or a nepotic link, such as a woman's [classificatory] brother's child.)

Fathers (both as *tata*s and as *kámlang*s) are prominent in Sursurunga thought and action. One's *tata* is the quintessential caregiver, and emphasized among the Sursurunga as demonstrated by the practice—quite reminiscent of the Trobriands (Mosko 1995:766–777)—of referring to an opposite-moiety big man as *tata*. This is an individual who performs *kebeptai*, or long-term (as in parental) care. The village as domestic unit writ large is obvious here. Somewhat less obvious is the acknowledged debt owed to anyone referred to as *tata*. This is a person who sacrifices for the good of a group that includes individuals of other lineages, whether it be his household or his village. To refer to a person as *tata* is a public acknowledgement of gratitude.

Jackson, in his Sursurunga ethnography, notes that there might even be said to be a Sursurunga "preoccup[ation] with the paternal [provisioning relationship]" (1995:96). He argues that the Sursurunga recognize food, land, money, semen, and pigs as but some of the manifestations of a father's contributions to his children's growth (1995:96). Jackson notes that although there is a balance in Sursurunga life between this provisioning and "maternal sustenance," "there is constant reference to the provisioning side of the division. . . . fathers providing for their children in the sense of 'looking after,' keeping in mind,' and 'giving to' their offspring" (Jackson 1995:97–98). In short, paternity is a relationship in which the direction of the flow of good things is from father to children. It is characterized by perpetual inequality and the presence of indebtedness, obliga-

---

4. More than one male informant also glossed *kámlang* as "male opposite-moiety friend."

tion, and accountability. Attention to these aspects of one's relationship with *tata* is prominent in specialized contexts such as Sursurunga ritual.

One example of ritualized attention to the debt owed one's father is the "harassing" of dancers in which rotted or leftover food, lime, and/or the buttocks of infants are wiped or slapped on the backs and shoulders of dancers by kin of the matrilineal group of a dancer's father. This practice is known as *bokur,* and was explained to me in the following way:

If you and I were brothers, our father's lineage will hit us [while we dance] with lime used for chewing betel nut. Then they owe us perhaps K2.00 as compensation. We are then required to return that amount with an additional payment of K0.20 to K1.00.
   Hitting us with food rubbish is the same thing. A father's thought is that a young man has grown up strong as the result of his and his clan's work. So now, here's some more food that they provide for us.

Another explication of *bokur* comes from Jackson (1995:105):

If one of my children were in a *singsing* [a dance], I would get my brother and whoever else of our clan was around. We would go inside the *singsing* and hit his (the child's) back with [lime] or with a banana. Or we might put the banana or [betelnut] in his mouth. We can also put the ass of one of our (children) on his shoulder or head. We do this because he is big now and can *singsing* and we have given him food. Our children are small and he is big now.

Recognition of debt to the father and his matrikin show up not just in ritual contexts such as *bokur*, but also in contexts such as everyday decisions and ordinary speech, thus showing the ubiquitous relevance of the notion of paternal provisioning among the Sursurunga. Consider the following case, which shows the importance of a father-husband (compared to a woman's brother) with regard to his importance in a matrilineal system.

In about November of 1991, Elizabeth, a widow with a young child, began to show her pregnancy. The overriding concern of those people with whom I spoke was not the identity of the genitor, but that a pater be named so that he could be economically responsible for her to go to Namatanai for weekly obstetric check-ups. Elizabeth's matrilineal kin were seemingly unconcerned about the matter.

To be sure, some of this apathy can be seen as a passive form of disapproval of Elizabeth's behavior, but matrilineal kin typically seem indifferent to a pregnancy of one of their own, married or not. If a father is not "logically required," then Elizabeth's male enates should have happily paid the money to ensure the success of her pregnancy and the health of their prospective lineage member; they did not. Rather, the importance of *paternal* care is so marked that it is expected to take place long before a child is even born.

The patrifilial relationship also appears in common speech. It is not uncommon to hear the phrase *"aratámán Topiknat"* ("the children of Topiknat"). The *ara-* prefix is rendered "those in the relationship," whereas *támán* can be glossed "one who has fathered children" (*tam* is the intransitive verb "to father"). The precise affective nature of this connection is not expressed in the term, but the social group is. The wife/mother may be a part of this group, or she may not. It is the case that, lexically, it is the *mother* who is out of the picture in this familiar expression.[5]

Another piece of the "matrilineal puzzle" is the assumption that husband and brother are to be viewed as equal contenders for a woman's compliance; that is, it is taken as axiomatic that in the relationship between conjugal and fraternal authority, one increases when the other decreases. Besides the problem of operationalizing what is meant by "strong, lasting, or intense solidarities" in a marriage (Schneider 1961:16), it simply has not been demonstrated that these solidarities or loyalties exist in a zero-sum relationship such that sibling devotion is inversely proportional to spousal devotion. "Husband" and "brother" are different types of relationships erotically, and also along other lines as well, so it seems infelicitous to conjoin them in this way. The same is, of course, true for men in their relationships with "wife" and "sister" as well.[6]

If siblings and spouses are not in a zero-sum relationship, then there is no need to expect the institutionalization of special limits on the "authority" of husbands over wives (Schneider 1961:19). There is no need to require that descent and domestic spheres of influence be delineated and complied with. Limiting the authority of husbands over wives would mean that it is important to know and keep straight just which male (a child's father or mother's brother, a woman's husband or her brother) has "authority" in which circumstances. But a husband who, for example, insists that his wife sell more produce in the market so that the children's school fees can be paid is aiding both *his* household and *her* descent group. Schneider's analysis fails to consider the possibility that men normally have nothing to lose by allowing their sisters' husbands to retain "authority" over their sisters. This is because, as noted above, it is father-husbands who are expected to provide much of the everyday nurture of another man's junior lineage mates, fathers who thereby enhance their children's lineage(s). It should therefore be expected that the father's important contributions are emphasized and

---

5. It is worthwhile to note here that when Sursurunga use Neo-Melanesian, they distinguish between *pamili* ("family") and *pikinini* ("children"). The former, when spoken by a man, excludes his children, and refers to enates—most commonly his lineage.

6. The Sursurunga language captures the difference quite nicely by a difference in noun classes, a difference discussed in detail in Chapter 6. The term for opposite-sex sibling, *kukung*, is an inalienable noun—a classification into which body parts and other intrinsic features of a person fall. The terms for spouses, *wák* and *pup*—wife and husband, respectively—are alienable nouns. These fall into a class of nouns that are characterized by their lack of inherence—possession is not innate. The difference between a spouse and a sibling represented in Sursurunga noun classification illustrates what is almost certainly true in other matrilineal systems as well: a brother is not like a husband, and an attempt to equate them as two components in a zero-sum scheme is contrived and facile.

acknowledged, rather than limited and denied, and this is precisely what we see in the *tata* relationship.

This failure to heed the differences between a woman's husband and her brother, and a man's wife and his sister, results in other mistaken notions. For example, matrilineal descent groups are said to have special problems in the organization of in-marrying affines with respect to each other (Schneider 1961:20). The point here is that since a man has authority in a sphere outside of his wife's natal domestic group (i.e., in his own descent group), he is not required to be entirely submissive to his WF. In addition, the domestic authority of the WF is ostensibly limited anyway, so his power is limited in any household-based relationship. In other words, Schneider asserts that a man has little control over his DH in a system of matrilineal descent.

This "special problem" (Schneider 1961:20–21) intrinsic to matrilineal descent recalls the earlier discussion of the circumscription of the authority of the father, in which a number of assumptions are made: (1) the existence of a zero-sum relationship between household and descent-group authority; (2) that women are subject to the *same* kind of authority by two conceptually *distinct* sorts of people—brothers and husbands; (3) that men retain the *same* kind of authority over two *different* types of women: wives and sisters; and (4) a man's domestic authority extends beyond wives and sisters and includes his married adult daughters. This is an unwarranted extension and unnecessarily complicates the discussion.[7]

But it is not only issues of authority that rely on a zero-sum assumption. A similar error occurs with the assertion that "the bonds which may develop between a child and his father tend to be in direct competition with the authority of the child's matrilineal descent group" (Schneider 1961:21). It seems, rather, that authority and positive affect—however these may be defined—cannot be assumed to exist in a zero-sum relationship.

Schneider's argument is based on the assumption of two kinds of "bonds" between children and fathers: bonds of authority, and bonds of affection. The bonds of authority are extensions of the authority that a husband has over his wife (cf. Schneider 1961:16–19). But the children are also ostensibly subject to the authority of their enatic elders, which excludes their father. As he did with a woman's relationships to her husband and brother, Schneider equates two different kind of links, placing authority and positive affect in a zero-sum relationship, so that the increase of one in a relationship necessarily means the decrease of the other.

The assumption that a child's relationship with her or his father is a function of the ebb and flow of "authority" and "positive affect" (and that these two aspects of a relationship are substitutes for each other) leads to the corollary that in

---

7. To be sure, fathers-in-law and sons-in-law are in conflict around the world. The point here, however, is that such conflict is not necessarily (i.e., logically) exacerbated as a result of matriliny.

matrilineal descent groups the "emotional tie" of a child to the father might translate into allegiance to and/or membership in the father's descent group (Schneider 1961:22–23). This deduction is spurious for two reasons: first, there is nothing to indicate that the kind of "emotional tie" that one has to a parent is commensurate with an emotional tie to collateral kin. Second, there is no reason to believe that an "emotional tie" necessarily becomes attachment (in the sense of recruitment) to another descent group. One Sursurunga man who tried to create a descent group link out of patrifilial affection for his children discovered that the "emotional tie" of a father to his children is quite different from the "tie" to a descent group. Here is the case:

Sian of Himaul village was a divorcé with two children, Sera and Saimon. The children's mother was from New Britain and had returned there to live. Sian is a member of the Tokbol matriclan and Kongkong matrimoiety, and his ex-wife was of the appropriate opposite ("small bird") moiety. Sera was nearing marriageable age, and would soon leave home, but Saimon, who was around 10 years old, and his father had several years left together.

Sian felt that given Saimon's mother's absence and the lack of any support from her or her enates, he needed to incorporate Saimon into a local descent group: his. His plan was to make a public announcement of his intentions, sponsor a feast for the entire village of Himaul, complete with several pigs, and thereby transfer Saimon's position from "son" to "brother." (I asked Sian why "brother," rather than "sister's son," and he replied that there was too much hierarchy entailed in a sister's son/mother's brother relationship, and that the nature of his relationship with his son was much more egalitarian and brotherlike.)

Upon hearing of Sian's plan, a number of Malai (the Sursurunga representative of the "small bird" regional matrimoiety) members in Himaul and nearby Nokon village strongly remonstrated with Sian, saying that he simply could not abrogate Saimon's moiety membership. Note that no one was going to directly benefit from Saimon's being retained as a Malai; it was simply thought that nothing could overcome the reality of Saimon's moiety membership, not even Sian's paternal affection. Sian eventually abandoned his scheme.

The case of Sian and Saimon shows that to Sursurunga sensibilities, paternal affection and matrilineal descent group membership are not inimical in that the former is seen to undermine the latter. Rather, the "emotional tie" between a father and his children is a qualitatively different phenomenon from the tie a child has to her or his descent group, as Sian discovered.

Segmentation and the "Matrilineal Puzzle"

Beyond the household, "the processes of fission and segmentation in matrilineal descent groups do not precisely replicate those of patrilineal descent groups" (Schneider 1961:24). The point here is that in a patrilineal descent system, unilineal descent groups are spawned when men diverge from other related men by living elsewhere and then marrying each other's daughters and sisters. In a matrilineal descent system, segmentation would be expected to take place when women diverge from other women. Furthermore, the likelihood of matri-lineal fission due to allegiances to different fathers is less than the likelihood of patrilineal fission due to different mothers since in the latter case, only one sib-ling is needed (Schneider 1961:25). In other words, segmentary fission is less likely in matrilineal units because at least two people—a brother-sister pair—are required.

But matriliny is not the mirror image of patriliny, and as I have noted, mar-riage does not have the same functions within each system. In patrilineal de-scent, segmentation and marriage are inseparable; in a system of matrilineal de-scent, segmentation and marriage are only tangentially related to each other, but segmentation and burial are inseparable. Consider the following case:

In May 1998, Tovina died. Born in Samo, Tovina had lived much of his adult life in Tekedan at Barbar *kuranu*. Himself a widower, Tovina had married the widow Prikila around 1970, caring for her children by her first husband and then, later, the four children that he and Prikila had.

Tovina was a member of the Sahwon clan, and after his death, a controversy over where to bury him emerged. To the people of Tekedan, to whom Tovina had been a leader, Tekedan, the location of Tovina's finest years as a *kabisit*—a big-man—was the natural place for burial. The Sahwons at Samo, a numerous group, disagreed and eventu-ally had their way, much to the consternation of the people at Tekedan.

The people of Tekedan were so unhappy about this decision that they took the un-heard of step of boycotting Tovina's funeral at Samo. A week after the funeral, three trucks carried the people of Tekedan to Samo to pay their respects at the site, and they were given a small meal by Tovina's Sahwon enates.

To the Sahwons of Samo village, the prestige of Tovina in their cemetery and the retention of the integrity of their group were the same thing. To have allowed Tovina to be buried at a Sahwon cemetery at Tekedan would have cre-ated an offshoot lineage, and more Sahwons from Samo might be buried in places other than Samo. Temporarily, at least, the Sahwons of Samo have re-tained the unity of their matriclan.

If men control wealth and power, then a matrilineage's men would be re-quired to support any split; that is, a woman *and* her brother—as wealth and power broker in the matrilineage—both need to be involved in the fission proc-ess. But the case of Tovina's burial had little to do with men and women coop-erating; the fact of the matter is that the Sahwons of Tekedan are few (and gener-ally elderly), whereas those at Samo are many. Schneider's deduction is based on the character of male authority. I have already suggested that his use of "authority" involves some slippage, and this feature illuminates the difficulty. Whatever is meant by "authority," Schneider assumed that the process of seg-mentary fission is impossible without it, and herein lies the rub. If, as Schneider said, male (that is, a mother's brother's) authority is a necessary condition for segmentary fission, then it follows that the absence of such authority means the absence of segmentary fission: that is, the lack of a mother's brother to lead a segment results in the lack of segmentation. But in the case of the two burials at

Barbar, segmentation does happen in the absence of male lineage leadership; and in the case of Tovina's interment at Samo village, segmentation is prevented not by an absence of males, but sheer numbers.

Schneider claims that a mother's brother's descent-group authority and a father's household authority keep each other in check; the absence of the mother's brother's political control allows the dominance of the father's household authority (1961:19). This would mean that a household in which a father has dominant authority is *less* likely to be the stem of a new descent group segment. Note, however, that the type of descent-group rupture initiated by an elder enate (segmentation) and by a father ("disruption" [1961:19] of the system) are different.

A "weak" enate does not necessarily entail a "strong" father, and a "strong" father does not necessarily entail erosion of the matrilineal segment. In other words, contrary to what Schneider had argued earlier in his essay (1961:14ff.), the logical entailment of what he says about segmentary fission (1961:24ff.) is that father/husband authority contributes to, rather than erodes, the integrity of the matrilineal segment, since the presence of a father/husband offers children the best chance for complete socialization. It is Sursurunga fathers who, for example, cite matrilineal dogma as the basis for brother-sister avoidance and respect for enatic elders.

Schneider's interest in matriliny, to recapitulate, is limited to understanding a system's "logic"; how the meanings of its symbols are interconnected. His theoretical orientation views "father" as a symbol, and limits the unit of inquiry to the local meanings/understandings that a community attributes to that symbol, and how those meanings/understandings are interwoven with other meanings/understandings about mothers, mother's brothers, children, and so on. His point is that although groups *may* have the symbol "father," that symbol is not essential to a set of symbols that can be called matrilineal descent. In other words, "father" and all that it connotes is detachable from a complex of symbols known as matriliny without doing any damage to the integrity of the complex.

SUMMARY

This chapter has provided an alternative general theoretical statement regarding matrilineal descent groups that relies on the kinds of theoretical constructs eschewed by The New Kinship. In my view, an approach to kinship and descent that ignores the realities of filiation in favor of abstracted ideational systems adds little to the study of anthropology in general and kinship in particular. For reasons made clear in this chapter, I cannot agree with Schneider that "biological relatedness, *used as an analytic category in terms of which kinship systems may be compared and analyzed,* has been as much of an impediment as a useful tool in understanding kinship in general" (Schneider 1961:2; f.n.2; emphasis in original).

Part of Schneider's antipathy to "old" kinship studies is that "over 100 years later we still do not know how these ideas [about kinship terminologies] relate to conduct" (1983:402). Schneider is wrong: there is a nonrandom, systematic relationship between terms and conduct, and between anthropological constructs and local cultural systems, as I have shown here and will discuss in the final chapter. I agree with Shimizu that Schneider's works, "in undermining leading theoretical frameworks of kinship studies, have unduly denied the pertinence of kinship itself for anthropological theories of social phenomena" (1992:377). To be sure, the analytic constructs that accompany us affect our analyses, but they also contribute to them. The Sursurunga data presented here within the outline of Schneider's essay reveal much more about how people within a matrilineal descent context operate on a day-to-day, on-the-ground basis. On the other hand, it seems to me that the symbolic study of kinship tells us more about the intellectual and rhetorical prowess to be found among anthropologists than the ways in which real people behave in and conceptualize their social worlds.

In the past two chapters, I have addressed the state of anthropological thinking about matrilineal descent, showing that (1) matriliny should not be seen as a monofunctional institution, and that (2) understandings about the sociology of matriliny are in need of adjustment. The stage is now set for the focal argument of the book, namely, that mortuary feasting among the Sursurunga is the result of a number of different kinds of understandings, and that matriliny itself is a result of the mortuary feasting complex. In the following chapters, I describe the Sursurunga mortuary feasting complex (Chapter 5), its antecedents (Chapter 6), and its consequents (Chapter 7).

Men from Himaul Village arrive at Tekedan for a feast.

A pig and taro loaded to be taken to a feast.

Siantokbol with the author's son.

Puspalai with husband Patrik, an immigrant from the Sepik Region.

Eriel and Kepui, her HZS, bring firewood to Tekedan.

Elsi and her firstborn.

Toateli (r) and his ZS Alex (l) along with Himson (m).

Vini (foreground) and other women with the author's daughter.

Topiknat readies food packets at a small feast.

Saku readies a bark covering for a food packet.

Suffocating a pig prior to a *ngin i pol* feast.

Chapter 5

Sursurunga Mortuary Feasting

Since the 1930s, anthropologists have written about mortuary feasting as a principal feature of social life on New Ireland (Powdermaker [1931], Groves [1933], and Bell [1934, 1937]). More recently, Clay (1975), Wagner (1986), Jackson (1995), and Eves (1996) have argued that key cultural symbols are instantiated in mortuary feasting on central and southern New Ireland, and Foster (1990a, 1995) showed that mortuary feasting on the island of Tanga reconstitutes the clan as a fully functioning unit in the aftermath of the death of one of its members. What Foster says about mortuary ritual on Tanga is also true for the Sursurunga: "Through the performance of mortuary rites, a lineage periodically "changes its skin." By sponsoring a sequence of mortuary feasts . . . lineages acquire a kind of continuity. . . . Feast makers define themselves as permanent collective individuals (or matrilineages) and effective agents of their own regeneration" (1995:143).

I have already noted my preference for "matrilineage" over "collective individual" in Chapter 1. Terminology aside, however, this is an accurate portrait of Sursurunga mortuary feasting: such events summon forth the prominence of the matrilineage in a display of its ability to be like other matrilineages in its viability and vitality.

As noted in Chapter 2, the ethnographic accounts of New Ireland and East New Britain societies show that mortuary ritual is an important social institution in the region. In this chapter, I describe the Sursurunga mortuary feasting complex and other memorial events. Recall that Sursurunga mortuary feasting will be shown to be a consequent of a number of values and social relations in Sursurunga society; this will take place in the following chapter. Then, in the penultimate chapter, mortuary feasting will be shown to activate and make salient matrilineal descent among the Sursurunga.

THE SEQUENCE OF MORTUARY FEASTS

As I have written elsewhere (Bolyanatz 1994a), "mortuary feast" refers to any one of the feasts within the sequence described below; "funeral feast" designates that particular feast held at the time of the burial of a corpse. The following description of the sequence of mortuary feasts is a composite. The length of an entire sequence is such that I was not able to witness an entire cycle of feasting. I have, however, participated in more than 20 mortuary feasts held in honor of a dozen individuals, and it is these feasts, along with statements from informants, and Jackson (1995), that provide the substance for this description. Indeed, Jackson's caveat is worth repeating here:

It is completely arbitrary . . . to write a "schematic" order of feasting. Indeed, there is "order," but it does not necessarily follow from any linear understanding of "stages," one after another. People can tell you an order, start to finish, if you are inclined to ask, but it is not how they conceive of the feast necessarily. Should someone talk of a feasting order they recreate it in their minds, working the feast from inception to completion. . . . That is, they conceive of acting it, participating in it, moving through it. One definitely senses the movement of the feast. Going to a feast for me, and arguably for the native participants as well, was exactly this image—start to finish unconsciously, without pause, then . . . [ellipsis in original] suddenly over. There is no definitive beginning point, nor ending. The pigs are delivered the morning of the feast, or the night before; the guests begin arriving early in the morning; the pigs are displayed, killed, cooked, everyone will eat and then slowly drift away (1995:183–184).

I, too, felt that my questions about mortuary feasting caused people to articulate an order and an orderliness that was the result more of my question than any "feasting template" that may have been in their minds. It was like asking questions about grammar: hearing rules articulated is experienced as unfamiliar by both a fluent speaker and an uninformed investigator, even though the rules are in fact unfamiliar to only one of them. Nevertheless, as Jackson notes, people *can* tell you about a progression of events within the context of a feast, and what follows is a synopsis of those events.

As I discuss mortuary ritual, the hypothetical deceased for much of the following description is an older man. I use an elderly male as the default case because, first, most of the mortuary feasts that I have attended were for older men, and second, Sursurunga informants (men and women) themselves treat the affairs of adult males as paradigmatic in Sursurunga society, with differences that arise in the cases of children or women mentioned as necessary.

Death is as unwelcome on New Ireland as it is anywhere else. Nevertheless, people die, and those who survive are left to contend with the physiological, psychological, and social aftermath. Bodies must be buried, grief dealt with, and relationships adjusted. Among the Sursurunga at Tekedan—population: about 120—death is not infrequent. In the six years between 1992 and 1998, five people died: four men (three elderly and one middle-aged) and one girl. Like the deaths that preceded them, each of these deaths initiated a series of events that begin with a rite known as *tataun*, an intransitive verb meaning simply "to bury."

Tataun

At Tekedan, a shell casing left over from World War II hangs from a tree in roughly the center of the village. As a bell or gong, it summons people to meetings of various sorts when it is struck repeatedly. When, however, three slow strikes are made, it means that someone has died. Normally, people know the identity of the deceased, since news about a person who is quite ill will be known up and down the coast. Even if the deceased is not from Tekedan, the bell will be rung as soon as the news of the death reaches the village.

Funeral arrangements are made quickly, often to take place on the following day. If a person dies late in the day, then the funeral is held two days later, with the intervening day used to spread the news and make preparations. Little or no effort is made to accommodate people's schedules: everything else gives way to a *tataun*.

On the day of the funeral, the widow and at least her oldest child (male or female) by the deceased are obligated to engage in all aspects of the funeral rituals. These two are known as *diar mokos*, meaning "those two who are widowed," referring to a widow and her firstborn. *Diar mokos* often becomes *di mokos*—"all those who are widowed"—because the lineage of the deceased will often invite all of the children, not just the firstborn, to participate in the formal aspects of mourning. This invitation is rarely spurned, out of respect for one's father, if nothing else. There are some noteworthy aspects of the expression *di* or *diar mokos*.

One is that *di* or *diar mokos* represents the widow and "orphan(s)" (*suisui*), at the very least, the widow's firstborn. The lexically marked emphasis is upon the widow and the (loss of) the conjugal bond. Another detail to notice is that the sex of the *suisui* is irrelevant; the firstborn represents all of the children of the deceased, an emphasis on the filial link. The combined emphases upon the conjugal and filial relationships show that conjugal and patrifilial relationships are quite important among the Sursurunga, a theme to which I alluded several times in the previous chapter.[1]

Another aspect of *di* or *diar mokos* to heed is the presence of the stem *mok-,* which also appears in the following words:

mokoi	to taboo something
mokmok	to fast in mourning
mokos	a widow(er)
mokson	a married couple
moksu	an old, nonproducing garden
mokdon	ancient ancestors

---

1. This emphasis upon the nuclear family among the Sursurunga in the *diar mokos* expression resonates with Spiro's reanalysis of Malinowski's explanation of the Oedipus complex in the Trobriands (1982). Spiro argues that the psychodynamics of the father-mother-son triad are not fundamentally altered by socio-structural variables such as matrilineal descent groups and ideology, and the Sursurunga focus on nuclear family relationships is consistent with this notion.

The Sursurunga language has many homonyms, and one must be careful not to make too much of them. Nevertheless, two semantic domains suggest themselves quite readily: one consisting of *mokdon* and *moksu*, and another with *mokoi, mokmok, mokos,* and *mokson.* The latter cluster may indicate that marriage and mourning are not seen, at some level at least, as disparate, unrelated events but as an initial aspect and a final aspect, respectively, of the same phenomenon: adult life itself.

The (at least) two *mokos* engage in formal mourning comportment: they don dark garb, dye their hair dark, and put on a *sawat,* or mourning necklace. Normally, only *diar mokos* are required to have their faces darkened, but others may if members of the deceased's lineage have no objections. The range of people who wear the *sawat,* however, extends to individuals who had called the deceased by the term "*tata,*" ("dad"), and other close, opposite-moiety kinsmen.

The *sawat*, which is the longest-lasting indicator of one's matrilineally informed social status, is made of braided strips of black cloth and is said to symbolize the viscera of the deceased father—the point being that because he provided for those who called him "*tata,*" his own belly went empty (Jackson 1995:208–209). The wearing of the *sawat* is a reminder to an outside observer that *sawat*-wearing, like any social status, may not necessarily be salient for a person at any given moment. A beholder of a *sawat*-wearer will necessarily know the person is in the category "mourner," but the wearer may not be experiencing bereavement at that moment. Attributing a *sawat*-wearer's behavior to mourning would be a mistake if the wearing of the *sawat* were the only datum at one's disposal. Similarly, since the wearing of a *sawat* is importantly informed by matrilineal group membership—an enate of the deceased cannot wear a *sawat*—it would be an error to assume that matrilineal group membership is necessarily salient in explaining the behavior of a social actor. In this regard, a *sawat* is perhaps the best mirror of matrilineal descent among the Sursurunga: especially meaningful and salient in the context of mortuary ritual, it is virtually forgotten in the everyday exigencies of routine life.

An enate of the deceased serves as the feast sponsor, or *kálámul a tataun* ("the man who buries"). *Di mokos* each present a pig to him. These pigs are designated as *bingbingpul,*[2] the term referring specifically to those pigs provided by *di mokos* in the event of a death. The live *bingbingpul* pigs are laid at the entrance of the *bang* of the deceased, at which point they become the property of the lineage of the deceased. *Bingbingpul* pigs are explicit compensation to the matrilineal descent group of the deceased for the energies and resources expended as he nurtured and raised his children[3]—children who are members of someone else's descent group.

---

2. The Sursurunga word *bingi* means "to kill something." I asked a number of people whether *bingbingpul* referred to killing something, but only two suggested that it referred to the killing of pigs. For the moment, I find these two people's interpretation to be counterintuitive, since (1) pigs are killed at other feasts and not designated as *bingbingpul*, and (2) *pul* is Sursurunga for bêche-de-mer or trepang.

3. Recall from the last chapter that among the matrilineal Sursurunga, a man's "family" (*pamili* in Neo-Melanesian and *kabinun* in Sursurunga) is different from his

This compensatory aspect of the *bingbingpul* prestation is to *"para talsai"* or to "speak (in order to) clarify" on behalf of *di mokos*. In other words, the pigs provided as *bingbingpul* represent an awareness of the debt owed to one's *tata* and to the lineage that contributed one's *tata*.[4] A Tekedan man offered this description of the character of *bingbingpul* pigs and other prestations:

They [i.e., the widow and her firstborn] provide money in addition [to the *bingbingpul* pig]: two kina for paying back the head of the widow, and two kina for paying back the head of the child. So, the child gets his money and with one shilling [i.e., a 10- or 20-toea piece], at a time he counts all the things that his father has done, because *tata* brings sugarcane, because *tata* brought water for my bath, because *tata* brought food from the bush for me to eat, because *tata* climbed for green coconuts which I ate, because *tata* planted bananas that I ate, for taro, yams, everything like that. The child hits them all, and comes with money equal to 10 kina with which to buy the mouth [that is, what the mouth has ingested].[5]

As the morning proceeds, people from neighboring villages gather at or near the *bang* of the deceased and the sponsor of the *tataun*. *Di mokos* typically sit inside the *bang,* surrounding the corpse. The stench of the corpse can become nearly intolerable inside the crowded *bang,* so some mourners bring aerosol air fresheners and fragrances which are used generously on the bedsheet-wrapped corpse. Tears flow occasionally, often stimulated by the wailing of women who arrive on foot together, usually as village groups. Even if they ride from their village, protocol requires that women walk the last few hundred yards, connoting intentionality and effort on their parts. These women will, as they approach the *bang*, commence conventional mourning formalities by forming a queue. Then, with head back and the back of a hand on the forehead, and eyes mostly closed, they enter the *bang* single file and wail, keen, and weep around the corpse, *di mokos,* and any other mourners who happen to be in the *bang* at the time. Each woman customarily wails for about two to three minutes, producing a generally high-pitched nasal howl, sometimes punctuated by short streams of speech referring to the deceased as kin rather than by name, as in, "Oooooo *tataaaaa*," or "Oooooo *kokoooo*." Sometimes women will remain in the *bang* for quite a while, comforting and weeping with *di mokos*; most of the time, however, they exit the *bang* after wailing, find a group of friends or kin, and spend the remainder of the funeral with them. Genuine or feigned grief is not the issue here; a woman either wails or fails to wail, and those who do have

---

"children" (*pikinini* in Neo-Melanesian and *rang natun* in Sursurunga). This differs from patrilineal usage, in which a man's family and his children are overlapping groups.

4. There is more to *bingbingpul* than the acknowledgment of debt; there is also the avoiding of unfavorable consequences: in the words of one person, *"bingbingpul* is given so that there will not be talk [i.e., gossip] by others, and there will be no shame."

5. I am grateful to Sharon Hutchisson for her help in translating this and other narratives.

their names recorded by an enate of the deceased.[6] These women will be compensated at the subsequent *ngin i pol* feast.

As the women wail, men chat, smoke, and chew betel nut. By late morning, most of the women who have come to wail have finished. By midday, the number of mourners swells and perhaps a few hundred people assemble in the general vicinity of the *bang*/cemetery—recall that *bangs* and cemeteries are adjacent to each other—when it is time to bury the corpse. The Sursurunga verb "to die" is *mat*; the term for "cemetery" is *matmat*, which could be glossed both as the "burial place" and "dying place."

The *kálámul a tataun* oversees the burial. The labor of interment—transferring the body into the casket, digging the grave, the burial itself, and backfilling the grave—is the work of men of the moiety opposite that of the deceased. There is little formality or decorum to this process: anyone of the appropriate moiety between the ages of about 13 and 50 who happens to be nearby is conscripted.

Let us return now to the activities of the *kálámul a tataun*. The pigs and other prestations such as money—known as *lulsit*—that had been presented to him are kept on behalf of his lineage. Sometime in midmorning, after most mourners have arrived, but before it gets to be too late—that is, too late to kill, butcher, cook, and eat the pigs and still make sure that everyone gets home before dark—the *kálámul a tataun* begins the process of making ready the feast. As sponsor of the feast, he is responsible for designating an enate to be in charge of cooking each of the pigs. Those so charged are pleased to do so, for this entitles them to the viscera of the pig.[7] The pigs are then killed by suffocation, after which the hair is burned off and they are gutted, have their legs trussed up toward the body, and are placed on the hot rocks of an earth oven.

A few hours pass as the pigs and other victuals cook. Most people spend this period visiting and socializing, although *di mokos* and others most profoundly touched by the death do little in the way of mingling. By midafternoon, the pigs and other foodstuffs are ready to be eaten. Jackson provides a lucid description of the moment the cooked pork is lifted from the earth oven and placed on palm fronds in front of the *bang*:

it is time for *tahtah an bor*, "cutting the pigs." The host will approach someone renowned for their pig carving abilities (usually, but not always, opposite moiety) handing them a knife and a small coin. It is considered an honor to be singled out for the cutting. This person, however, is usually only responsible for the major pig to be eaten. Others

---

6. In the past, according to older people, before literacy, pencils, and paper, wailing women were kept track of by assigning members of the lineage of the deceased to be responsible for various villages. As the women from a particular village came to wail, the person (usually a man), would keep count by bending coconut fronds. Later, the number of women who wailed from that particular place would be easily recalled and compensation for their wailing made easier.

7. After consuming the meat from the pig's head, the jawbone of the pig will be returned to the men's house of the deceased and hung up in that men's house as an index of the prestige of deceased lineage members, and of the lineage itself.

will lend a hand in carving any remaining pigs meant for distribution, attacking each pig with machete, knife, axe, or whatever else is handy. The initial cuts are always the same; beginning just behind each ear, a long lateral cut down each side ending just at the hind quarter. Starting again at the ears, cut perpendicular to the long cuts are made across the back. The truly master carvers are able by look and feel to cut between each vertebrate, the large separate chunks lifted up to be distributed. While the cutter is working, if he knows any magic he will employ it at this point. The magic is said to lessen the appetite of the feasters, or make the provision too large to consume completely, so that there will be plenty of pork left over for distribution and make the host clan appear "big" in their ability to provision. (Jackson 1995:196)

In this way the makings of the entire feast are exhibited for all to see. After this has been done, the serving of the food begins. This point is the consummation of the investment of time, energy, and resources of those putting on the feast; the community witnesses—and, significantly, admires—the obvious competence of the sponsors, even at this time of distress.

As the pork is being cut up and divided, the servers begin distributing the nonpork food cooked by the women in the *pal* ([women's] cooking area). In funeral feasts, this will often include rice as well as tubers. Traditionally, of course, rice was not a part of this feast, but since normally funeral feasts can come up at unexpected times and on short notice, rice has become a favorite means of providing large amounts of food that does not require several days of preparatory work in the garden, seashore, or village. By the time rice, tubers, and sprigs of betel nut have been distributed by the servers—a group made up of members of the "host" moiety, that of the sponsoring lineage—upon the plates (several breadfruit leaves placed on the ground), the pork begins arriving. Approximately three to four pounds of pork is placed upon each plate in two or three chunks. When all of the food has been distributed, a local United Church leader often offers a short prayer of thanksgiving, after which the food is eaten.

Generally there is not much conversation during the consumption of food. I never heard an extended conversation during eating at any one of the 25 or so feasts (of all sorts) that I attended. Eating does not take long, and after about 15-20 minutes, there is very little left on the plates. There is a certain amount of gaiety, including, for example, good-natured ribbing of someone for taking too much—or too little—food, or for cutting the pork into pieces that are too small. Leftovers are bundled up in breadfruit leaves and placed into personal baskets (known as *rat*) to be taken home. The sprigs of betel nut are broken up and distributed to those who ate, and betel chewing and smoking begins almost immediately.

At this point, the *tataun* is formally over. Most visitors to the village will remain for an hour or two before returning to their homes, although a few will remain for days. The next day or two will see "echoes" of the *tataun*, in which those unable to be present for the actual burial will come wail at the *matmat*, provide *lulsit* or perhaps *bingbingpul*, and visit with the bereaved, depending on sex and moiety membership. For enates of the deceased, these few days entail a lot of time around the *bang* providing hospitality for well-wishers, grieving, and discussing the timing of the next feast, known as *ngin i pol*.

Ngin i pol

Older informants say that the *ngin i pol*—which means "drinking a (green) coconut"—feast should normally, and used to, take place within a week or two of the *tataun*. These days the timing is quite flexible, however, and the feast can be delayed for any number of reasons, such as a dearth of food in the gardens, other responsibilities such as church feasts that cannot be rescheduled, or waiting for school holidays to begin so that students will have returned home. The stated preference is, however, to perform the *ngin i pol* feast sooner rather than later. The reality is that sometimes years pass between a *tataun* and a *ngin i pol* on a person's behalf.

Although the literal gloss of *ngin i pol* is "drinking a coconut," the connotation is, as one man said, "time to eat pork." It is at this feast, more than at any other mortuary feast, that the most pigs are killed—a number said to be up to 40 for a renowned big-man (although I never saw more than 20). Such a number of pigs is practically impossible for one person to provide. The result is that the acquisition of pigs on the part of the feast sponsor (the same person who sponsored the funeral feast) can be very complex. I describe the strategies for acquiring pigs in the following chapter. All that is necessary here is to point out that the ability to organize and coordinate a feast of any magnitude is an index as well as a determinant of leadership.

Jackson describes the treatment of the pigs:

On the day of the feast the pigs will begin arriving early in the morning, unless they have come from a distance, in which case they will most likely have arrived the night before to "sleep in the man's house." Traditionally they would have been carried live on a wooden platform called a *soa*. Now they simply arrive by truck, always with a coterie of youth on the back to assist in holding the trussed up pig still by sitting on it.

When all the pigs have arrived, but not necessarily all the guests, the pigs will be laid out in the *pelbut*, the courtyard, or more specifically in the *kamiansit*, the feasting area, for viewing. (Jackson 1995:187–188)

The bound pigs lie on their sides, "generally the largest pig first followed by the next largest, etc. with their heads facing the door of the men's house" (Jackson 1995:188). The sponsor of the feast then conducts the observance known as *suka bor* ("stepping on the pig[s]"), in which the sponsor "places a foot on each live pig in line and calls out a name, whether or the purchaser or the supplier, depending apparently on the discretion of the host" (Jackson 1995:189). Either way, the names called out are those of the men (and, less often, women) responsible for the presence of the pig at the feast. Also at this time, the pigs' destination is announced: some will go to feed the men at the *bang*, some to the women at the *pal*, some to those who gave *bingbingpul*, and some to be cut up and placed in baskets to be carried off by those women who wailed at the burial and whose names were recorded.

If a person has provided a pig for the feast, she or he is designated by the sponsor as the person responsible for cooking the pig in the earth oven. Women who provide pigs designate this responsibility to male enates. Having been designated by the sponsor of the feast as the provider of a pig, the person retains rights as the pig's *de jure* owner. He, or, much less often, she, will in practice, surrender large chunks of pork to the feast sponsor to be used for the feast. As in the funeral feast, the person responsible for cooking the pig receives the per-quisites of the liver and other tasty bits of the viscera.

One important function of the *ngin i pol* feast is to compensate those men of the opposite moiety of the deceased for their work when handling the corpse, digging the grave, and burying the corpse at the *tataun*. In addition, women (of either moiety) who came to wail are compensated, as are those who helped bring food or cook. Now, at the *ngin i pol*, and contrary to the burial, these men of the opposite moiety are "guests," and protocol requires that they abstain from mak-ing an effort to help with the work of the feast in any way (although I have seen it happen).

After the food has been cooked and assembled for exhibition, the sponsor of the feast recapitulates the *suka bor* procedure. Standing over what were once live pigs, but are now cooked pork, the sponsor takes a tuber, usually either a yam or sweet potato, and goes along the row of pigs laid out at the *bang*, striking each one in the forehead with the tuber, and calling the name of the deceased. One alternative to this is tweaking the ear or ears of each pig. Either (but never both) of these procedures is done to formally mark the cooked pigs as pork to be eaten in honor of a dead enate and whose mandibles are destined to hang in the rafters of the *bang*.

Also at this time, the purchases of the pigs are acknowledged and com-pleted. Individuals who provided pigs are recognized with a green coconut and a sprig of betel nut, a part of the feast known as *ratis bu*[8] ("betel nut for the bas-ket"). During this phase,

> a feast worker will approach the front line of pigs, pick up a branch of betel nut and a shelled coconut and take it to a person who has provided a pig for the present feast and who will later receive payment. . . . It is always persons who are not members of the hosting clan that are publicly paid. Any pig provided from within the hosting clan is considered clan business and is not handled in public. After each person has been *radis bu*, payments begin. The amount will have been agreed upon by those involved prior to the delivery of the pig. The feast worker will approach the person who has just been marked, and will count out the payment one bill at a time, or one strand of *reu* (shell money) at a time, so that all assembled guests can count for themselves. The strands of shell money, given before the cash, are held up in the air one at a time so everyone can see the length (an important characteristic). This is perhaps the quietest moment in the entire feast, as everyone is concerned with who gets paid what for which pig. (Jackson 1995:194–195)

The actual consumption of the food at the *ngin i pol* feast varies little from the funeral feast. The two most notable differences are that rice is not normally a part of the *ngin i pol* feast, while, on the other hand, green coconuts are. Be-fore eating commences, the sponsor of the feast—with some solemnity—breaks open a green coconut against a house post, tree, or stone and tosses the shattered

---

8. Jackson (1995) renders this expression as *radis bu*.

coconut into or toward the cemetery where the body of the deceased is buried. The purpose of this gesture is, in the words of one man, to tell the deceased, "We are now eating pork on [i.e., as a result of/in the name of] you." (On several occasions, I asked the men who performed this coconut-shattering rite about its meaning. No one ever articulated anything more than the that's-the-way-we've-always-done-it response so frequently—and frustratingly—encountered by anthropologists.)

After the typically 20–30 minutes of chewing betel nut and talking that follows the consumption of the food, two important aspects of the *ngin i pol* feast take place. I will describe the two in sequence, although in fact they often occur, at least in part, simultaneously.

As noted above, not all of the pigs for the feast were to be eaten that day. Those that were kept aside are now carved up by the sponsor of the feast or someone designated by him. Overseeing this process are the older women of the lineage of the deceased, who are responsible for putting pieces of pork of perhaps four or five pounds each and tubers into baskets that had been prepared previously and laid out for this occasion. When the baskets have all been filled, the women, after consulting the list of wailers that was made on the day of the funeral, hand out the food baskets to each of the women who came and wailed. Informants say that a woman who did not wail at the funeral will not receive a basket, even if she is closely related to the deceased (although others are free to share the contents of their baskets with her). The only exceptions to this standard are when women are kept from attending the funeral because of illness or the one-month post-parturition period of staying indoors. But even in these cases, to receive a basket a woman will be expected to have wailed in front of a close kinsman of the deceased who perhaps lives in her village or whom she happened to see on the road.

Either after or during the distribution of baskets to the women who wailed at the *tataun*, the large chunks of pork that were not eaten are tied with rope vines and laid out in front of the *bang*. The men of the sponsor's lineage convene and discuss the distribution of the remaining pork. During this time, old debts of pork are reciprocated, and new pork debts are initiated. These transactions are known as *kokos* and *utngin sál*, respectively, and informants assure me that these transactions of pork are totally distinct from the transactions by the same names involving the acquisition of live pigs described in Chapter 6. After the discussion, during which extant debts are considered, along with who has been particularly helpful in, say, the recent construction of a men's house or garden fence, the chunks of pork are ready to be distributed. The prestige of the recipient is considered, and is typically commensurate with the cut of meat given: the butt portion is considered to be the crème de la crème, followed by back and ribs, hind legs, forelegs, and head.

When the time for the distribution has come, each piece of pork is handled in the following way: A member of the sponsor's lineage shouts out, "Hua!" This is immediately followed by the sponsor calling out the name and kin term of the recipient, as well as what sort of transaction—either *kokos* or *utngin sál*— is taking place. These statements take the form, for example, "*Kámlang Toma-*

lar; kokos!" ("My father Tomalar; payback!") There is no prescribed syntactic order in these presentations. One could just as easily say, *"Utngin sál si Tokon, sinat!"* ("A new road for Tokon, my affine!") It is important to note that in the course of these prestations, matrilineal group membership is highlighted. Given that the moiety membership of the man making the prestations is known—and it cannot fail to be known with the use of a kin term—then the prestations also mark the moiety of the pork recipient. Although it is not impossible for pork to be presented without involving a reference to matrilineal descent, I never saw it occur. Whatever else might be said, the prestation of post-*ngin i pol* pork prestations draws public attention, through the use of kin terms, to matrilineal descent ideology.

These chunks of anywhere from three to 20 pounds of pork are held up by the sponsor as he makes his proclamations. He then gives the meat to one of his younger enates, who walks over and hands the pork to the recipient. When this is finished, the feast is over and the attendees break up and head for home, usually quite quickly.

As with all feasts, the jawbones of all pigs are returned to the *bang* of the feast sponsor, where they are hung up on rafters as a memorial to departed enates.

Táptápir and *Suka Bim*

In some ways, the *ngin i pol* feast culminates the series of mortuary feasts. *Táptápir* and *suka bim* are two other feasts that informants mentioned in interviews, but these seem to be quite different from *tataun* and *ngin i pol*. *Táptápir* is becoming something of an endangered species, and *suka bim* appears to be extinct. I will mention these two feasts, but they should be understood to constitute a distinctly different component of the mortuary feasting complex among the Sursurunga in and around Tekedan village.

Táptápir is a transitive verb meaning "to make a feast for." Meanings for *táptápir* feast given by informants include, "final act," "last feast," "final thinking of the deceased," and "the deceased has already turned into soil." This feast is the third in the sequence of mortuary feasts and is characterized by the eating of bananas. I attended fewer *táptápir* feasts than *ngin i pol* feasts and funerals. As with the *ngin i pol* feast, the readiness of food in the gardens, and the availability of pigs as evaluated by the feast sponsor (normally the same man who sponsored the *tataun* and *ngin i pol* feasts) will determine when the time is right to hold a *táptápir* feast. The timing of this feast is even more flexible than for the *ngin i pol* feast, and although it is supposed to occur within a few months of the *ngin i pol* feast, a *táptápir* feast may not occur for years, if—as I indicated, it occurs at all. Informants say that this is not good, and that only ne'er-do-wells will wait that long, but in fact, all four *táptápir* feasts that I attended took place years after the *ngin i pol*, and one person told me that a *táptápir* feast was not a part of the feasting sequence, so the moral force of prescriptions about *táptápir* feasts is quite weak. The details of the *táptápir* feast are like those of the first two feasts in the mortuary sequence: the sponsor names individuals who will be responsible for cooking the pigs, and, as in the case of the *tataun,* the small number of pigs means that usually there will not be enough leftover pork for post-feast prestations of pork.

Older informants tell of a now-defunct feast that normally transpired a few years after the *táptápir* feast, the *suka bim,* or "step on the ground." The "ground" in this case is what the corpse by this time has decomposed into, and "stepping on" suggests a lack of regard for or a sense of completion of grieving with regard to that ground. Descriptions of the *suka bim* feast vary, but by all accounts, it was a large-scale pork feasting extravaganza.

When a Woman Dies

There is no appreciable difference between men and women when it comes to the observance of mortuary ritual. As in the case of a man's death, more pigs are involved in the mortuary sequence for older than for younger women, and also as with men, the sense of loss with younger women who die leaving small children is indescribably profound.

The most significant difference in the case of a woman's death is at the *tataun,* in that (1) the category of *di mokos* includes different people, and (2) *bingbingpul* pigs are not accorded quite the same meaning. There are no noteworthy differences in *ngin i pol* or *táptápir* feasts that are conducted in honor of deceased women.

Di mokos. In principle, any person who is related to the deceased by marriage—that is, who is a member of the opposite matrimoiety—is eligible to be in the *di mokos* category. This is because of the rule of matrimoiety exogamy, which means that, irrespective of the sex of the deceased, the (opposite) group responsible for providing *bingbingpul* pigs at the *tataun* is always the same, as shown schematically in Diagram 5.1. But as in the case of a man's death, it is those most acutely affected by the death who are formally *di mokos.* When a woman dies, those most likely to be designated *di mokos,* then, are her husband and her brother's children (who will also be, at least in classificatory terms, her children's spouses).

Bingbingpul. Pigs are provided to the lineage of the deceased, but the rhetoric of paternal provisioning is, naturally, absent. Although these pigs are referred to as *bingbingpul,* it is in much the same way as references to women in North America who engage in traditionally masculine tasks, such as "woman taxicab driver," or "woman physician." That is, the pigs given in the case of a death of a woman are *bingbingpul* pigs, but informants invariably mention that they are not for the death of a man, but of a woman.

Other Ritual Memorial Events

There are other pork-consuming events associated with the dead, but they are much more sporadic and do not have the obligatory nature of the *tataun, ngin i pol,* or even the *táptápir* events. In principle, any activity that is related to the memory of the dead should be accompanied by the consumption of pork,

Cross-Moiety Relations
Diagram 5.1

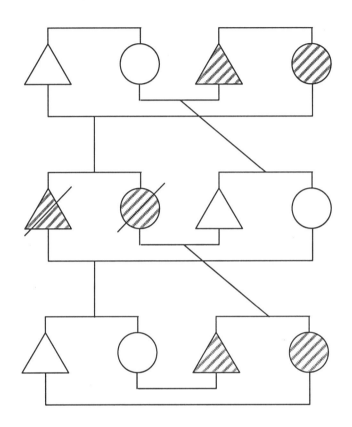

    Matrilineal descent group of deceased

    Matrilineal descent group related to deceased by marriage

even if only a pig or two. Because they are not part of the sequence of mortuary feasts but are related to honoring the memory of the dead, I refer to these other rites as *memorial* rather than *mortuary* events. One of these memorial events is formally known as *aso i rat*, or "burning the basket." Other events are unnamed (at least as far as I could tell), perhaps because they are relatively mundane activities: the repair of a *matmat* fence; the weeding of a *matmat*, or the destruction of a dilapidated house whose former occupant has recently died.

Aso i rat. I attended only one of these events (in Samo) and was told that burning a personal basket and a favorite stool of a man who had died years earlier was a way to remember him. There seemed to be little in the way of scripted order to the event; a number of us from Tekedan simply sat in the appropriate *bang* at Samo, talked, smoked, and chewed betel nut. The event was explained to me simply as something done with personal possessions of the dead. Jackson provides more detail:

Asoi rat . . . serves to provoke memory of the deceased just at the time of its imminent dissolution. That is, it is done "when everyone has nearly forgotten the bigman." This feast generally marks a remembrance between bigmen, at the same time that it marks our forgetting. The current bigman might see the basket or ceremonial axe of the last bigman hanging in the rafters of the men's house and have "worry" over the deceased "because he worked kastam for us and fed us at feasts and everyone is forgetting him." To mark this "worry," to show that we are (in a positive sense) forgetting, a small feast to burn the deceased's personal possessions will be organized. The person is dead and we are forgetting him, but we always know him and his work. Thus we forget someone in these terms, it is not an activity "misplacing" thoughts or even redirecting those thoughts, projecting them onto some other activity, like feasting. To feast is not to be unable to remember a specific person, but to positively conceive the schema out of which all persons are produced. (Jackson 1995:182–183)

What Jackson says for the *aso i rat* memorial event is true, as far as I can discern, for the destruction of other property of the deceased, such as tearing down an old house.

House Demolition. When a dilapidated house needs to be torn down so that a new one can be built in its place, and when the old house was the longtime domicile of a somewhat recently deceased person, a small feast is held, often consisting only of a pig or two along with the obligatory tubers. The rationale is quite like that of the *asoi rat*, but because houses (unlike baskets and other personal possessions) are often used by other people, and can be replaced only with some difficulty, such memorial events are not common or required.

Matmat *Maintenance.* On occasion, a cemetery becomes overrun with weeds or has a bamboo fence that is in disrepair. Unlike other parcels of land, however, a *matmat* retains a supernatural vigor by virtue of the people buried there, and work in or around a *matmat* cannot be undertaken cavalierly. For most *matmat*s, the consumption of pork is adequate, as long as weeders and/or fence-repairers conduct their work with a certain amount of sobriety. Piknat cemeteries, however, are different because of the supernatural power attributed to members of that matriclan—power attributed both by Piknat and non-Piknat alike. This power is said to be manifested after death in that any non-Piknat who walks on or near the ground of a Piknat *matmat* will get blisters on her or his feet. I also heard stories that Piknats have risen from the dead. The source of and reason for this supernaturally imbued power seems to be unknown, even to Piknats, and it seems to provide living Piknat with no particular political or economic advantages. Piknat power, then, is merely the most pronounced version of the supernatural aspects of death and burial.

Matmat maintenance itself typically takes much less time and energy than the preparation of the pigs. These events are small scale (only those in the matrilineage of the deceased and their immediate affines are included) and sporadic (sometimes even spontaneous), and in one case, provided the ritual "excuse" when a domesticated pig had to be killed because it had been terrorizing village dogs.

SUMMARY

The Sursurunga mortuary feasting sequence involves the energies and resources of a large number of people. In the following chapter, some of the reasons behind individuals' choices to invest their energies and resources in mortuary ritual are discussed. Although matrilineal descent-based obligations are part of the motivation for participating in mortuary feasting, I will leave these to the side and emphasize those "causes" of involvement in mortuary feasting that themselves may have little to do with descent but entail a mortuary feasting complex that in turn reinforces the salience of matrilineal understandings and activates matrilineal descent groups.

The following chapter describes some of the reasons for individuals' continuing commitment to the mortuary feasting complex. Chapter 7 then details the ways in which mortuary feasting makes salient (often otherwise latent) matrilineal descent understandings. The current chapter and the next two form an array that is logically counter-intuitive, but conventionally standard in that the facts of feasting are presented first here, with the analytical antecedents and consequents presented second and third, respectively. Although the description and analyses of the mortuary feasting sequence are presented serially, the reality of Sursurunga mortuary ritual is much more of a simultaneous happening.

Chapter 6

The Antecedents of Mortuary Feasting

In this chapter, I describe the ways in which complexes of understandings, values, and social relations cause individuals to devote the necessary time, energy, and resources required for mortuary feasting. As I noted in Chapter 1, matrilineal descent is both effect and cause of mortuary ritual. As cause, it plays a subsidiary or indirect role related both to the avoidance of shame and to political allegiances. Sursurunga do not perform mortuary feasts so that matriliny might be accentuated; rather, matrilineal understandings are made salient, and social relations resulting from these understandings are activated, just before, during, and after mortuary feasts as unpremeditated results of the practice of mortuary feasting. The issue, then, is if matrilineal obligations are not all that make for mortuary feasts, then what else is? Why do people such as the Sursurunga engage in mortuary ritual?

The answers to these questions begin with a section on grammar and cognition, in which Sursurunga noun classification is presented as representative of Sursurunga cognitive categories. These categories play important roles in Sursurunga notions of food and eating, which is the topic of the ensuing section. After the food and eating section is a discussion of the affective bases for behavior, including, importantly, the desire to avoid shame, followed by sections describing the understandings and social relations that involve reciprocity as well as leadership.

OCEANIC NOUN CLASSIFICATION

The Sursurunga language is a member of the Oceanic sub-sub-subfamily of the far-flung Austronesian language family. Oceanic grammars often include nouns that are not infrequently classified into two (and sometimes more) categories, often called "alienable" and "inalienable." Mortuary feasting is consistent with cognitive constructs—understandings—that are parallel to, if not influenced by, Sursurunga grammatical understandings of noun (in)alienability.

Sursurunga grammar classifies nouns into categories of inalienable, alienable, and, within the alienable category, food-related and non-food-related kinds of nouns (Hutchisson 1986). Not all Oceanic languages conform exactly to this pattern. Macintyre, for example, cites a third "semi-alienable" category in the Tubetube language (1984), and Pawley and Sayaba suggest four noun classes for Fijian (1990:150). Some linguists use different terms; Hollyman, for example, uses "permanent personal" possession and contrasts it with "non-personalized" possession (1991:147). Edwin Hutchins (personal communication) also eschews "alienable" and "inalienable" as useful descriptors, preferring "distal" and "proximate" to refer to Trobriand nouns.[1]

There is, then, no one Oceanic noun classification system. Nevertheless, there is a set of Oceanic noun differentiations with "near universality" (Keesing 1988:117) which, while varying in their criteria, can be discussed together as evidenced by the similarity of the terms that are used as descriptors: for example, "alienable," "distal," and "non-personalized." The Sursurunga version of the Oceanic noun alienability and inalienability is represented by Diagram 6.1.

Diagram 6.1
Sursurunga Noun Classes

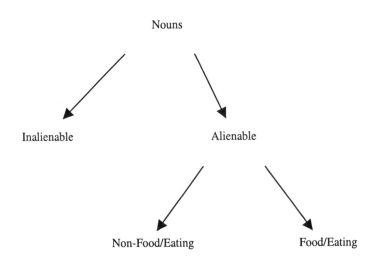

---

1. Lichtenberk 1985 is a useful general treatment of the subject of noun possession.

The distinction between alienable nouns and inalienable nouns is indicated by the labels used. Inalienable nouns refer to those things that are inherently possessed—that is, things that cannot be alienated from a person or another thing. A person's arm (*limán*), for example, is not normally separate from a person, and *limán* is an inalienable noun. An example of an alienable noun would be *unsis* or "turtle." Turtles can be "alienated" or separated from people, or the sea. The alienability of nouns is marked by the use of grammatically different possessive forms. It is, for example, not possible merely to say "arm" in Sursurunga. The term must have a possessive attached to it, so that one must say "my arm" (*limang*), "your arm" (*limam*), or "her/his/its arm" (*limán*). On the other hand, one can say *unsis* either with or without a possessive. In this case, the possessive is a free morpheme, so that "my turtle" is *kak unsis*, "your turtle" is *kam unsis*, and "her/his/its turtle" is *kan unsis*.

Below are some examples of alienable and inalienable nouns in Sursurunga:

Alienable Nouns		Inalienable Nouns	
asir	"guest"	*arung*	"my face"
dan	"water"	*buang*	"my clan"
garap	"bamboo slit drum"	*gárán*	"its song"
inbul	"yam"	*kaungam*	"your voice"
kalik	"child"[2]	*lusang*	"my clothing"
manu	"sore"	*mutwán*	"river's mouth"
nguk	"mosquito"	*ninsin*	"one's manner"
pap	"dog"	*rákán*	"tree branch"
sál	"road"	*tanyang*	"my spirit"
tas	"salt"	*wán*	"outcome"
wak	"wallaby"	*yátin*	"the top of"

As indicated above, alienable nouns can be possessed, but they require an unbound morpheme to do so, according to these rules:

"my [alienable noun]" = *kak* [alienable noun]
"your [alienable noun]" = *kam* [alienable noun]
"her/his/its [alienable noun]" = *kán* [alienable noun]

The rules above refer only to non-food-related alienable nouns. The other subclass of food related alienable nouns, has these possessives, which differ from the first set only in that they do not have the initial /k/:

ak (1st person)
am (2nd person)
án (3rd person)

---

2. *NB: kalik* is "child" or "young person." *Natung* ("my child") refers to a genealogical relationship. With an actual S or D, *natung* is almost always used, but I have recorded instances of "*kang kalik*" and "*natung*" being used between the same alter and ego. My impression of the differences is that "*kang kalik*" (*kak* changes to *kang* before [k]) is used offhandedly or lightheartedly.

The choice of which of these different possessives to use with alienable nouns provides important information to the hearer. Consider the examples below:

ak bu = "the betel nut in my possession"
kak bu = "the betel nut tree that I own"

Literally, both *ak bu* and *kak bu* mean "my betel nut," but the betel nut carried around in one's possession is more immediately consumable. Indeed, perhaps the best glosses for alienable nouns used with the "edible possessives" include the phrase "for eating":

ak bu "my betel nut for eating"
kak bu "my betel nut"
ak bor "my pork for eating"
kak bor "my pig"
ak pol "my coconut for drinking"
kak pol "my coconut"

The choice of possessives can indicate intention. Here is a typical scenario with a typical Sursurunga question/greeting. Walking down the road, I encounter a person with a fish. To make conversation, acknowledge, and greet the other person, I might ask, "*Dáni u longpasi?*" (What are you toting?"). In response I might hear either "*Kak isu*" ("My fish") or "*Ak isu*" ("My fish"). With the former, I know that she or he is saying that there is no intention to eat it, but that it will be given away, or chopped up for use as bait. In the case of the second response, it is clear that she or he intends to eat it. In other contexts, when one person proffers betel nut to another, it is not unusual for her or him to accompany this gesture with the words "*Am bu*" ("Your betel nut for eating"). Similarly, at a feast, I have often heard, "*Ani am bor!*" ("Eat your pork!") to too-quickly sated feasters.

This grammatical focus on eating appears in Sursurunga terms for body parts. All body parts except one are inalienable, such as, *kiking* ("my leg"), *nihung* ("my hair"), *susung* ("my breast"), and so on. The one body part exception is *ak pongon* ("my throat"). When I asked one informant why a throat is different from other body parts, he shrugged that it is simply because a throat is "for eating."

One of the functions of Sursurunga noun classification is to mark the processes and elements of ingestion; another is to differentiate between alienable and inalienable nouns. But what does it matter? What difference do noun classes make? I will return shortly to the food and eating aspects of Sursurunga nouns; at this point, I turn to the significance of alienability and inalienability.

THE SOCIOLOGICAL RELEVANCE OF NOUN (IN)ALIENABILITY

Noun classifications like the one just described do have implications for the behavior of social actors. Kay and Kempton (1984) showed that there *is* something to the Whorfian way in which language can covary with perceptual differences, but their work also shows that these differences are far from profound. More recent work by Lucy (1993a, 1993b) addresses the same issue.

Lucy notes that Sapir-Whorf and other linguistic relativity hypotheses involve the proposition that "linguistic classifications" ultimately contribute to "organizing experience into categories" and argues for the useful distinction between linguistic categories and cognitive categories. The difference here is straightforward: categories that are cognitive but not linguistic are those that influence nonverbal behavior (Lucy 1993b:101). This means that the conflation of linguistic and cognitive categories is not warranted "[s]ince the mere presence or absence of a specific grammatical category alone is not a sufficient basis for inferring a possible influence on thought" (1993b:103). If cognitive categories and linguistic categories are kept conceptually separate, it is possible to investigate the way(s) in which one might influence the other. Lucy notes that "the extent to which linguistic classification can be expected to have effects on thought is necessarily contingent on the degree to which and manner in which those classifications are actually brought into play as a matter of cultural practice" (1993b:126).

By "cultural practice," Lucy means frequent, routine behavior. Linguistic classifications are assumed to parallel useful and marked cognitive classifications if the linguistic classifications are reflected in, or otherwise related to, "reality." Language, thought, and reality therefore constitute the bedrock of Lucy's version of the linguistic relativity hypothesis, which asserts that "differences in morphosyntactic structure have detectable effects on thought about reality" (1993b:266).

It is important to distinguish between creative or sporadic thought—Lucy's "specialized thought" (1993b:272–273) and "habitual thought," which is defined as "certain everyday ways of apprehending and dealing with the world of experience characteristic of most normal adult members" of a society (1993b:272). This means that research attending to the relationship between language, thought, and reality should look to aspects of reality that "emphasize simple skills and everyday knowledge" (1993b:273).

Neither Lucy nor I wish to argue that language structure causes behavior. Language does, however, affect perception, and perception does affect behavior. What can be seen, then, in language, is an indication of "habitual dispositions towards, or ways of responding to, a referent" (1993a:91), or "characteristic cognitive responses" (1993a:148). Lucy's unwillingness to assert too strong a causal link between language and thought is due to his recognition that "the linkages of language and thought are often thought to be so pervasive and complex that no proof is possible" (1993a:153). Nevertheless, he notes that "correlational evidence can be extremely suggestive of a causal role for language if the relationships are strong and distinctive and if no other explanation for the contrasting cognitive patterns seems plausible" (1993a:85).

In short, Lucy has made the case that linguistic structures make certain aspects of reality seem more "natural" or less counterintuitive. Sursurunga kinship terminology is one type of "everyday knowledge" leading "habitual dispositions" and "characteristic cognitive responses." Kin terms among the Sursurunga are the best examples of this naming system because they are a commonly used genre of nouns that includes both alienable and inalienable forms, and kin terms provide a clear case for showing how noun alienability is consistent with and, in part, constitutive of social reality. The Sursurunga linguistic categories of alienable and inalienable nouns affect the way people think—and importantly, act[3]—in the real world of social relations.

Sursurunga kin terms have been stable except for the grandparental terms, which have undergone some changes recently. The terms traditionally used, and still used by many people, are:

wakang	MM
pupung	MF
lapung	FM
tuang	FF

A number of younger people, however, rely on only two grandparental terms, *wakang* (vocative form: *wowo*) and *pupung* (vocative forms: *pupu*, *titi*), for grandmother and grandfather, respectively. I found this to be very confusing since not everyone was using the same set of terms. In one instance, I was asking Penias, a middle-aged man, about the reasons for the changes in grandparental kin terms. He said he was not aware of any such shift. I then turned to Peril, a neighbor boy—about seven years old—and asked him what he called Tovina (the boy's FF). He replied that he called him "*Titi*." Penias looked at me and said, "Hey, you're right!" The newer forms are:

pupung	FF, MF, and m.s. CC
wakang	MM, FM, and f.s. CC

Because of this ambiguity, I do not use the grandparental terms in the following analysis. Not all Sursurunga kin terms are inalienable nouns such as those listed above; some are alienable. The list of inalienable kin terms, along with basic kin types, is:

kakang	F, FB
mamang	M, MZ
kawang	MB, ZC
kukung (lik)	m.s. Z, f.s. B
tuang	m.s. B, f.s. Z
yanang	HM, SW
natung	C
kámlang	m.s. opp. moiety male

Alienable kin terms are:

---

3. The link between language and cognition is the focus of my attention in this section. The link between cognition and behavior I take to be axiomatic.

kak tau	FZ, f.s. BC
kak kokup	m.s. MBD, FZD, f.s. MBS, FZS
kak sinat	WZ, WB, HZ, HB
kak pup	H
kak wák	W

Matrimoiety membership is an important consideration in social organization, and moiety membership is also related to kin terms. In the following 2x2 grids, I offer a chi-square analysis, even though the number of cases is too small for the test to be valid. Nevertheless, as a means of demonstrating the strength of the association, the chi-square result is provided:

For a male ego:

	Same Moiety	Opposite Moiety	
Alienable Nouns	0	4	4
Inalienable Nouns	5	3	8
	5	7	N = 12

$\chi^2 = 4.286$; P-Value = 0.038

For a female ego, the numbers are even more telling[4]:

	Same Moiety	Opposite Moiety	
Alienable Nouns	0	4	4
Inalienable Nouns	5	2	7
	5	6	N = 11

$\chi^2 = 5.238$; P-Value = 0.022

These data strongly suggest that there is a non-random relationship between the alienability of kin terms and moiety membership—and the important social relations that are influenced by moiety membership. The examples that follow show that the use of alienable and inalienable kin terms is reflected in actual social relations.

The connection between social relations and terminology is exemplified by the use of different terms for some persons as a result of marriage. A marriage changes the uses of certain kin terms. In one change, two friends from opposite moieties who had enjoyed referring to each other as *kámlang* must, upon the marriage of one to the other's sister, alter the relationship to brothers-in-law. The biggest difference here is that ego is no longer interested in hearing ribald stories of alter's sexual exploits once alter has married ego's sister. In general, there is expected to be a reserve—even avoidance—between brothers-in-law, a reserve marked quite neatly in the shift to an alienable kin term, *kak sinat*. To be sure, not everyone conforms to the idea of affinal avoidance, but those who flagrantly violate the principle are made the subject of gossip. There does exist the understanding that close affines should have little to do with each other, and this understanding is encoded in the alienable/inalienable distinction.

---

4. The difference between the Ns of the two grids is that men have the additional *kámlang* term.

The shift among women from *kak tau* to *yanang* is the structural reverse of the *kámlang* to *kak sinat* change. In referring to her new mother-in-law as *yanang*, a woman uses an inalienable kin term where an alienable term had been appropriate in the past. Upon marriage, a woman's link to her mother-in-law changes from a generalized opposite-moiety relationship to one characterized by a structural connectedness. There is the avoidance that infuses all affinal relationships among the Sursurunga, but this affinal restraint is overshadowed by another understanding: the debt owed to one's father and his enates, as described in Chapter 4.

Bridewealth connects a woman to her mother-in-law. Whether the resources given to a woman's group came from the groom's lineage (as was traditionally the usual case) or whether from the natal family of the groom (as more often happens these days), the mother-in-law stands to have an economic stake in the daughter-in-law. This economic linkage is fortified by the contemporary preference for virilocal residence. It is not uncommon to find women helping their mothers-in-law in the gardens, or to have mothers-in-law care for children when women are away from the village.

Men experience *terminological* distancing from their brothers-in-law whereas women experience its opposite with their mothers-in-law; and changes in behavioral patterns in these relationships parallel the use of alienable and inalienable terminology: men, for example, exercise restraint around their former *kámlang*s, whereas women are often found in economic cooperation with their mothers-in-law. When I asked people what they thought about these changes, men said that they now had to "respect" their brothers-in-law, and that jocularity—if there ever was any—would have to cease between them. Two men said that they regretted the change; both felt that they had lost a friend in gaining an affine. One of these men said, "I only think about it once in a while, so it is not too bad." In these cases, the terminological shift from the inalienable to the alienable signalled an unpleasant sociological reality.

The women that I interviewed on the matter were either less forthcoming with me or more fatalistic. They only offered the view that a woman's lot was hard, and that cooperation—with anyone—was an asset in gardening, housekeeping, and child care. Any links between them and their mothers-in-law were expressed as necessities; one should not trouble oneself to worry about whether one liked it that way or not. For both women and men, the alienable/inalienable distinction is more than a linguistic contrivance; it reflects a cognitive orientation that is importantly associated with everyday sociological realities.

I turn next to the classification of nouns and the concomitant cognitive constructs and understandings that serve as an index of social relations in the area of food and eating.

FOOD-AND-EATING AND FEASTING

Several aspects of Sursurunga culture and social relations center on food and eating. These features are expressed in a wide range of Sursurunga activities, and point to a significant emphasis or "hypercognition" (Levy 1973) on edibles and their consumption, an emphasis consistent with Sursurunga noun categories.

The dominant theme of Sursurunga food and eating ideology is that food is an index of congenial social relations—especially those relationships characterized by care and nurture. This emphasis on good social relations also finds expression in the Sursurunga hyperbole that equates food with feces and waste. *Namnam* is a Sursurunga word that is used both as noun ("food") and as intransitive verb ("to eat"). When I refer to "food-and-eating" with hyphens in this section, it should be understood as a means of capturing in English both of these aspects of *namnam*. Recall that Sursurunga noun classification marks not only alienability, but ingestion as well. This highlighting of eating in Sursurunga grammar is found in other Oceanic languages, and is not unique by any means (see Macintyre 1984). Nevertheless, when taken as a component of a widespread emphasis within Sursurunga society and culture, this grammatical feature suggests a marked prominence for the understandings about good social relationships that are articulated below.

Sursurunga understandings about food-and-eating can be inferred from folklore, as well as both routine and ceremonial activity. The linguistic emphasis on food-and-eating does not, in itself, "mean" anything. Rather, it marks food-and-eating as substance and behavior of especial importance. In other words, language amplifies or emphasizes the meanings of food and eating, serving as a form of cultural italicization for the meanings that are found in a variety of domains. This variety in itself reinforces the argument that for the Sursurunga, food-and-eating are pervasive considerations—considerations that go beyond their rational aspects; that is, there seems to be no shortage of food that might generate or maintain a marked attention to food and/or eating. There is, for example, plenty of land available for gardens.[5] The reef is replete with shellfish and smaller fish, and the ocean is full of pelagic fish. The availability of cash from copra and cacao sales also provides people with a means of feeding themselves. Furthermore, feral pigs can still be hunted in the bush, and young men will occasionally bring one or two home. The prominence of food and eating in myth and social life, and the grammatical focus on food and eating are probably not due to a shortage of food, either now or in the past. Indeed, as Mauss suggests (1967:29–31) and as Kahn (1986:1–10) argues, it is perhaps the somewhat ready availability of food that makes it so useful as an index, or "currency" of social relations.

Sursurunga understandings about food are importantly informed by the source of the food; that is, whether the food was garden-produced or store-bought, and whether the food required much or little work in the garden. *Namnam musuan,* or "true/real food" is *til songsong,* or "from sweat." A proper feast is a direct product of the energy, effort, and labor—evidenced by perspira-

---

5. No one from Tekedan has to walk more than 45 minutes to their nearest garden. (Of course, many people have claims on more distant land as well.) Beyond 45 minutes, much land is available, but it is not used, since there is enough land for gardening, as well as for coconut and cacao trees (for cash).

tion—of those contributing to a feast. In effect, this means that tubers should be a part of every feast. Rice and bananas, although tasty, do not constitute real food since they require relatively little effort to provide and are not the product of long-term care (read "sweat"). Of course, rice is not free and bananas are not magically delivered to one's front door. There *is* effort (and, normally, *song-song* as well) involved in the acquiring of cash to purchase rice and in carrying stalks of bananas from gardens. The difference is in the amount of time allocated to an endeavor. Rice requires only that one go to the nearest trade store and buy it; bananas require almost no care other than planting and harvesting. Time is care; little time spent represents little care, whereas much time spent represents much care. In this respect, nurture is transitive, in that the nurture provided the tubers is passed along to the guests at a feast, who themselves enjoy the fruits of the nurturing capabilities of the sponsor and his lineage.

Folklore and Food-and-Eating

Of the 25 Sursurunga stories in my possession,[6] food plays a role in all but three. The provision of food is an index of close relationships, and includes the use of food as a reward, as an enticement, and as defining nurturing behavior. Here are some examples:

Food as a reward:

Long ago they closed up a woman; she was *kámgu* [a girl initiate]. The *kámgu*, even if she came out [of the initiation hut], she returned there. One day she went to bathe down in the river. While she was bathing a woman named Tinkulkultatekenbor ["One who rubs pig feces on her body"] came and said, "*Kámgu*, let's splash each other." The two of them splashed each other for a while and then Kulkulta got up and stuck *kámgu* up in the inside of a rock.

So, Kulkultatekenbor returned to the girl's village. Her mother and father looked for her, that girl that Kulkulta had stuck to the inside of a rock. The parents gave the leafy part of a ginger plant to the birds from all over. The birds came to try to release the girl, since the parents had said that the one who released her would marry her. All kinds of birds came and tried and tried. Very large birds tried, but they could not do it. Another day they returned and tried.

Then, two little birds named Támtektektilingtiling ["One characterized by small things and big things"; possibly referring to its voice] and Támlislisdáránbor ["One characterized by sprinkled pig's blood"] decided that they would follow the large birds. They (the other birds) cursed the two of them. The two of them went alone and tried but did not succeed. At that time when they went to split open the rock to get the woman, her father and her mother were baking in an earth oven and eating pig [as at a *tataun*].

On another day Támtektektilingtiling and Támlislisdáránbor decided to try the rock. They went and sat up on a tree branch. Then Támtektektilingtiling said that he would try. Then he flew from up above, from the tree branch and threw out his foot and made a noise as he hit the rock like, "teng." The rock broke. Then he returned up above. Then Támlislisdáránbor in his turn flew and threw out his foot at the rock and it made a "teng" noise and the rock broke. The two of them did that and kicked the rock and it broke and

---

6. I am grateful to Sharon and Don Hutchisson of the Summer Institute of Linguistics for providing me with these stories and their translations.

revealed the arm of *kámgu*, her feet, her stomach, head, face. They took hold of her. They took *kámgu* and went with her, and went and hid downcoast in a stand of shrubbery behind her father's men's house.

They went like that and they sat and sat and sat and it was a bit dark. The two birds appeared from nowhere with her, and her father and mother were very happy and her maternal kin and relatives there were happy. They praised those two and they cooked pig and they gave those two food, making a feast with lots of food and the two of them ate. At that time they explained that Támtektektilingtiling and Támlislisdáránbor had gotten the woman from the river. The large birds were angry with the two smaller ones, and did not speak to them. And the parents said that they will give the woman to the two of them. So, the two of them both married that woman.

Gratitude is manifested with food, which results in marriage, the closest relationship that can be achieved—that is, the only relationship in the natal or conjugal family that is not ascribed by birth. In the following story, food is an enticement, and is in fact a disingenuous use of food as an index of close relations; the little people used food to get the man's guard down, so that the man, after eating, believed himself to be safe.

A man woke up in the morning and led his dogs up to the bush. He wandered around here and there but did not encounter any wild pigs. Well, his belly was angry because he had wandered around for nothing having seen no wild pig and then he thought he would return. He decided he would get up and then the rain started to blow a lot and he was not able to see far. So, he wandered around not knowing where he was in the bush and not eating or finding any good things to get shelter under. He just wandered blindly through the bush. He wandered about and then came upon a small *kamkam* bird [a starling?] and then he caught the bird and carried it through the bush. Then he walked a little also up there and then he arrived at a village of the little people. Well, the little people saw him and felt very sorry for him. So, they fed him with food and he ate it. He had finished eating it all and then the little people said to him, "Let's *arsiut*" [a diversion in which people sit on a bench and sway back and forth until the people on one side fall off].

The man said, "Whatever you all want to do." He continued to carry his little *kamkam*. That man sat in the middle and the little people sat on both sides of him. They counted, "One, two, three," and they all crushed him, and the man was close to dying there in the middle. He rose just a little and shook his small *kamkam* until it cried. All the little people were startled and all of them fell into a large, deep hole. The man returned to his village. He did not know that the men and women in his village had cooked pig [that is, conducted a *tataun*] for him. The women cried a lot for him because they thought he had died. But no, the man had been staying up with the little people. They were startled at his arrival and they were then very happy and praised him to his skin. That's it.

In the story below, the provision of food as an index of congenial social relations is taken a step further by its use in marking a specific kind of relationship, one of care and succor:

An unmarried woman lived and bore a set of twins—both boys. The three of them, mother and children, lived and lived and the two children were big and the mother said to them, "If I die you two will see a tree growing from my eyes and you two will take good care of it. Every day you two will clean the ground away from it."

The three of them lived and lived and lived and then the mother died and the two brothers buried her. And they remembered their mother's words. When seven days had passed they went and looked at their mother and saw a tree growing there in their mother's eyes, and they cleaned the ground around it. Every day they went and cleaned the ground around it. When the tree was big and bore fruit the two of them did not know what kind of tree it was. So, it bore fruit and one fruit dried, and one of them saw it and he got one fruit and tried to eat the fruit of that tree. When he ate it was very tasty and he carried it down to his brother and he ate it and it was very good. The coconut grew up there. And some fell and many coconuts grew. Today we have coconuts because the coconut grew out of the head of their mother. We see that coconuts have a mouth and eyes; today we see it.

In this story, a mother continues her care for her offspring even after death by providing them with food. In another "origin of coconuts" story,[7] two brothers out in a canoe are attacked by a large shark. One brother allows his body to be thrown into the sea to mollify the shark so that the other brother might live. The surviving brother then plants the head—all that remains—of his deceased brother, whence come coconuts. Here succor becomes self-sacrificing protection.

Food is an index of close social relations in Sursurunga stories. Importantly, the provision of food often demonstrates a particular sort of close relationship, one of nurture and care.

Social Relations and Food-and-Eating

The ways in which the provision and consumption of food are performed also indicate something about the nature of social relations. For example, a land transaction is not considered formally concluded unless a pig has been consumed by those involved. In such an instance, the buyer of a parcel of land must also provide (in addition to the purchase price itself, usually in the form of *reu*) a pig to the seller, who would normally be the oldest active male in a matrilineage. After having been baked in an earth oven, the pig is cut transversely. The seller eats the hindquarters of the pig at the time of the transaction, and the head and forelegs are taken back to his lineage and other local clan members so that they might share in the proceeds of the sale, since, after all, as enates, they had a nominal claim to the land. At least one land transaction at Tekedan has not yet involved a pig as part of the transaction, and some enates of the seller are threatening to reclaim the land upon his death. The pending sale was to the seller's son, and the use of eating (or, in this case, not eating) signals an incomplete transaction—and, by the way, a less-than-harmonious relationship—and is at least a nominal basis for a future dispute over a land transaction.

Eating together is an act that is something more than an index of good relationships; it also creates good relationships. Consider the following case.

---

7. Interestingly, the second, aquatic story came from a member of a clan that had traditionally always lived along the beach. The first, land-based story came from a member of a "bush clan." Neither had heard of the other's version.

At a small feast made possible by Makis's killing of a rather large feral pig, Tovevel (Makis's younger brother; about 14 years of age) and Devit (also about 14) were sitting with a group of boys and young men as the pork was being sliced by some men and cooked tubers were brought to the men's house by some women.

As is normally the case, on this particular occasion, this group of boys and young men was the source of much noise, laughter, shouts, and general cutting up. At one point, however, Devit said something to Tovevel, which the latter found not to be funny.[8]

Within moments, Tovevel and Devit were exchanging insults, and the altercation escalated into blows in seconds. (Young men in the group did later say that they thought the two were just mimicking anger until the blows actually began.) Separated by others after the first few fists landed, the two boys were led away to the edge of the feasting area in order to recoup. Minutes later the two were enjoined to shake hands—a process that clearly was enjoyed by neither, each looking away and shaking the hand of the other rather lethargically.

Order having been restored, the processes of feasting continued. Breadfruit leaves were provided as plates, and village leaders, including Tovevel's father Sokip, called for a woven coconut frond mat upon which Devit and Tovevel were instructed to sit together as they ate their food. At first, they sat on either end of the mat, staying as far as possible from each other while still complying with the mandate. As in normal feast protocol, one plate of food was served to the two boys, who then had to sit closer to each other in order to reach the food. Older men sitting in and around the men's house muttered comments such as, "They'll have to sit close now [as the food was being given to them]"; "That's right, sit close and eat together"; and "The anger is finished now."

The act of moving closer together to be able to eat from the common plate illustrates the broader Sursurunga notion that eating together is equated with harmonious social relations. Making the two boys sit together to eat was an attempt to provide a resolution to their conflict. At the same time, two men sitting together and eating from the same plate (and also, but less significantly, sharing betel nut and tobacco[9]) in the men's house signifies an already harmonious relationship, creating an ambience surrounding eating that is generally festive. Eating together, then, functions both as something of a cause and an effect of good social relations.

Sometimes, however, relationships can become (or appear to become) *too* close. In providing food, betel nut, and tobacco, a giver is understood to posit a close(r) relationship, including relationships between the sexes (of roughly the same age). To provide food, betel nut, and/or tobacco to a member of the oppo-

---

8. I never found out what was said. This event occurred within my last 10 days on New Ireland in 1992, and attempts to pursue the matter were rebuffed. Perhaps talking about it so soon after it happened was too painful. In 1998, people recalled the incident, but no one remembered the details.

9. The use of tobacco and especially betel nut in this regard are not to be overlooked. I was walking to a feast and stopped to purchase some betel nut at a roadside stand watched by two women from Tekedan. "What!" exclaimed one. "Are you going to chew all of that?" "No," said the other, replying for me in the typical patois blending Neo-Melanesian and Sursurunga: *"Awuh, kápte; askim saplai, be?"* ("Oh no; a supply for those who ask, right?").

site sex is flirtation, and includes innuendo of sexual suggestion. Two brief cases make the point: In one case,

A woman went to the orderly at the government-sponsored aid post at Tekedan and asked him for some food. In addition to the sexual innuendo, this woman was also sending a strong message that her husband does not meet her needs.[10] According to those in the village who knew what happened, the orderly provided this woman with some food in the afternoon. Later that night, he visited this woman in her house and was caught *in flagrante delicto* by the woman's husband. The orderly was later required to pay a fine of K50 to the cuckolded man.

Note that it was the request for and acceptance of food that signaled quite clearly the intentions of both the orderly and the woman. In another case,

A man proffered some betel nut to a woman he barely knew. The woman's husband flew into a rage (a rage exacerbated by the several bottles of beer he had consumed that day), chasing after the man shouting in Neo-Melanesian, *"Em i laik traim meri bilong mi!"* ("He wants to make an attempt on my wife!") The following day, when settlements were made, no one questioned the husband's understanding that the man's offer of betel nut to his wife had sexual implications.

Perhaps the most telling datum on the matter is a statement made by a man about brothers and sisters providing betel nut for each other. Recall that there is a strong brother-sister taboo in operation in Sursurunga society, and the relationship between the two is expected to be a staid, distant one. I asked an informant whether a sister had ever asked her brother for betel nut, and the reply was, "No; if she ever did, he'd ask her where her shame was." Again, the sexual innuendo of offering something to eat is understood to be a part of social life.

Scatology and Food-and-Eating

The full significance of food and eating among the Sursurunga cannot be fully explored without addressing its scatological connections.[11] One common Sursurunga epithet is, "Your head is full of food!" The point is that food, once digested, becomes feces, and this epithet is best glossed in English as "shit for brains." The relationship between food and feces is understood to be one of equivalence; that is, there is change in the form, but not in the essence of the substance.

---

10. By my lights, this man is a hard worker and a good provider, so it seems that his wife's claim that he does not provide for her is spurious. On the other hand, he probably does fail to meet her sexual needs, as he prefers to sleep in the men's house. I do not know whether his preference for the men's house is primarily cause or effect of his wife's renowned interest in other men.

11. A. Epstein's analysis of Tolai anality (1979) is not inconsistent with Sursurunga scatology. Clark (1995) argues that scatological associations with food and wealth are not limited to the Tolai.

When expressing deep gratitude, or upon greeting a close friend or kinsman after a lengthy separation, Sursurunga will sometimes use the expression, "*Ak tikim!*" This means literally, "My (for eating) your feces!" More freely, this sentence is rendered, "Give me your feces to eat!," the idea being that one is so grateful to, or elated to see, the person that even that which is most repulsive about her or him is relished. Here, food equals feces/waste within the context of a good relationship. This equivalence is the most hyperbolic indicator of good social relations; being willing to consume *anything* offered by another also suggests a high degree of trust and solidarity within the relationship.

Note that the noun for "my feces," *tiking*, is inalienable. This may seem incongruous, since people normally alienate themselves from their feces in the process of elimination. Furthermore, there is a grammatical clash in the expression "*ak tikim,*" since an alienable possessive is used with an inalienably possessed noun. Informants were unable to shed much light on the matter. The best explanation for the classification of feces as inalienable is that it is a grammatical representation of the transformation of a meal from alienable food to inalienable feces; that is, the process of digestion (or of "feces-izing") makes food one's own.[12] The point is that for the Sursurunga, feces is a form of food, and even in this form, food is an index of social relations. On the Lelet Plateau of New Ireland, north of the Sursurunga region, feces-ized food is especially salient in that pre-feast magic is performed so that feasters will see the food provided them as feces, thus reducing their appetites, creating a food surplus, which upon rotting and stinking, will be an index of the sponsoring group's magnanimity (Eves 1996). Although no Sursurunga ever articulated this to me, I do not believe that it would be rebutted, either.

A final example of this "equivalence" of feces and food appears in another form in *bokur*—the convention of harassing dancers. Recall that "harassing" involves members of one moiety wiping rotted food on dancers of another moiety as they perform. In the clearest demonstration of food-feces equivalence, infants are sometimes lifted and their buttocks wiped on the heads or shoulders of dancers. In fact, as noted earlier, this harassment is a friendly gesture; it would not be done to a stranger, or to one with whom one is not on good terms. The aggressive component is not altogether absent—young men are often pelted quite ferociously—but neither is it mandatory: children and older women are merely tapped. Wiping food waste or a baby's buttocks, yet another form of food (cf. Jackson 1995:105), then, is a friendly/joking action.

Recap: The Symbolism of Food-and-Eating

The points made thus far are (1) the linguistic focus on food and eating in Sursurunga social life cannot be attributed to a shortage of food, and therefore

---

12. This explanation is not without its own problems. Although some forms of body exuviae are alienable nouns, such as *tul* ("ear wax"), *songsong* ("sweat"), and *mismis* ("urine"), others are inalienable: *bingin* ("one's snot"), *ngair* ("one's semen"), and *dár* ("one's blood").

must have other sources; (2) the provision and sharing of food both connotes and creates good social relations; (3) food and feces/waste are seen as essentially the same thing; the body makes food its own—that is, it "inalienable-izes" food—in the course of digesting it and turning it into feces; and (4) the equivalence of food and feces in the expression "*Ak tikim*" is a hyperbolic statement about the solidarity of social relations, an equivalence also expressed in *bokur*.

Food-and-eating expresses solidarity in social relations. In the examples and cases above, food-and-eating defined social relations, whether they were nurturing, restorative, flirtatious, or appreciative. The grammatical focus on eating highlights food as a central feature of social life without marking the nature of the importance of food. This expression of the role of food in social life is accomplished in myth and in the ideology of feasting and food (and in food's transformed state, feces).

The question of why food rather than other substances should be symbolic of social relations still lingers. The least complicated answer is that food has always been culturally affiliated with relationships—that is, other people. The processes of creating a garden, sponsoring a feast, and hunting pigs necessarily entail other people. And the allocation of surplus food to other people in a hot, humid climate with no refrigeration is merely avoiding waste (again, the connection between food and refuse), and, importantly, setting up or reinforcing reciprocal obligations on the part of others. Jackson summarizes this perspective nicely:

Production and consumption for [the Sursurunga] tend towards moral, rather than (as for us) merely functional, activity. As a moral activity, production becomes a process of exhibition, inseparable from consumption. It elicits the latent potentiality of "public" participation which encompasses the simple idea of subsistence. Production is public in that it is open to the knowledge and, more significantly, the judgment of others and therefore implies community attention. In a real sense, what we call production is an arena for revealing cultural value, explicitly the value of *artangan*, social help and challenge. (Jackson 1995:64)

The Sursurunga focus on food and eating may be best understood as a natural outcome of the processes of procuring and consuming food. An emphasis on food and eating does not require a feasting complex, and, in itself, does not, however, account for feasting as a social institution. The mortuary feasting complex, then, employs, but is not necessarily exclusively due to, Sursurunga understandings about food and eating. Such understandings are part of the cultural setting in which feasting takes place, but they do not make up all of the setting. Other cultural, psychological, and sociological aspects combine with the symbolism of food, eating, and relationships to make the mortuary feasting complex among the Sursurunga an important and resilient social institution.

SHAME, GRIEF, AND FEASTING

People's involvement in mortuary feasting is also partially due to emotional factors. The two most important of these factors are best glossed "feeling shame" and "grieving."[13]

What I have glossed "feeling shame" is the Sursurunga word *rumrum*, an intransitive verb. This is a generic term and can also be glossed "shyness" or "embarrassment."[14] *Rumrum* is unpleasant affect and has as a central concern anxiety about what others might think or say. There is good reason to see *rumrum* as the Sursurunga equivalent of the nearby Tolai *vavirvir*, glossed by A. Epstein as "embarrassment-shame" (1992:221–229). According to Epstein, Tolai find unpleasant the "awareness of the gaze of others" in the context of risking "one's breach of custom or propriety" (1992:221).

Many Sursurunga men speak of the anxiety they feel about whether their lineage will be able to organize and sponsor a proper feast. These men, who are normally carefree and/or fatalistic, fret about their ability to fulfill their feast-related obligations. In fact, most of the times that I have seen Sursurunga men experiencing anxiety of some sort is when a prearranged pig transaction has fallen through or failed to materialize for one reason or another. The sense of panic that engulfs men in such circumstances suggests that the provision and acquisition of feasting materiel, especially pigs, is deeply rooted in the psyches of individual Sursurunga males. Although sometimes unavoidable (and not all that uncommon), this type of episode often results in curtness with others and facial expressions that transmit worry and frustration. To my question about what motivates them to invest the time and labor and resources into feasts, men responded with answers that were a variation on the theme of avoiding *rumrum* (or, often, the Neo-Melanesian *sem*). As I noted in the previous chapter, some men specifically mentioned that the purpose of providing *bingbingpul* pigs was to avoid gossip, which shows that an important motivation for contributing toward a successful feast was to avoid unpleasant affect associated with believing that others were evaluating them in negative terms. "We would feel shame if we didn't have a proper feast," are the words of one informant, summarizing what many men said about feasting. Anxiety over avoiding *rumrum*/"feeling shame" by failing to perform the appropriate behaviors and being thought of as niggardly is a strong psychological basis for participating in mortuary feasting. Conversely, the successful organization and performance of a feast, climaxed by the impressive display of food just prior to eating, is a way of experiencing the pleasurable *laes*, or "feeling pride."[15] Although normally articulated as the avoidance of *rumrum*/"feeling shame," the competent and successful sponsorship of a mortuary feast also generates *laes*/"feeling pride." There is no evi-

---

13. I have addressed some of the psychological functions of mortuary feasting elsewhere (Bolyanatz 1994a). This section cites heavily from that discussion.

14. In this regard, the genitals can be referred to as *náin rumrum*, "the shameful place." *Rumrum*, then, is to be avoided if possible.

15. Most Sursurunga emotions are said to have their source in the *bál*, the belly. *Laes*, as a noble emotion, springs from the *mátán mansin*, the center of the breast.

dence for a competitive feasting complex such as found on Goodenough Island (Young 1971), but Sursurunga do find that the sponsoring of a successful feast in the eyes of others is a source of pleasant affect.

The other affective factor is grieving. The Sursurunga (intransitive) verb glossed "to grieve" is *tang i bál*, or, literally, "the belly cries." Crying (*tang*) is the most unmistakable part of one's behavior when one is grieving, and to say that a woman cried without providing any other context is a euphemism for mourning.

The mortuary feasting complex functions as a defense mechanism for Sursurunga men. Mortuary feasting provides men with an expression for otherwise un- or underexpressed grief. In terms of psychological function, the mortuary feasting complex does for men what institutionalized wailing does for women: it is a culturally constituted setting that allows the expression of affect that results from the death of a member of the community. In saying that mortuary feasting functions as a defense mechanism for men, I do not mean to say that it cannot or does not serve that function for women, nor that it always effectively reduces intrapsychic pain for men. Rather, mortuary ritual provides for men the same structured opportunity for affective expression that wailing at a funeral does for women. Although the opportunity for displacement is provided, it is not always realized by all men all the time. Along the lines of Epstein's argument, close attention to mortuary feasting serves as a way of acting out unpleasant affect for Sursurunga men, who are bereft of one culturally approved form of catharsis, weeping. (There is one other affective motivation for participation: *mámnai*, or feeling sorry for someone. People demonstrate their compassion for bereaved friends and kin by attending funerals and subsequent rites.)

RECIPROCITY AND FEASTING

There is a vigorous concern with the exact repayment of debts and obligations among the Sursurunga. Examples from a variety of sociological contexts support this assertion. One such exemplar is the practice of *bokur*, mentioned in Chapter 4. Recall that dancers are harassed by having rotted food and other matter wiped or slapped on them by members of their father's lineage.

Another example is that services performed outside of the lineage are monetized. This might include a commercial service such as the use of someone else's copra-drying house (usually for a kina or two). Even a relatively minor service, such as the cutting of pork to be distributed at a feast, will require a token payment of perhaps 10 toea. Money provides a way to achieve perfectly balanced reciprocity. Donations from other villages for church-related feasts are paid back to the toea. In traditional times, exact repayment was also the norm: as they still are today, pigs exchanged for feasts had their girths measured with rattan so that they would be reciprocated with a pig of precisely equal size.

Understandings and values regarding marriage are heavily informed by a notion of reciprocity and repayment of debt. An analysis of marriage among the Sursurunga allows one to see how marriage conventions, cognition, and a concern with reciprocity work to influence individuals to participate in mortuary feasting.

Traditional marriage rules among the Sursurunga included prescribed moiety exogamy and a preference for classificatory cross-cousin marriage. (I know of no cases of actual cross-cousin marriage.) The moiety exogamy rule is still in place, and 31 out of the 33 marriages in Tekedan village conform to this pattern, a practice that indicates that the exogamy prescription is still intact. Reciprocity appears even in the exceptional cases: each of the four individuals involved in the two *yom* (intramoiety) marriages at Tekedan were required to pay a small amount of cash compensation to their spouse's families to "pay for the shame" of their new affines. Finally, reciprocity was offered to me by a group of women as the reason given for a preference for MBD/FZS marriage. A woman marrying her classificatory FZS "repays" her father's clan for the energies he expended for the benefit of members of another clan and moiety—that is, his children.

Many of the components of the mortuary feasting sequence are explicitly portrayed by the Sursurunga themselves in reciprocal terms. Women who wail at the funeral are given food at a subsequent *ngin i pol* feast, as are those men who handled the corpse and dug the grave. The wish to settle a debt, along with the wish to receive settlement, cannot be overlooked as reasons that induce people to participate in mortuary feasting.[16]

LEADERSHIP AND FEASTING

Political leadership and feast sponsorship are closely linked. In general, the latter is a necessary condition of the former. That is, political authority rests, at least in part, on the ability to organize and sponsor mortuary feasts. This means that another reason men are motivated to participate in mortuary feasting is that competence and significant contributions to successful feasts are means to the end of prestige and authority.

A person with the ability to organize a feast is accorded the term "*kabisit.*" The word includes the morpheme *kabin*, which means "source" or "root." Informants sometimes provided the more literal Neo-Melanesian gloss "*as bilong kaikai*" ("the source of [the] food"), and often used *kabisit* and the Neo-Melanesian "*bikman*" interchangeably.

Another aspect of the expression "*kabisit*" is made clear by the following anecdote. I was once traveling with an older man from another village near the end of my time on New Ireland when he told me that I must most certainly be a *kabisit* by now, having gone to so many feasts and seen how they were done. Leaving to one side the issue of Sursurunga notions of epistemology, perception, and learning (i.e., seeing = knowing = doing), it is worthwhile to note that the man's comment shows that an important qualification for *kabisit* status is

---

16. Jackson also notes that a sense of moral obligation in the form of *artangan*, or "helping" (1995:225), and the wish to garner public recognition for helping in certain ways (1995:236) are also important reasons for participation in mortuary feasts.

knowledge. This knowledge includes all aspects of feasting in general, from the sorts of feasts to be organized for various purposes to the steps involved in performing a specific feast, from initial introduction of the idea of a feast to potential supporters, through (most clearly in the case of the *ngin i pol* feast) the final prestations. Perhaps most important, however, is the ability to get people to conform to one's ambitions by performing the labor necessary to provide food and other feasting paraphernalia. This ability is not represented as a characterological advantage, or a perquisite of wealth, but simply as knowing how. It may seem tautological, but the Sursurunga version is formulated in this way: *kabisit*s sponsor feasts because they know how; they know how because they are *kabisit*s. Knowledge is demonstrated by performance; performance is made possible by knowledge. In this regard, "knowing" how to sponsor a feast entails much more than memorizing of the steps involved. It also involves the sociological knowledge required to exercise power over others (Jackson 1995:336–344). A *kabisit* is known by the feasts that he sponsors (although many feasts are organized by men not renowned as *kabisit*s). This is the point made by Clay when she notes that "a big man is recognized when people experience what he has produced, when they see a dance performance, receive pork or observe a ritual" (1992:723).

Recall also that some informants glossed this expression as "*bikman.*" The aspects of authority and prestige of *kabisit*s are not to be ignored, and it is to these that I now turn.

From around the early 1980s until the early 1990s, political leadership at Tekedan had fallen to two older men (as it happens, one from each matrimoiety[17]), Sam and Tovina (Tovina has been married to Sam's uterine sister since about 1972.). Sam died in 1994, Tovina in 1998. (As I write this, there is something of a leadership vacuum at Tekedan, and it is felt by many people. One of Tovina's sons, Topiknat, is one of the more likely candidates to help fill this void.)

Both of these men were heeded at weekly community meetings, and I am unable to think of an instance in which their wishes were not at least partially fulfilled. Each of these men were referred to as *kabisit*, and their prestige and leadership were unsurpassed within Tekedan village. Even beyond Tekedan, they were sometimes called upon to adjudicate disputes—which means that their recommendations were expected to be followed. Unfortunately, neither of these men organized a feast during my stay on New Ireland, so I have no firsthand knowledge of their prowess when it comes to sponsoring feasts. The point can still be made, however, that two of the men resident at Tekedan known as *kabisit*s were also known throughout the area as having political authority and prestige. The relationship between authority, prestige, and *kabisit* status is, as in the tautology above, also circular: Sam and Tovina were *kabisit*s because they

---

17. Although I never heard anyone say that each moiety was required to be represented by a local leader, the balance that is achieved by having leader of each moiety in the village recalls Errington's (1974:49) point about the Duke of York Islands in which such a balance was explicitly required.

had authority and prestige, and they had authority and prestige because they were *kabisit*s.

The organization of a feast involves getting others to do what one wants them to do. Prestige and authority are exercised by *kabisit*s (and, on a lesser scale, by any feast sponsor) by determining a day for a feast (other than, obviously, a funeral feast), and by recruiting support for the feast by asking individual clan[18] members, "*Arwat turpasi bor?*" ("Are you able to acquire a pig?"). If enough positive responses are forthcoming, the onus of feast sponsorship abates somewhat; individuals who have committed themselves to providing pigs now face the pressures of complying with their promises.

The sponsor of a feast will first look for pigs from members of his own lineage, then to members of his clan before looking to members of other clans of the same moiety who are closely affiliated through residence and/or friendship. If a large number of pigs are needed, the sponsor of the feast will have to extend himself to find members of his clan who are willing to contribute a pig in accordance with one of the three approaches described below. The sponsor and those helping him will then attempt to acquire pigs from any source through one or more of three avenues: (1) *utngin sál,* (2) *kokos,* and (3) *turpasi.*[19]

Utngin sál ("new road") is the establishment of a new debt of a pig. In this case, there is no extant pig debt, and the owner of a pig may prefer to establish a new pig debt rather than selling the pig outright to the person trying to obtain one. The arrangement is made in advance, and upon delivery of the pig a day before the feast, the length and girth of the pig are measured by lengths of rattan. These rattan lengths are kept at the men's house of the feast sponsor so that when the time comes for him to reciprocate, he will provide a pig of the same size.

Kokos ("to answer; to reciprocate"; transitive verb) is a second means by which a pig can be acquired. In the case of an extant pig debt, the sponsor of a feast can collect the outstanding pig. *Kokos* is, naturally, the other side of *utngin sál*—the repayment and initiation of a pig debt, respectively. Upon receipt of a pig that was owed, the debt is terminated, and there is nothing like the incremental ongoing sequence of debts found in the Highlands of New Guinea (e.g., the *moka* and *te* complexes; A. Strathern [1971]; Meggitt [1974]).

Turpasi[20] ("to stand hold" or "start"; transitive verb) is a third means by which a pig can be acquired. In this case, a man seeking one will go to a man— or, not at all infrequently, a woman—and inquire about a pig. The owner will

---

18. A smaller scale feast may entail only lineage members. A larger feast may entail members of other clans (but of the same moiety) who are closely affiliated with the sponsor and his lineage.

19. The individuals who provide pigs to members of the feast-sponsoring unit will be acknowledged in the *ratis bu* rite, public recognition of their assistance as well as a source of *laes/*"feeling pride."

20. The word for "buy" usually used to refer to the purchase of pigs is *tumai.* I was told that *huli,* a word for "buy" more generally used, can in no circumstances be used to refer to the acquisition of pigs. See Jackson 1995:234–237 for a discussion of pig acquisition.

state a purchase price, and the sponsor will either accept or reject the transaction, with no haggling or bargaining. As one person noted about the process of purchasing a pig, "The owner of the pig is the owner of the pig, and he knows the pig and how much it's worth; you can't argue with him." The purchase price of a pig is determined largely by two considerations: (1) the perceived ability of the buyer to come up with a particular sum, and (2) the size of the pig. The cost of a pig ranges from K10 for a piglet to well over K500 for a large pig that stands perhaps 30 inches high. More often than not the purchase price consists of a combination of cash and lengths of *reu*, or shell money. (One five-to-six foot length of *reu* is worth K30.) Also, it is not uncommon for a larger pig to be acquired by a combination of *utngin sál* or *kokos* and purchase with cash and/or *reu*.

The current needs of the pig's owner determine the mode of transaction. If a pig owner is short of cash and needs some for, say, children's school fees, a new radio, vehicle purchase, and the like, she or he will ask for cash only. If the owner needs just a bit of cash, a small amount of cash will be paid, and the remaining value of the pig will become a debt. In one case, a huge pig, worth at least K500, was purchased for K100. But the transaction also involved a *utngin sál*, or new pig debt, for which the buyer of the pig is now liable. In this instance, cash was exchanged *and* the pig was measured with lengths of rattan. In order to be fully repaid or "answered," a pig of equal size and K100 must be handed over at some future date as *kokos*.

In Chapter 3, I indicated that feasting needs were taken into consideration in the construction of gardens. Likewise, the quality of the produce extracted, or soon to be extracted, from extant gardens influences the timing of feasts. This is the main reason that leadership—being a *kabisit*—is relevant beyond the feasting event. People who are likely to be called upon to supply garden produce know that even if there is no impending feast, the extra work required to construct a larger or an extra garden will likely pay off in that one can avoid the *rumrum*/"feeling shame" of having to tell a *kabisit* in the process of recruiting support for a feast that one is unable to provide, for example, feast-quality taro.[21]

In the days before the feast, tubers, green coconuts, and other foods and the paraphernalia of food preparation[22] are collected. On the day before the feast, the pigs that have been arranged for are collected and brought to spend the night at the site of their eventual demise.

The threat to the prestige of a sponsor—and to the renown of an aspiring *kabisit*—is that too many people will respond to "*Arwat turpasi bor?*/Are you able to acquire a pig?" that they are unable to provide a pig at the time the would-be sponsor wishes. When a man is asked if he can provide a pig, he must

---

21. Recall that ideally, the *ngin i pol* feast should take place as soon as possible after the funeral, especially in the event of the death of a prestigious elder. Surviving kin who delay the *ngin i pol* feast not only risk shame for themselves, but also undermine the memory of the deceased.

22. This category includes banana leaves for covering foods that will be steamed, bark to wrap the banana leaves, rattan for tying packets of food, coconut leaves for making baskets, and so on.

consider a number of variables. What are the consequences of failing to comply? If the feast proceeds anyway, one is faced with belatedly providing a pig, or not providing a pig at all. Either option entails a reduction of prestige vis-à-vis the sponsor, although the former option is less likely to be construed as outright rejection. If, for example, a potential feast sponsor, A, is unable to get an adequate number of people to comply, then a refusal by B puts B at an advantage vis-à-vis the would-be sponsor, and A's position as someone who knows (or ought to know) how to organize a feast is undermined. Also, B's unwillingness to comply with A's wishes are construed as an indication that perhaps B knows more about feasting than A.

Complying with a would-be sponsor's request indicates at least a minimal level of political allegiance. A successful feast allows a man to "ride the coattails" of the sponsor: the sponsor and his lineage are seen as capable, and *rumrum*/"feeling shame" is avoided. Furthermore, the ability to organize and coordinate a mortuary feast is both an index and a source of prestige for the accomplished or aspiring *kabisit* who is sponsoring the feast. On the other hand, a feast that fails to materialize can leave a man stuck with a pig for which he has arranged—at perhaps considerable personal cost—and no feast. This sort of leadership—and its risks—recalls the classic "big man" of the New Guinea Highlands. Recently, the "big man" model has been juxtaposed with that of the "great man."

The distinction between "big man societies" and "great man societies" in Melanesia was first proposed by Godelier (1986). His point was that the standardized Melanesian big man was not a particularly useful model for understanding political leadership among the Baruya, a Highlands Fringe group. M. Strathern later summarized the differences between the two in the following way:

Big men are produced in systems that promote competitive exchanges, the transfer of women against bridewealth, and war compensation procedures that allow wealth to substitute for homicide. Great men, on the other hand, flourish where public life turns on male initiation rather than ceremonial exchange, on the direct exchange of women in marriage and on warfare pursued as homicide for homicide. (1991:1)

By these criteria, modern Sursurunga society is best represented as a big man society, but the Sursurunga do not fit well into either category. Using Strathern's criteria above, the Sursurunga show little in the way of the characteristics of great man society. But neither are the big man guidelines altogether fulfilled: I have already noted that the competitive aspects of feasting such as those found on Goodenough Island are absent among the Sursurunga. Still, bridewealth is used as a means of exchanging women (although, as I have mentioned, it is not always clear that bridewealth in a patrilineal system and in a matrilineal system are analogous institutions), and wealth is used as a means of redressing homicide.

Liep has suggested that among some Massim societies, the colonial experience has engendered a process he calls "bigmanization" (1991:46–47). This process is a result of pacification (in that homicide-for-homicide resolution is disparaged), missionization (in that male initiation and other ritual systems are discouraged), and capitalism (in that "gifts" become "commodities" [Gregory 1982; Foster 1995:25–66] and there is a concomitant interest in surplus/profit). But the fact that modern Sursurunga resemble more of a big man than a great man system is not necessarily due to bigmanization induced by colonialism. The extinct *suka bim* feast mentioned in the previous chapter suggests elements of competitive exchange. There is no evidence that bridewealth was ever absent or that sister-exchange marriage was ever present among precontact Sursurunga. Finally, wealth-for-homicide substitution seems to have been present, if not prominent, in the report of a parcel of land at Tekedan—Kankapgam—that was given by a member of the Rongol clan to a member of the Kárpápus clan as compensation for the death of a Kárpápus at the hands of a Rongol in an event that I estimate to have taken place in about 1880.

It is certainly true that although the influences of pacification, missioniza-tion, and capitalism have altered many aspects of Sursurunga society, these in-fluences cannot be said to have resulted in bigmanisation. At most, these influ-ences reduced the tendencies of great man-ism by making, for example, com-pensatory homicide more difficult. But it is a misnomer to call this bigmaniza-tion because it suggests that big men are a result of the colonial period, rather than independent of it. Although a big man system has been enhanced by Ger-man, and, more profoundly, Australian colonial control, the process is probably better called "de-greatmanization" because it inhibits strategies and directions that characterize great men societies.

This process of de-greatmanization is why mortuary feasting is the primary means of attaining political power, and why individuals participate in feasting even if they are not sponsors. Sponsors acquire prestige and, eventually, *kabisit* status, through the promotion of successful feasting rather than through talionic warfare or arranged marriages as (putatively) in the past. Political advantage also accrues to those individuals supporting sponsors since the provision of the stuff of feasts—either tubers or pigs—provides a person with political capital vis-à-vis the sponsor as well as vis-à-vis other feast-sponsoring supporters.

Clearly, then, the sponsorship of a feast cannot be divorced from its politi-cal implications. Consider the following case, in which standard procedure was modified, allowing a glimpse of the link between authority, prestige, and feast sponsorship:

In 1986, a woman named Teruko of Silbat clan and born at Huris village died in Rabaul. Teruko was survived by (among others) Niumai, a Z, and Tomaibi, a B (see Diagram 6.2).

In 1991, there was interest on the part of Niumai and Tomaibi to sponsor a *ngin i pol* feast on behalf of Teruko. Todus, the lineage's and clan's preeminent big-man was not himself interested in organizing the feast. Eventually, Tomaibi and Niumai were allowed to do so, and in October 1991, plans were initiated for a feast which was to take place 25 January 1992.

Tomaibi had originally asked Todus when he (Todus) was going to be able to spon-sor the feast. Todus declined to make any specific plans himself, but allowed Tomaibi to organize the feast—a privilege that Tomaibi is not necessarily guaranteed. Tomaibi em-

Diagram 6.2
Dramatis Personae of *Ngin i Pol* Feast

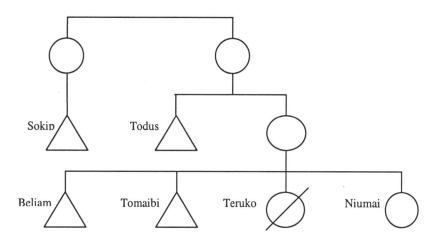

phasized that he was not in competition with Todus, but was organizing this feast "underneath" Todus, and that this feast was his "training" in "*kastam skul*" (Neo-Melanesian for "heritage or custom school") as he called it.

When asked, some people said that Todus was the feast sponsor, whereas others said that Tomaibi was. In fact, both views are accurate, since Tomaibi was the most active organizer, but the feast took place under the auspices of Todus. Observations of behavior at the feast were difficult to interpret without knowing the participants themselves. Todus said very little throughout and his participation was limited to a very un-*kabisit*-like digging of a hole. Beliam (Tomaibi's and Niumai's B) was also quite involved, although he was not centrally involved in the organization of the feast. More the extrovert than Tomaibi, he took centerstage at specific points.

Todus's role in the organization of the feast was primarily a clandestine one. He was responsible for asking his enate Sokip, for example, if he would be able to acquire a pig, just as other lineage leaders, after being informed of the feast by Tomaibi, asked members of their own lineages. Todus, then, served two purposes in this feast: first, he allowed it to transpire, as the designated Silbat clan leader in the area. Second, as a lineage leader, he was responsible for recruiting support for the feast on the part of members of his lineage. Tomaibi, in wishing to remain subordinate to Todus, first requested his permission to hold the feast. Todus, in allowing the feast to take place as Tomaibi asked, reinforced his position as clan head. By recruiting pigs for the feast (from Sokip and others), Todus reinforced his position as lineage head. In both regards, Todus, *qua kabisit*, gained prestige.[23]

This case shows that mortuary feasting cannot be divorced from politics. There is a linkage between authority and prestige, leadership, and feasting. Pacification, missionization, and capitalism have not yet dealt fatal blows to

---

23. I am grateful to Stephen A. Jackson for his help in gathering information about this case.

traditional patterns of leadership (and its concomitants, authority and prestige) among the Sursurunga: *kabisit*s still expect and receive the compliance of others in both routine and ritual activities. Sursurunga mortuary feasting thus can provide motivation for individuals with political aspirations to participate in and thereby maintain the institution of mortuary feasting.

Here is a case in which mortuary feasting is explicitly connected to leadership:

A pig at Tekedan village had a reputation for ferocity and, just as many had warned would happen, one day killed a dog belonging to someone else. The owner of the pig happened to be away at the time and was unable to represent his interests during the ensuing discussion of what was to be done about the pig. The pig owner's mother and mother's brother were both aged and not able to overcome the consensus that the pig should be killed to prevent further property damage.

After they executed the pig, the young men sought out Singong, an older man who, they figured, would know what to do with the pig. The death of a pig was not to be wasted: there were ceremonial needs to be met, and Singong would know just how to apply the pork that would be forthcoming.

Singong knew that his wife's lineage in nearby Nokon village were contemplating doing some repair work on the lineage cemetery—work that entails a small (one or two pigs) feast. Singong then made a gift of the pig to his wife's enates in order to repay an earlier similar gift to his lineage.

In this case, a feast was performed as a result of Singong's acknowledged leadership. Singong transformed the mundane death of a pig into a ritual exchange—an act made possible by the authority that he has. Although it may be stretching the point to say that without Singong's leadership there would have been no feast, it is the case that Singong's authority and prestige influenced the way the pig was to be used: his leadership created a ceremonial event, a clear example of how authority and feasting are linked.

SUMMARY

The responses of people to the question of why mortuary feasting has been retained in the face of the sorts of changes affecting much of Papua New Guinea at the end of the 20th century were usually permutations of, "That's the way our ancestors did it." I take such a response to be, in part, evidence of the fact that the reasons for involvement in mortuary ritual are not only complex, but also not entirely conscious. Both of these attributes are to be found in this chapter.

In addition to being represented in matrilineal descent, the understandings that inform much of mortuary feasting are represented in an Oceanic grammatical feature. Do the Sursurunga—or anyone else—emphasize mortuary feasting because they have a system of alienable and inalienable noun classes? The answer is clearly no. Nevertheless, grammar may be seen as reflecting a set of understandings that themselves function to reinforce the social institution of mortuary activity by impelling individuals to participate. The cognitive constructs emphasized in Oceanic noun classification are integrated culturally and sociologically in mortuary feasting in that mortuary activities are importantly informed by understandings about alienability. The grammatical "rules" used by individual actors are consistent with the cultural "rules" that deceased fathers' groups need to be compensated, and that this compensation best occurs after the father's death. The cognition of (in)alienability represented in Sursurunga grammar that finds social relevance in combination with matrilineal descent is a prominent aspect of Sursurunga social life. Sursurunga grammar seems to have changed little since 1616,[24] and to the degree that it is connected to mortuary feasting, it contributes an intuition of propriety to mortuary ritual, as well as to other aspects of social life that it informs.

The presence of mortuary feasting among the Sursurunga can in part be accounted for by the fact that individuals are impelled by values, understandings, social relations, and emotions that have to do with (1) grammatical and cognitive constructions of alienability, (2) a deep concern with balanced reciprocity, (3) food and eating—*namnam*—as an index of congenial social relations, (4) the avoidance of *rumrum*/"feeling shame" and the function of feasting as a defense mechanism, and (5) leadership evidenced by authority and prestige as exemplified by the expression *kabisit*. None of these five sources of mortuary ritual is dominated by matrilineal descent understandings, and the first three might be safely said to be effectively unrelated to matrilineal descent understandings. As noted earlier, Sursurunga mortuary feasting is also in part governed by matrimoiety, matriclan, and matrilineage membership. There is, for example, the issue of the avoidance of *rumrum*/"shame," in which group membership matters because people will experience bad feelings if one of their enates acts shamefully, even if they do not. Also, leadership and political authority concerns are largely conducted along the lines of and within the auspices of the matrilineal descent group. The aspiration to leadership, however, is not itself related to matriliny, only the exercise of it.

Now that I have discussed the causes of mortuary ritual, I move to the effects, which include the heightened salience of matrilineal descent understandings and the activation of matrilineal descent groups.

---

24. Possessives from a word list elicited in 1616 suggest that inalienable and alienable possession worked very much like it does today (Lanyon-Orgill 1960:25ff.).

Chapter 7

Consequents of Mortuary Feasting: The Salience and Activation of Matriliny

In the previous chapter, mortuary feasting was shown to be the result of a number of different concerns, interests, and understandings, including understandings that had little to do with matrilineal descent. In this chapter, I discuss the effects of mortuary feasting, drawing attention to the ways in which matrilineally informed social statuses are emphasized throughout the mortuary feasting complex. One of the outcomes of mortuary ritual is that it makes salient matrilineal understandings and statuses, and activates matrilineal social relations, producing the lineages, clans, and moieties found at ritual mortuary events. The Sursurunga do not try to create matrilineal descent groups through mortuary ritual, but they are made nonetheless. In the previous chapter, I looked at what impels Sursurunga individuals to engage in mortuary feasting; in this chapter, I look at what they accomplish through it.

It is at mortuary feasts, more than any other aspect of Sursurunga social life, that matrilineages qualify as corporate descent units. Mortuary feasts mobilize matrilineal descent understandings for all participants, not just sponsors, since many aspects of mortuary feasting require individuals to be identified primarily, if not solely, on the basis of matrilineal group membership. Sponsorship of mortuary feasts requires summoning assistance from enates. This assistance involves not a little expenditure of time, resources, and labor on the part of matrilineally related individuals. Matrilineal descent understandings and their concomitant social relations also appear in the designation of "host" and "guest" moieties, funerary obligations and proscriptions, *bingbingpul* and *lulsit* providers and recipients, feast sponsorship, pig services (killing and butchering), and pork prestations.

Before describing the ways in which the salience of matrilineal descent understandings is a largely unintended consequence of the mortuary feasting sequence, I turn to a description of Sursurunga descent ideology. When I say that matrilineal descent understandings are made salient though feasting, I mean more than merely group membership, since descent group membership is but part of a larger complex of descent ideology. To be sure, not all Sursurunga are conscious of all of the aspects of descent ideology every last minute of every feast. It is the case, however, that (outside of a probing ethnographer) mortuary ritual is the most likely regular set of circumstances to evoke these kinds of notions. I did not ask people what they were thinking in between bites at feasts. I did, however, listen in the men's house and watch during rituals such as *suka bim* when older men told young adults clan stories and how and why feasting is done. Mortuary feasting thus provides the best context for passing on descent ideology to the next generation. In a sense, these teaching moments are the activation of matrilineal descent groups writ small in that matrilineal descent group membership is the focal point in the articulation of descent ideology.

SURSURUNGA DESCENT IDEOLOGY

Among the Sursurunga, descent is commonly characterized in the idiom of a banana plant. A *kabinun* ("stem of a banana plant") refers to a matriclan (and rarely, a matrimoiety). Members of lineages who consider themselves to be part of the same clan, but cannot demonstrate that connection genealogically, are referred to as the shoots or suckers that grow from a banana plant. Quite often, the actual origin of these shoots are under the ground, and therefore the places in which they connect to the main part of the plant are unseen. This is why I utilize the convention of referring to Sursurunga matrigroups as lineages and clans: clan members are assumed to be connected with each other, just as the shoots from the banana plant are known to come from the plant, even though the connection is hidden.

Another implication of the *kabinun* metaphor is that a common (extended maternal) origin is the Sursurunga basis for shared descent group membership. Unlike other parts of Papua New Guinea in which, for example, blood is seen to come from the mother and bone from the father, Sursurunga descent ideology is not grounded on shared substance between enates, only shared origin. Clan origin stories, for example, focus on pedigree and shared location of that origin rather than substance as the basis for connectedness.

This emphasis on origin rather than substance can be seen in the most complete set of clan origin stories in my possession. These stories were collected by Lesli of Poronbus village, having been written down in Neo-Melanesian as he dictated them to a younger enate some years earlier. My English translation of the written account follows; my comments are in square brackets.

History of the Piknat Clan

A bush spirit in the form of a snake named Teu[/Tew] (Gulembek) bore three children: two boys, Rewa and Rewkai, and one girl, Terew.

Terew married a man from the Hantahi [Antalis] clan. The two of them lived together and made a garden for themselves. In their garden they planted yam known as "*kanih*" [which also means snake] and *mami* [a type of yam] known as "*kah*" and taro.

The two of them planted all of these things because they were in the habit of getting the greens from the taro leaf and the *kah* for the purpose of giving them to Tirew's mother, Tew (the snake).

When giving these things to Tew, only Tirew was involved. Her husband did not see; she simply gave clandestinely.

Once, Tirew's husband looked back when his wife wanted to give her mother, Tew, the shoots of the taro and *kah*.

At this time, Tirew's husband saw his affine Tew, Tirew's mother.

So Tew became embarrassed and cried. Then came rain, wind, earthquake, lightning, and thunder. And the village became completely dark.

She cried, and her house, the base of a bamboo stand known as *Wán,* fell down a huge precipice. She spiraled down to the ground.

[The following passage has been crossed out]

Tew then traveled to Kudukudu to look for Kárnatew.

Tew then got going and traveled to Kudukudu. And she went to stay at a village known as Raputraput. And she again went, going from Raputraput to Lihir.

The Twelve Children of Tinul and Tinhol:

Kabinwol (m)	Sulam (m)
Kolnák (m)	Tinbilam (f)
Manian (m)	?
Gowirwir (m)	?
Kangus (m)	?
Ritang (m)	?

Kabisit: Chiefs [in English]

1. Rewa
2. Rewkai
3. Támanmátlang
4. Rewtang
5. Kolnák
6. Manian
7. Gowirwir
8. Ritang
9. Kangus
10. Sulam Rewtang

Tumbuna [Notation in Sursurunga: *kabisit*]

1. Rewa [crossed out]
2. Rewkai
3. Támánmátlang
4. Rewtang [crossed out] Kasngew [sic]
5. Kabinwol
6. Kolnák
7. Manian
8. Kangus
9. Gowirwir
10. Rewtang Sulam [crossed out]

Diagram 7.1
Generations of the Piknat Clan

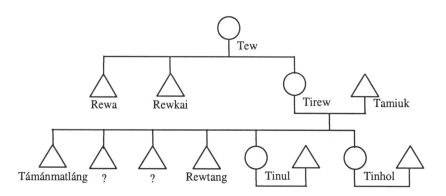

The Generations of the Piknat Clan

Tew was a bush spirit in the form of a snake who bore the forerunners of what is now known as the Piknat clan.

Tew came up at a village known as Poronbim. She stayed at this place. Later, she bore two boys. Their names were Rewa and Rewkai. Tew also bore a girl; her name was Tirew.

When the two boys Rewa and Rewkai grew up to be men, Tew gave the two some responsibility. The two of them went up to Ngádámá mountain. There the two of them learned how to do wrong things. And the two of them stayed at Ngádámá mountain.

And their sister Tirew bore four children: two males, Támánmatlang and Rewtang, and two females, Tinul and Tinhol. These two women bore 12 children.

Each one of them [presumably the 12] lived at the places here: Rataman, Kansilibor, Kandamau, Sokulihárám, Kanálápát, Pákángorgor, Kabinbunbun, Beroimoran, Poronbáláu, Tártárál, Lipelik, Hipungan, and Kanbulimahan. [These are *kuranu* and other land parcels in the interior.]

The Story of the Bigmen of Piknat Clan

This is the story of the ancestral spirit Teu (a snake).

Teu came from Poronbim. She bore three children, two males—Rewa and Rewkai, and one female, Tirew. And they all stayed at Poronbim.

Subsequently, Rew and Rewkai went to the top of Ngádámá mountain. And Teu taught the two of them how to do all of the bad things of traditional life.

During this time, Tirew went to Rataman. And she married Tamiuk, a man of the Antalis clan. And the two of them lived at Rataman. The two of them had six children, four males and two females.

And these two females later on bore 12 children, and now, they are a large number. Subsequently, their big man gathered them and they all went to live at Kanbulimahan.

Afterwards, there was a large number of them at Kanbulimahan. At this point, their big man divided them up and sent them around to various places: Kanbulimahan, Kansilibor, Kandamau, Sokulihárám, and Matanaboroi; and another group they sent to live at Kabisimir as fighters for the Seruai [clan].

Most people do not know their clan's origin account to this degree of detail. The application of this kind of knowledge, however, does show up now and then in the attribution of kin terms.

Clan Histories and Kin Terms. Although two individuals may be of the same kin type vis-à-vis a particular ego, they can be called by different terms as a result of membership in different clans. This system of kin term designation is a phenomenon that, to my knowledge, has not been noted in the ethnographic record. Sursurunga consanguineal (to use Morgan's word) kinship terminology resembles the Iroquois pattern, with merging in the +1 generation, and parallel cousin terms merged with sibling terms. Sursurunga affinal kinship terminology is dynamic: as I have shown, kin terms used between two individuals can change as a result of a sociological change.

My discovery of variation in Sursurunga affinal designations came rather late in my initial period of fieldwork. Before departing New Ireland in 1992, I spent much of my time double-checking information, including kinship terminology. During the course of an interview with a middle-aged man, I asked him what he called Tinpai, his SW. He responded that he called her *wowo*. I then suggested that he must then also call Tinkus, another SW, *wowo*. That was incorrect, I was told; Tinkus he calls *nana*. Now, I knew the women involved, and could see no reason for these women, who occupied the same kin type, SW, to be called by different terms by the same ego.

The relationship in focus is affines in adjacent generations; for males, this is SW (but not DH; see the following paragraph). For female egos, the relationships are BSW and BDH. On the basis of matrimoiety exogamy, a (m.s.) SW will be a moiety mate of ego, as will a (f.s.) BSW and BDH. See Diagram 7.2.

Affinal Kin Terms
Diagram 7.2

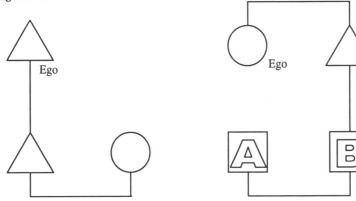

Quite often—and understandably so, given the Sursurunga preference for village exogamy—the spouse-to-be is relatively unknown, and kin terms need to be established for him or her upon marriage. This term will be a consanguineal term emphasizing the same-moiety relationship between ego and the newly married affine. The possibilities are:

kukung: m.s. Z; f.s. B
natung: f.s. C
koko: MB/ZC
wowo: MM
nana: M

The following cases show how knowledge of descent ideology and clan histories affect the use of kinship terms. Some stories that detail the birth and growth of clans often include other groups. Some of these stories include a common origin for different clans, whereas others include mention of groups that assisted or supported each other.

Case 1. Tovina's son Toateli married Tinirwán. Tovina is a member of the Sahwon clan, whereas Tinirwán is a Tokbol. According to the origin story of the Tokbol group, they were originally part of the same root or *kabinun* as the Kámrai clan, which itself has close ties to the Sahwons. This makes Tokbols and Sahwon's "brothers." (Indeed, as an adopted Tokbol, I was always enjoined to refer to all Sahwon men my own age as *tuang*, "my brother.") The result is that Tovina the Sahwon and Kwin, the mother of Tinirwán, are "siblings." And since Tovina is the "MB" of Tinirwán, they began to refer to each other by the reciprocal *koko* (MB/ZC). See Diagram 7.3.

Diagram 7.3
Case 1

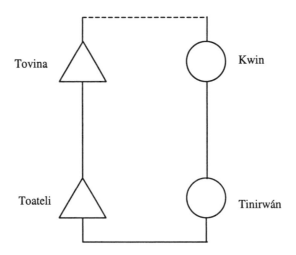

Case 2. In another case, Tomilen's son married Laisa, a Sahwon clan woman. Tomilen himself is a Sahwon, although of a different *rákán*, or "branch" (in anthropological terms, a lineage) than Laisa. Because Tomilen "came from" (that is, had the same origin as) a Sahwon woman, and Laisa is a Sahwon woman, Tomilen now calls her *nana* (M). See Diagram 7.4.

Diagram 7.4
Case 2

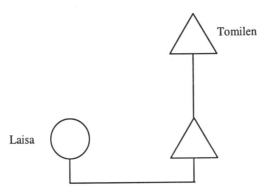

Sometimes, events within living memory inform the relationships between clans. All such histories depict harmonious relationships between clans. These are also "brother" groups. As brothers, they are therefore genealogically equivalent. When asked if there were groups that did not get along well, informants allowed that there were, but that such things are not well remembered.

Case 3. Sokip is a Silbat clan member whose son Makis married a Piknat woman, Elena. The Silbats were traditionally a beach group, occupying the coastal lands in the Nokon-Huris area. The Piknats, on the other hand, traditionally resided in the bush areas in the hilly hinterlands, migrating to the coastal areas only under German, and, later, Australian mandate. The Piknats, upon arriving at the coast, were, understandably, short of land, since they had no traditional basis for claims upon land. Some Silbat clan members offered land to the Piknats, and Topuku and Torengen, Piknat and Silbat big men, respec-

Diagram 7.5
Case 3

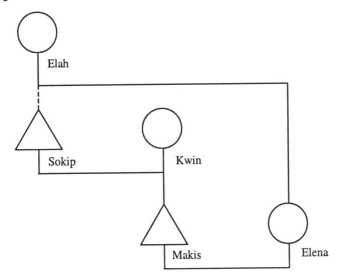

tively, became friendly allies and "brothers." This genealogical connection has been retained to this day with the result that Elena's mother, Elah, is Sokip's classificatory mother, or *nana*, making Elena Sokip's classificatory sister/grandmother, or *wowo*. See Diagram 7.5

Case 4. Toap, a Tokbol man, married Tinko, a Kárpápus woman, and lives in Hilalon, his wife's natal village. Toap's father is Sokip, a Silbat. Many of Tinko's ancestors hail from Himaul, which is Tokbol and Silbat territory. At Himaul, the relationship between Tokbols, Silbats, and Kárpápuses is well known, and Sokip is seen as a classificatory child of Ting, Tinko's mother. Sokip and Tinko are therefore "siblings," and he refers to her as *wowo* (MM). See Diagram 7.6

Diagram 7.6
Case 4

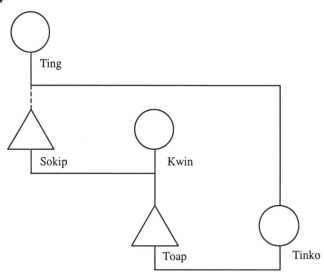

In the Piknat clan stories, as well as the cases exemplifying the attribution of kin terms, there is no reference to substance; rather, the focus is on pedigree—common origin—and shared location. Note that "common origin" here can be seen to refer to being of the same womb, which means that Sursurunga descent ideology entails understandings about conception and gestation.

Sursurunga Gynecology

There is among the Sursurunga the notion—so prevalent in Melanesia—that women, because they menstruate, are dangerous creatures.[1] Sursurunga ethno-

---

1. As in many other places in Melanesia, food that has been stepped over by a woman becomes tainted and possibly poisonous. For example, a man was peeling a betel nut at a large feast. The betel nut slipped out of his hand and fell to the ground. We then looked knowingly at each other, and I said, "Well?" He shook his head and said, "Nah, too many women have walked around here."

gynecology holds that women are most sexually receptive during the time that they are most dangerous: when they are menstruating. A woman is also seen to be at her most fertile at the height of her flow since she has plenty of reproductive fluids (*ngair*) and will conceive a girl and possibly twins at this time; at other times of the month a woman is "dry," and boys are conceived.

The basis for the belief in males, females, and fluids is the notion that a woman needs water and other liquids, so an abundance of menstrual fluid is a necessary condition for the conception of a girl. Evidence for this position is that women do not sweat in the gardens as much as men do, since they conserve their bodily fluids for milk and menstruation. Men are "dry" and have no need for such fluids; therefore they can also be conceived in "dry" wombs. Note that this "wetness" of females is not a substance, but a characteristic of their reproductive abilities. The Sursurunga view of women is related to descent understandings in that the state of the uterus is the variable in question. Being of the same uterus is the only criterion for descent group membership. Uterine origin, like the shoots of a banana plant, is obvious.

ACTIVATED SURSURUNGA MATRILINY

Matrilineal descent-based statuses are made salient and matrilineal social relations activated as a result of mortuary feasting. Other aspects of Sursurunga life also emphasize matriliny, so I am not making the argument that matriliny is the result of feasting only. The argument is simply that, as a consequence of the components of feasting described below, matrilineal descent-based social statuses are most salient for most Sursurunga in the context of the mortuary feasting sequence. Activated matrilineal descent groups emerge when people together engage in social relations that are importantly informed by matrilineal descent understandings.

Mortuary feasting among the Sursurunga is the activity par excellence that brings descent group membership into focus for most adults. I have already described the manner in which the support of lineage members is recruited by feast sponsors sometimes months in advance of a feast, and how the economic solidarity shown by a lineage in preparing for a component of the mortuary feasting complex is unmatched in any other area of Sursurunga social life. The economic requirements of feast sponsorship for a lineage are substantial, especially on the death of a respected person.

For most Sursurunga most of the time, participation in a mortuary feasting event emphasizes one's membership in a matrilineal descent unit. It is at these times that the salience of matrilineally informed social statuses is greatest. Although matrilineal social relations are activated for many people, especially the sponsor and his lineage, in feast preparations, it is during a feasting event that matrilineal descent understandings are most prominent for the entire community. This is true even when the motivation for participation on the part of those attending a mortuary feast is not directly related to matrilineal descent, such as a sense of reciprocity or a wish to consume pork, as I described in the previous chapter.

The Activation of Matriliny at a *Tataun*/Funeral

As I noted above, I did not make it my practice to ask people in the middle of eating, *lulsit* giving, coconut drinking, or any other feasting activity, "Are you thinking about the fact that you are a Sahwon clan member right now?" or "Is your membership in the Malai moiety salient at this moment?" Not only would it have been inappropriate, but the responses may not have been very useful.

The recent processual approaches to mortuary ritual that I addressed in Chapter 1 make it clear that matrilineal descent groups *do* exist in a qualitatively different way at a feast. My claim is that a detail of this emergence of matrilineal descent "groupiness" (to use Foster's term) has as a necessary condition the salience of group membership. And since direct query was impractical, I think inference based on words and actions are the best indicators of salience, so I attend to words and actions as evidence of matrilineal descent group salience in this section.

I have already described the ways in which giving and receiving *lulsit* monies and *bingbingpul* pigs to the lineage of the deceased at a funeral is an explicit compensatory payment for the labor and care provided to people in another lineage by the deceased. Social statuses made salient in the exchange of *bingbingpul* pigs include those individuals in the same matrilineage of the deceased—the *bingbingpul* recipients. In addition, there are the *bingbingpul* providers: those individuals who are matrilineally related to an affine of the deceased, that is, the brother's children of a woman—their *tau*—and, the widow and children of a man, their *tata*. Even if the individuals who provide *lulsit* and *bingbingpul* have grief as the only consciously salient mental state, the giving of these prestations publicly reminds everyone around of matrilineal group membership.

Also at a funeral the names of the visiting wailing women must be recorded, and this task falls to an enate of the deceased. Normally, this bookkeeping chore is given to a person (always a man, by my observations) who was not so close to the deceased that his grief would keep him from performing the task with competence. The only other criterion is that the man be matrilineally related to the deceased, because this group of people is already—by virtue of recording these names, if nothing else—looking ahead to sponsoring, as a lineage, the subsequent *ngin i pol* feast. The wailing and keening is women's analogue to the actual burial of the corpse: it is what women contribute to the making of a proper burial. Unlike the handling of the corpse, wailing is not moiety-specific, but the compensation for wailing, made possible by the recording of names, is.

Before the burial of the corpse, a spot must be selected in the lineage cemetery. The choice of location is the result of the information provided by older lineage members who are consulted on the basis of their status as matrilineage elders—men who have witnessed a large number of burials in the same lineage cemetery and recall the positions of other graves. The expertise of these men is a function of their having witnessed multiple burials at a particular *matmat*, which itself is a function of their matrilineal descent group membership. Again, even if an individual does not experience group membership as salient, all those who witness the procedure are reminded of a heightened awareness of matrilineal descent ideology and group membership.

The corpse will have been handled, cleaned, and prepared for burial by members of the moiety opposite that of the deceased. The body is lifted into the casket by men fulfilling the same criteria, who also lower the casket into a grave dug by men of the opposite matrimoiety of the deceased. These services are considered *artangan*, or "helping" the members of the bereaved, person-losing lineage. By the time the corpse has been buried and the pigs are ready to be eaten, a number of matrilineal social statuses have been made salient: *bingbing-pul* givers and receivers/cookers; those keeping track of the wailing women; *di mokos*, the *sawat* donners and others in mourning garb; and those opposite-matrimoiety individuals who provided *artangan*/"helping" by attending to the care and burial of the corpse.

At all mortuary feasts, the food is assembled at the men's house of the sponsoring matrilineage. The cooked pigs are laid out by men, and women bring rice and/or tubers. The mass of food and other trappings of feasting (such as betel nut) laid out in front of the men's house is a conspicuous demonstration of the capabilities of the sponsoring matrilineage—even at such a difficult time. During these moments, the sponsoring group's *bang* is the center of much activity, and as the physical symbol of a matrilineal descent group, keeps matrilineal descent in the consciousnesses of many, if not all present. The men's house of the deceased and its sponsoring lineage retain components of the feast even after the feast is over, in that the jawbones of the *bingbingpul* pigs used—as the mandibles of all pigs used in all of the mortuary feasts—end up in the men's house of the feast-sponsoring matrilineage. Like the *sawat*, the importance of the symbolism of the men's house is at its greatest during a mortuary event. And, like the wearing of a *sawat*, even though the day-to-day utility of the men's house is usually little more than a shady place to sit and talk (except for the feasting context), the observers of these symbols are always going to be mindful of matrilineal descent.

The Activation of Matriliny at a *Ngin i Pol* Feast

The funeral feast cannot be planned in advance, of course, but the subsequent *ngin i pol* feast is always the subject of careful planning. Variables that influence the timing of the *ngin i pol* feast work both for and against an expeditious feast. All of these variables are taken into consideration by the matrilineage of the deceased, as well as by leaders of other matrilineages in the same matriclan who will be under some obligation. The scheduling of the *ngin i pol* is the subject of discussion on the part of members of the clan at the end of the funeral, and, if no satisfactory date is arrived at, for days and weeks to follow.

The most important variable that moves people to delay as little as possible is the posthumous prestige accorded a deceased individual—and by extension, the lineage and the clan—if the delay between the funeral and the *ngin i pol* feast is short—that is, a month or less. Almost always, however, the delay becomes months and sometimes years, often because the people who make the decision—matrilineage elders who live in dispersed villages—are seldom in the same place at the same time, except for a mortuary or church-related feast. Also, the resources required to sponsor a feast are considerable, and, as discussed above, necessitate the coordinated efforts of a number of matrilineally related individuals. All of this is to say that for a number of people, especially prominent people in the matriclan and members of the matrilineage of the deceased, attention to the scheduling of mortuary events brings into focus the matrilineally informed relationships that a member of a would-be *ngin i pol* sponsoring group has with others.

At the *ngin i pol* feast, matrimoiety membership is especially marked in that individuals are either "guests"—that is, not members of the moiety to which the feast-sponsoring lineage belongs—or "hosts." Among the "guests" are those who attended to the corpse and dug the grave. Members of the "host" matrimoiety—especially young men—are responsible for providing betel nut, coconuts, and heavy labor, such as carrying pigs to and from the pit ovens. The "guest"/"host" status distinction—grounded in matrilineal descent understandings—is made salient by the fact that even young men known as *kalilik*, who cavort and gambol together under normal circumstances, comply with the protocol of "guest" and "host" roles. Horseplay is not absent, but even in the midst of the frolicking, "hosts" still serve to their sitting friends who are "guests."

The payments for the pigs—in the form of cash, *reu* shell money, or both—are made by representatives of the feast-sponsoring matrilineage. In some feasts there is more pomp attached to these transactions than at others. During those feasts at which there is much ado about the pigs, the focus is on the payment by the sponsoring matrilineage to those who provided pigs. The process is a visible symbol of the salience of matrilineal descent group membership: a member of the feast-sponsoring lineage walks across the men's house area and methodically places kina bills and/or strands of *reu* across the outstretched palm of the person who provided the pig and is being compensated by the sponsoring group. There is a certain amount of pomp in the public display of wealth, which is matrilineage wealth, and as if making sure that no one misses the point, a representative of the sponsoring group will announce to those assembled at the *bang* just what kind of outlay was entailed—in *reu* and cash—for pigs, plane tickets for distant kin, and so forth. The hundreds and sometimes thousands of kina that are exchanged and then announced constitute one of the clearest examples of a matrilineage conspicuously being a corporate descent group.

The food exchanges that take place at a *ngin i pol* feast provide a demonstration of the viability of the group. Besides being able to feed hundreds of people, the ability to disperse perhaps a ton of pork in baskets and post-feast prestations emphasizes, more than any other moment, the matrilineal descent group. The provision of food baskets to the women who wailed takes place under the auspices of the women of the feast-sponsoring matrilineage. The baskets—scores of them—are constructed out of palm fronds by women of the matrilineage and sometimes have the names of the recipients attached to them.

This work is done by individuals whose matrilineal descent based statuses are salient.

The prestations of pork made after eating takes more planning than the baskets. The matrilineage's men discuss the prestations to be made, and in the course of the presentation of the pork, the matrimoiety of the recipient is highlighted by the use of a classificatory kin term in the announcement.

Discussion

Many of the behaviors at a mortuary ritual make certain social status memberships salient that are otherwise dormant in daily life. In the course of a mortuary feast, matrilineal descent understandings become prominent for everyone present, even if only in terms of being a member of the "guest" matrimoiety. For many people, however, a particular feast provides much more than a script for conventional comportment, especially if one is a member of the "host" matrimoiety. Furthermore, since mortuary feasts in the area take place at the rate of perhaps one per month, an individual will regularly find her- or himself in contexts in which membership in matrilineally based social statuses is marked.

If a properly executed mortuary event makes salient and activates matriliny, then an *im*properly executed event might be expected to affect the salience of matrilineal social statuses and/or the degree of activation of the matrilineal descent group. The following case is such an instance of a mortuary feasting sequence gone awry. This aberrant case is highly diagnostic. Even in the failure of mortuary ritual to be properly carried out, matrilineally informed social statuses are still made salient, but the activation of matriliny—matrilineal social relations—are much less marked. One of the points to be made in the presentation of the case is that the failure to perform acceptable mortuary ritual is disruptive, and that this disruption includes a reduced level of social relations informed by matrilineal descent understandings. The case:

In November 1991, Edward Pitili of Nokon village died. The last surviving member of his lineage, Pitili (as he was known) had been estranged from his enates for years, arguing that they had never helped him in any way. Indeed, Pitili had the letters "T.K.V.K." (which stands for "*tu kes wat Koris,*" or, "The last Koris clan [lineage] member") emblazoned on both his cargo truck—his primary means of income—and his house as a statement to others about his independence from his clan, and his intentions to take care of his children, rather than his enates when it came to naming heirs.

Pitili had gone to the district headquarters at Namatanai and signed a document legally preventing his enates from benefiting at all from his resources after his death. He enjoined his children to refrain from providing *bingbingpul* pigs to his clan at his death (as they are traditionally bound to do) and requested that he not be buried in a Koris cemetery.

After Pitili's death, his grown children adhered to his wishes, much to the irritation and anger of Pitili's enates.

When I left New Ireland three months after Pitili's death, people were still discussing the inappropriateness of his and his children's actions. Jackson, who lived at Nokon, extends the narrative:

Certain Koris members from Kápsál, a village several kilometers south, had desires on the accumulated goods, and were adamant about hosting the funeral feasts. But because the announcement had been made, and one prominent Nokoner in the Provincial government was there to see that it was enforced, the children and wife of the deceased performed all the feasting [instead of the Koris clan]. The final coup de grace was when the news reached everyone that the deceased had requested that he be buried in front of his house. That is, he requested explicitly that he not be buried in the *matmat* (cemetery) of the Koris clan *bang*. He was, in effect, disassociating himself with clan ancestors and with current clan members by not being buried in clan grounds, further removing any claim that extant clan members might try to exercise on his property. [Jackson adds the following insightful footnote:] Of course, one can imagine in future generations someone from Koris claiming the land in front of this house where the Koris bigman is now buried, saying that if he is buried there then it surely must be clan land; a bigman of such prominence certainly would not be buried on another clan's land.

In the end, the Koris clan members from Kápsál, feeling they had legitimate claim on the property in question, came and, with threat of force, took the truck now belonging to the children of the deceased. They also wanted the houses on what they said was clan property. The confrontation threatened to become nasty when a group of men from Kápsál showed up in Nokon one day with the intent of tearing down those houses and the Koris men's house. Only with the considerable number of men from Nokon standing in front of the houses was the issue resolved, or postponed. The matter would be taken up in the Provincial court in Namatanai. Eventually, with the persuasion of the Namatanai police, the truck was returned to the family of the deceased in Nokon. (Jackson 1995:110–111)

The motivations of Pitili's enates seem transparent enough: they are upset about not receiving the pigs to which they believe themselves entitled. Their expectation is founded upon traditional expectations and practice. Recall that *bingbingpul* pigs and *lulsit* monies are explicitly intended to compensate the lineage of the dead man for the strength, energy, and effort that he expended on behalf of children not of his own lineage—namely, his own children. The transfer of *bingbingpul* pigs, then, is a public display or manifestation of matrilineal descent understandings: children are pointedly not in the lineage of their father, and his labors on their behalf must be acknowledged.

To be sure, their not receiving the *bingbingpul* pigs bothered members of the Koris clan greatly, and their annoyance and anger are related to a heightened awareness of rights and obligations informed by matrilineal understandings plus their being deprived of resources. In short, members of Pitili's lineage were quite angry over their not receiving the *bingbingpul* pigs, and they invoked matrilineal descent-based status rights and privileges as the justification for that anger. (In 1998, my latest visit to New Ireland, the sons of Pitili were using Pitili's land and truck. No one indicated that Koris clan members were doing anything other than accepting this fait accompli.)

But what of those not so immediately involved? Some people in the Nokon area eschewed the funeral on the grounds that the arrangements were odd. I was unable to get people to tell me precisely what they felt to be so odd about Pitili's funeral other than the fact that it was not normal. This inability to be explicit is consistent with (although does not, of course, prove), that the "logic of actors' situations" includes at least the cognitive and psychological motivations that I articulate for social actors in Chapter 6.

And what of Pitili's offspring? Why would they attend to their father's wishes in the face of the kinds of resistance that such behavior could be expected to—and did—elicit? Their[2] explanation of their actions is illuminating: they argue that since they received nothing from their father's lineage, they owed his lineage nothing. The estrangement of their father from his lineage had a transitive effect: Pitili's children are also estranged from his lineage. From the perspective of Pitili's children, the "debt" owed to their father's lineage—normally acknowledged and reciprocated with *bingbingpul* pigs—was negated because of the fact that their father himself had little significant interaction with his lineage. Structurally, Pitili's children are blameless in that they did the proper thing: they followed the wishes of their father. The relationship that Pitili's children have with their enates is unchanged as a result of their actions; indeed, one person even admired Pitili's sons for their ability to utilize the advantages that they had (such as, for example, not becoming encumbered with costly exchanges with their father's lineage). It is probably not a coincidence that the admirer was a clansman of Pitili's children. From the perspective of Pitili's children, the patrifilial link is to be retained, and in so doing, they are not necessarily endangering their linkage to their matriline.

The Pitili case shows that complementary filiation is best seen as a connection between ego and ego's father rather than between ego and ego's father's enates—that is, the link is a patrifilial one, rather than a generic patrilateral one. This means that the father's group-acknowledging behaviors such as *lulsit* money, *bingbingpul* pigs, and *bokur* backslapping are done because of the logic of the situation for each individual actor. And if this is so, then people's decisions to acknowledge their father's matrigroup is a conscious choice made within the context of salient understandings about the father's—and one's own—descent group.

Recall also the ambivalence for many people toward Pitili's funeral. Here some people eschewed the funeral because matrilineally oriented protocol was flouted. Here, matrilineal descent understandings are certainly salient, but groups were not activated, since it was individuals, rather than groups, who made the decision not to attend. For everyone, then—Pitili's enates, his children, and disinterested others—the circumstances surrounding Pitili's funeral made matrilineal social statuses salient, but matrilineal descent groups were not activated in the ways that they normally are. The Pitili funeral is the showcase datum marshaled on behalf of the key argument of the book: that participation in a sequence of mortuary feasts for a variety of purposes results in an increased salience of matrilineal descent understandings, the statuses that those understandings inform, and the activation of the matrilineal descent group.

---

2. By "their," I mean the oldest child, a grown man, and two young adult sons whom I interviewed.

ACTIVATED MATRILINY AND THE SYMBOLISM OF MORTUARY RITUAL

Mortuary ritual also makes salient matrilineal group membership in ways that go beyond the specific concerns of people that are highlighted when seen from the perspective of methodological individualism. Aspects of the structure of mortuary ritual evoke matriliny as well. The ethnographic record shows that societies that stress mortuary feasting can be found beyond the Bismarck Archipelago, most notably in the Massim (cf. Damon and Wagner 1989). Most of these societies also have matrilineal descent groups. An exception supports this assertion: the Yela on Rossel Island in the Massim region speak a language quite unrelated to Oceanic languages; they also do not perform mortuary rituals that resemble those of their Oceanic-speaking neighbors (Liep 1989; Wagner 1989:255).

There is a strong correlation between matrilineal descent and an emphasis on mortuary ritual (Damon 1989:11), although little seems to have been made of it. This connection is all the more striking when compared with the patrilineal New Guinea Highlands, in which marriage ritual and exchange have long been known to be of central sociological and cultural import.

Let me pause to say that mortuary rituals are not absent from the Highlands of Papua New Guinea (see, for example, Levin 1977), nor are marriage exchanges absent in Island Melanesia (see, for example, Battaglia 1990:109–111). Likewise, I am not saying that bridewealth payments are always higher in the Highlands. My point is that, in general, when viewed in terms of pomp, ostentation, and ethos, marriages in the patrilineal Highlands parallel mortuary activities in matrilineal, Oceanic-language, Island Melanesia: they are analogous although not homologous social forms.

Two recent bridewealth exchanges that I know of at Tekedan village totaled K100 and two strands of *reu* each. The exchange of these resources in both cases took place surreptitiously, with one at night. The de-emphasis on the exchange is bound to be remarkable to anyone familiar with Highlands ethnography. Indeed, one man offered that he knew of an instance in which a man dropped off a bridewealth payment while leaving the motor running in his vehicle. Another individual offered the following explanation for such covert activity: "If we stand up and make a big deal by giving bridewealth to another line, then we are doing the equivalent of shouting, 'Our brother wants to screw your sister!' And nobody wants to hear that sort of thing, right?"

Contrast this with marriage exchanges found in the New Guinea Highlands in which publicity—even showmanship—is a necessary feature of the exchange. It is because patrilineal descent understandings in the Highlands are more consistent with an emphasis on marriage and its concomitant exchanges, and patrilineal descent evokes—and is evoked by—elaborate marriage exchange in the same ways that matrilineal descent is made salient in mortuary activity by being structurally commensurate with it. Here is what I mean by "structurally commensurability": there are structural similarities between patriliny and marriage exchange on one hand, and matriliny and mortuary exchange on the other.

It is generally noted that in surrendering bridewealth, a man and/or his group compensates the woman and/or her group for the fact that the woman's offspring will not be members of her group (Lemonnier 1991:13). This explanation is consistent with patrilineal understandings since bridewealth establishes a *de jure* patrifilial connection, which is used as a condition of patrilineal descent group membership: a child is a member of the group that surrendered resources to the group of the child's mother, and a woman's reproductive capacities are an important object of the exchange. But bridewealth in matrilineal societies is not a mirror image. Indeed, were it not for the functions of bridewealth,[3] there would be no reason to expect the institution in a society with matrilineal descent groups. This, then, is the reason for the relative lack of attention to bridewealth where there is matriliny, as among the Sursurunga: there is no need to compensate the woman's group for the loss of the woman's children.

Mortuary events, on the other hand, in which the descent group of the deceased receives goods from affines, are more understandable. In patriliny, what is needed most is an uncomplicated means of social and biological reproduction for the descent group; this is normally legitimated if not provided by bridewealth. In matriliny, mortuary exchanges also provide for the social and biological reproduction of the matriline—but *after the fact*. It is only after a man dies that his descent group is compensated—after the man has spent his energies providing succor and support for children of another descent group (cf. M. Strathern 1984:50). For the Sursurunga, this is the explicit purpose of the *bingbingpul* pigs, as well as the giving of *lulsit*, the money given to the sponsor in the name of the paternal indulgences of the deceased.

Why should this compensation take place after a man dies? Recall that a patrilineage loses an out-marrying woman and the rights to her children. This is qualitatively different from what a matrilineage loses in an out-marrying man: his care for the matriline's children. Sursurunga grammar/cognition and attention to reciprocity provide an insight.

Recall that children are classified by the Sursurunga as an inalienable noun (*natun*). The labor that a man puts forth, on the other hand, is an alienable noun (*kán him*). Recall also that inalienable nouns refer to items that are more proximal, more immediate, whereas alienable nouns refer to distal phenomena. The Sursurunga use a grammatical system which, consciously or not, describes the relationship between a person and his or her offspring as more closely connected than a person and his or her labor. When, for example, my family was away from Tekedan for weeks, and I was able to spend more time at my work, both men and women commented that I must be sad to be away from my children (but never, I noticed, my spouse), and that I must miss them. No one ever observed that I must be pleased to have the extra time to do my work. Men invariably say that the hardest part about plantation labor away from the village is

---

3. For example, the solidarity of lineages as bridewealth collecting and receiving groups; and the solidarity of marriage in the eyes of bridewealth receivers (see Goody and Tambiah 1973:2–17).

being separated from their children. I once asked a man with a sick child if he was going to his garden that day. No, he answered, his child was still sick and a child was more important than a garden. Their children are the reason that men at Tekedan work. To refer to a child with an inalienable noun and work with an alienable noun represents a quite real—and striking—aspect of Sursurunga social life.

This means that, certainly for the Sursurunga, and I imagine many other places as well, the patrilineal Highlands emphasis on marriage is viewed as extraneous: filiation and descent group membership are not what is at issue in major exchanges; paternal care—the work of a *tata*—is. In such a context of understandings about alienability and descent, mortuary feasting is experienced as a good and proper expenditure of time, energy, and resources. This conclusion exists among the Sursurunga, and it appears that a similar dynamic also obtains throughout matrilineal, Oceanic-language-speaking Papua New Guinea.[4] A. Weiner (1992) suggests that those resources that are perceived as inalienable[5] are protected and not freely given up to exchange. She notes that pigs used in exchanges such as the *moka* and *te* in the New Guinea Highlands are not seen as Maussian inalienable possessions and are therefore easily disbursed for exchange purposes (1992:27). The point is that what is viewed as inalienable in a Maussian sense is more difficult to relinquish.

Grammatical inalienability reflects a cognitive orientation or worldview that appraises some "possessions" as more reluctantly alienated, or less easily surrendered. These more reluctantly surrendered "possessions," being dear to their owners, require immediate rather than delayed compensation. Thinking in Sursurunga terms, the relatively higher value placed on children than on labor means that the surrendering of a woman's (potential) children (as in patriliny), being inalienable (in both the Maussian and grammatical senses), to another lineage should exact reciprocation immediately—that is, bridewealth in which much ado is made over quite something: the next generation. A matrilineage, on the other hand, loses "only" labor, comparably distal and alienable, when a man marries out, and, given the relative unimportance of labor, need not be compensated until the performance of labor has been completed—that is, in the form of (in the Sursurunga case, *bingbingpul*) mortuary payments. When a woman dies, the Sursurunga response—as throughout much of matrilineal Melanesia—is that the widower's lineage is obligated to surrender pigs to the lineage of the deceased. Nurture is not a unilaterally masculine characteristic on New Ireland, even where it is emphasized. Husbands receive care through the *him* (alienable

---

4. Thurnwald (1938) describes a similar value on Bougainville Island represented in the payment used to "'buy' the strength of a man" (cited in Nash 1974:93).

5. A. Weiner's use of "inalienable" and "alienable" follows Mauss (1967:6–16, 41–43). She does note Marx's use of the terms but fails to mention the linguistic classifications noted here. One must be extremely careful not to conflate the terms and assume that Marx, Mauss, and linguists are all referring to the same thing. On the other hand, this homonymic circumstance serves as a reminder that there *may* be linkages between the concepts for some people, as I shall try to make clear. Unless noted otherwise, my use of "inalienable" and "alienable" will be in their grammatical sense.

labor) of their wives; indeed, a Sursurunga idiom used by men for "to get married" is "to have someone cook for me."

This, then, is why patrilineal marriage exchange is analogous to matrilineal mortuary exchange: each compensates a lineage for its most prominent loss. The reason, however, that the two are not homologous forms is based on the difference between what is being ceded: young human beings in the case of the patrilineal woman-losing lineage, but only labor for a matrilineal man-losing lineage. This difference, reflected in Sursurunga grammar, means that the most significant structural loss that a matrilineage will incur at marriage is the loss of its men's labor on behalf of others. If it is true that patrilineal marriage is importantly the entailment of many values and understandings, then the same must also be true of mortuary ritual in the matrilineal systems—as can be seen throughout New Ireland.

Differences Within Matrilineal Melanesia. Mortuary ritual within Melanesia has been most studied in the Massim and in the East New Britain/New Ireland (a region for which I will use "New Ireland" as a shorthand) areas of Papua New Guinea, and in general, Massim mortuary ritual has been the object of much more comparative scrutiny than has New Ireland mortuary ritual. Massim mortuary rituals are similar enough to their New Ireland counterparts that one can agree with Wagner (1989:255) in seeing a "strong overall congruence" in the mortuary rituals of the two regions. There is, however, one noteworthy difference between the two regions: the analogous relationship between food in the Massim and work in New Ireland.

The ideal of the nurturing father is present and recognized in both areas, and this nurture does paradigmatically take the form of provisioning. "Feeding" and "eating," however, appear to be hypercognized in Massim conceptions of patrifilial relationships (Battaglia 1985, Montague 1989, Lepowsky 1993:298) whereas (help in) "work" characterizes the ways in which New Ireland people refer to the same link. In the New Ireland region, in contrast, A. Epstein (1992:83ff.) discusses the importance of work among the Tolai, whereas Foster says that Tangan food giving is not "reciprocal nurturing but . . . unilateral force feeding" (1990a:444). As I have noted, rather than "feeding," Steve Jackson (personal communication) argues that the primary social fact or "core symbol" of Sursurunga life is *artangan* or "helping"—typically taking the form of assistance with some performance of duty. And the analysis of the bases for participation in Sursurunga mortuary ritual in Chapter 6 revealed labor/work (*him*) to be the principal contribution of men to their children.

The work : New Ireland : : food : Massim syllogism may be rooted in differences between New Ireland and the Massim. Food supply is perhaps the first place to begin looking for a way to account for the difference. The variety of microclimates enjoyed on the larger landmasses of New Britain and New Ireland provide for a greater likelihood of adequate food supplies in the event of climatic or disease catastrophe. It would be expected, for example, that Massim histories would include stories of hungry times (as in Young 1971; Kahn 1986) that would be absent or less common in New Ireland.[6] This would not mean that food is unimportant in New Ireland, only that in New Ireland, the labor involved in the process of provisioning others with food is seen as the fundamental symbol of paternal nurture.

Another difference between the Massim and New Ireland is the absence and presence, respectively, of exogamous matrimoieties.[7] By all accounts, men and women in the New Ireland region adhere in large part to the matrimoiety exogamy prescription. In addition, this prescription is perceived to have been more strictly followed in the past than it is today. Matrimoiety exogamy, then, can be assumed to have been a historical component of New Ireland societies, and to have co-occurred with this emphasis on labor rather than on, as in the Massim, feeding.

One of the most obvious and immediate results of the moiety exogamy rule is that half of a biologically qualified population is ineligible for marriage consideration. Another outcome among the Sursurunga is that half of the population is regarded as classificatory affines, and, more specifically in the matrilineal case, classificatory "fathers." If the notion of providing "labor" for half of the population is easier to comprehend than "feeding" half of the population, then it is easy to imagine that "feeding"—by any standard a more intimate sort of relationship than "laboring for"—would be a more dominant symbol in the Massim, where the people to be "fed" are one's father's lineage- and clanmates and are likely to be known than, as in New Ireland, one's father's moietymates.

These speculations suggest the need for comparative research that takes into account Massim and New Ireland mortuary ritual. Such comparison is likely to reveal other similarities and disparities between the two regions that can lead to conclusions about the functions of mortuary ritual and matrilineal descent.

SUMMARY

I have discussed Sursurunga matrilineal descent ideology and understandings and occupancy of social statuses informed by those understandings as often dormant, but made salient in the context of mortuary ritual. Another outcome of mortuary activity are activated, conspicuous matrilineal descent groups as group members conduct social relations in which matriliny is salient for them. The concept of varying salience and activation can also apply to patrifiliation, as

---

6. The El Niño pattern of 1997–1998 had terrible consequences for New Ireland. Many trees died, and gardens bore poorly or not at all. People *were* hungry, and aid from Japan and other countries did help alleviate the situation somewhat. It will be interesting to see what sorts of stories about this period will be told to children and in the men's house in another generation or two.

7. Foster notes that although there are no extant moieties on Tanga, there is a "submerged dual organization" (1990a:433). An older male resident at Tekedan who grew up on Tanga says that there *are* matrimoieties on Tanga. The best synthesis of the two statements is that there *were* matrimoieties on Tanga a generation or two ago, and that there is only residual behavioral and ideological evidence of such groups these days.

shown by the Pitili case. The complementary filiation link has always been a part of the Sursurunga behavioral environment, just as has matriliny. Attention to patrifiliation and matrilineal descent group membership as social statuses in which salience is high or not, and the group is activated or not, offers a new outlook on the changes in societies with matrilineal descent groups. According to the old models, Sursurunga matriliny is disintegrating. When viewed through the lens of methodological individualism and with attention to the variable salience of social statuses, matrilineal understandings are still vibrant, and although the functions of the matrilineal descent group may be different from what they were a century—or even a generation—ago, the sociological integrity of the group—at least vis-à-vis feasting—and the cultural integrity of matrilineal understandings are still intact.

It is likely that we will never know much more than we do now about the ultimate causes of matrilineal descent, but there of contemporary social life may provide some insight in answering the question of proximate cause—that is, of why people continue to view themselves in important ways as members of extant matrilineal descent groups. In the following, concluding, chapter, I have more to say about the implications of descent and filiation for the study of kinship, as well as discussion of other issues raised in the first chapter.

Chapter 8

Conclusion

The Sursurunga case contributes to certain conceptual and ethnographic issues within anthropology; specifically, The New Kinship and The New Melanesian Anthropology. The New School of Kinship and The New Melanesian Anthropology both have, near their centers, the idea that certain conceptual tools/constructs—"lineage," "clan," "group," "individual"—are outmoded and misleading.

I believe there to be excesses in both The New Kinship and The New Melanesian Anthropology. Even if the understanding of constructs such as lineage and group is enhanced by a processual perspective, this should not be taken to mean that these entities exist solely in the behavior of social actors, having no existence outside of their evocation. Kinship, at least in the form of filiation, *does* exist prior to cultural elaboration and anthropological understanding of those elaborations, just as matrilineal clans exist prior to their activation by events such as mortuary feasting. What is needed is a bit of theoretical restraint when it comes to using the insights provided by processual perspectives.

THE NEW KINSHIP

The Sursurunga attention to fathers is an example of the kind of elaboration of the tie of complementary filiation—and is, of course, no surprise to students of unilineal descent groups. Among matrilineal descent groups, the patrifilial connection is structurally indispensable. Among the Sursurunga, the relationship with one's father is characterized by gratitude: children owe the lineage of their father for his care. For the Sursurunga, matrilineal descent and complementary filiation dovetail from the outset of the mortuary feasting complex. The central component of a funeral is the presentation of pigs, known as *bingbingpul*, to the lineage of the deceased by the widow and children as recognition for the deceased's paternal care. When a woman dies, her children do not provide *bingbingpul* pigs; only a man's lineage receives *bingbingpul* pigs from the children of the deceased. This difference underscores the gratitude that one has toward one's father.

Given the exigencies of residence, the adult male who is likely to be around a child most of the time is the child's father. Therefore, if children are to grow up well prepared for adulthood as competent matrilineage members, fathers must make important contributions to their children's socialization. From the perspective of the future well-being of any matrilineage, the father of a matrilineage's younger members is vitally important. Matriliny, in short, flourishes where fathers are necessary and valued. The descent group and the domestic group are not necessarily in conflict, and husbands exercise "authority" over wives in ways that contribute to the *wife's* lineage, not the husband's.

In attending to the ideal dynamics of matriliny, Schneider's essay was too closely attentive to a synchronic perspective, and overlooked the necessity for a means by which a descent group can reproduce itself in ensuing generations. The Sursurunga take as fundamental that the future of a descent group is its children, and that a descent group's children are cared for by a representative of a different descent group. Schneider's logic neglects the fact that for part of their lives, members of a matrilineal descent group rely upon their father.

This is why there is no "matrilineal puzzle." Men are said to be subordinate to both paternal (i.e., household) and avuncular (i.e., descent group) authority early in life, only to be constrained later in life as fathers who must share household authority with their wife's brother, and as avunculi who must share descent group authority with their sister's husband. But this way of thinking about it suffers from an ill-advised assumption of a zero-sum model with regard to authority—that is, it is probably unwise to assume that fathers would consistently tell children to do one thing, and avunculi tell them to do another. Most individuals in most societies care for their children and do their best to provide for them. Among the Sursurunga, for example, fathers chastise their children in order to inculcate brother-sister avoidance behavior so that the children might grow up to be competent matrilineage members. Children benefit from a host of adults who are motivated to train and nurture them as a result of patrifilial as well as enatic affections. This is hardly a social order riddled with "tension," and "stress" (Richards 1950:207–210). The difficulties that had been identified as indicative of the matrilineal puzzle have been, for example, conflicting requirements on a man *qua* husband/father and *qua* brother/uncle. But of course, the larger ethnographic record tells us that such conflicts are not unique to matrilineal descent groups—descent and affinity are well-known mutually antagonistic forces.[1] Going a step further, there are as yet no data in the ethnographic

---

1. To be sure, there *are* instances in which patrifiliation is in conflict with matriliny (e.g., Tolai cacao groves; see T. S. Epstein 1968), but these conflicts are not institutionalized or systemic, and they are certainly not a "logical" condition of a matrilineal descent group.

record showing that the "tension," "strain," or "stress" of the matrilineal puzzle can be attributed to matriliny rather than to the exigencies of life as an affine.

Schneider's description of the "matrilineal puzzle" and other dynamics of matrilineal descent groups was an early effort in the symbolic study of kinship. In this approach, the actual behavior of real people is ignored, and the constructed meanings of relationships are the objects of analysis. Quite clearly, the approach I have taken in this book is antithetical to Schneider's, who once wrote that

Our aim is not to explain individual acts treated as the acts of an individual, nor the ways in which collectivities can be observed to act, but instead our special sphere is precisely the cultural, and this sphere is not "How the system really works," and neither is it "What goes on in society" nor is it "What is actually going on in the social group." It is, in brief, the symbols and meanings of that collectivity, its culture. It is, therefore, the native model itself that is the subject of my study and the object of my enquiry and the problem for me to explain. And it is so on the premise that it is no more possible to reduce the behaviors of a collectivity to the psychology of the actor than it is possible to reduce culture to social systems. (from a letter to Claude Lévi-Strauss dated 28 August 1972)

For Schneider, the task of the anthropologist is to demonstrate that culture is an integrated symbolic system. In the matter of matriliny, data from actual matrilineal descent groups are irrelevant—whether they support his argument or not. He wishes only to elaborate on the organization of the cultural symbols found within matrilineal systems. In Chapter 4, I showed that understanding matriliny as a collection—a "coherent," "logical" system—of symbols and meanings actually tells us very little, since that approach rests on certain fallacies. Notwithstanding Schneider's opposition to "what is actually going on," the Sursurunga case is itself a critique of an abstracted, symbolic analysis of matrilineal descent groups.

We are now face-to-face with the matter of just what the advantages are of a Schneiderian approach to kinship. What is the point of being interested in the logic of such systems divorced from social reality? Schneider once offered the following answer: A ghost and a dead man are both cultural constructs. The fact that one is more empirically knowable is irrelevant: what is important is to know the understandings about ghosts and understandings about dead men, how they are related to each other, and how they are related to other cultural constructs (1968:2ff.). Since then, there has been some refinement of this position: "I do not mean that reality does not matter. I mean that it does not matter in the ways in which Morgan and others since . . . say or imply that it does" (Schneider 1989:165). In other words, Schneider does not treat "reality" as anything like an independent variable in his investigation of kinship (or anything else) as a cultural system.

This, of course, represents a particular perspective in contemporary anthropology. It is a perspective, however, that is not merely a shift from cultural grammar to cultural semantics or from social *langue* to social *parole*; it is a perspective that radically reorients anthropology. This perspective is based on an antireality notion that makes anthropology's primary, if not sole, purpose a form of cultural commentary (Birth 1990; Spiro 1986, 1996).

Schneider cites Morgan as the founder of an approach to kinship that takes, a priori, biological relatedness as a real, supracultural phenomenon—a phenomenon that then becomes reconstituted in various cultural configurations. These configurations vary according to cultural information (knowledge about paternity, for example), and are represented in a circumscribed lexical domain called kinship terminology: "[F]or Morgan, the mode of classification of kinsmen derives from and describes the peoples' own knowledge of how they are actually, or most probably, related to each other" (Schneider 1984:98).

Since then, according to Schneider, authors of kinship studies have unthinkingly assumed that there is an ontological reality to that thing called "kinship" (minimally the biological parent-child link), and that all cultural systems "do something" with this link. Schneider views this as the conceptual split in the study of kinship: "The crux of the problem [i.e., the differences in the study of kinship] is the different ways in which the facts of sexual reproduction . . . are held to be related (or in no way related) to the cultural constructs of kinship" (1984:95).

Schneider asserts that the root of the problem is that Western anthropologists suffer from an unarticulated presupposition that "blood is thicker than water," a dominant value in the West, and therefore, a source of skewing in the anthropological treatment of kinship. This is because, according to Schneider, anthropologists have not been able to pull themselves away from the notion that there *is* something fundamental to "blood." He believes this to be an essentialist error (1983:400), and argues that a kernel of belief that all societies have kinship leads to other fallacious assumptions about the existence and nature of clans, matriliny, affines, and so on. Schneider's call, then, is for the anthropological treatment of kinship to assume *no* commensurability between societies—that is, to assume that there is not necessarily such a thing as "kinship" (or "clans," or "matriliny," or "affines," and so on) that can be compared: "If kinship is not comparable for one society to the next, then it is self-evident that comparative study is out of the question" (1984:177). The following syllogism reveals this approach: KINSHIP THEORY : GERM THEORY :: LOCAL NOTIONS OF RELATIONSHIP : LOCAL NOTIONS OF ETIOLOGY (Schneider 1992:629–630). Just as anthropologists do not normally enter a society asking what local people "do with" the "real," bacteriological understanding of disease, so also anthropologists should not, according to Schneider, ask what people "do with" the "real," biological reproduction-based notion of kinship. The focus of the anthropologist should be, according to Schneider, to describe the complexities of the cultural system, rather than comparing that system with cultural constructs formed in the West.

Taken as precautionary remarks, Schneider's argument does have value. It is indisputable that entities that receive labels such as "matriliny" are not identical around the world. Goody, for example, pointed out that "the presence of a genealogical structure of a unilineal kind signifies little in itself" (1990:53). This does not, however, logically entail Schneider's position, namely, that such labels are necessarily Procrustean boxes into which incommensurate social forms are collected. Recall the discussion from Chapter 1: the belief that an account of unilineal descent groups necessarily means that the researcher was duped by her or his a priori unilineal assumptions is a fallacy.

A public debate between Warren Shapiro and Schneider that took place not long before Schneider's health began to fail portrays "old" and "new" in the anthropological study of kinship. Schneider (1989) chastised Shapiro for his (1988) a priori assumptions about the existence of kinship, procreation, and genealogical relations, accusing him of the fallacy of assuming "that the relations which can be imagined to arise out of the facts of procreation are universally built into systems of cultural constructs" (Schneider 1989:165). Shapiro's rejoinder defended his use of these analytic constructs and the anthropological tradition from which they came. He also pointed out the irony that Schneider is from the intellectual tradition—elsewhere labeled by Schneider as Western and ethnocentric—by which Shapiro is ostensibly hamstrung:

The gravamen of his argument is that we are locked into this [Western, Judeo-Christian] tradition, whereas Schneider has somehow managed to escape it. It is precisely this profound conceit which, I submit, underlies the exaggerated modesty of "postmodern" thought. (Shapiro 1989:167)

There is, I think, a way out of this conundrum. It involves a rejection of Schneider's epistemological relativism (Spiro 1986) along with an attention to his warnings. This approach is exemplified by Barnes's (1962) article in which he showed that what might be mistaken for (African) patrilineal descent was much better described as cumulative patrifiliation in the Highlands of New Guinea. Barnes showed the disadvantages of relying exclusively on theoretical constructs such as "patrilineage," while eschewing the epistemological relativism of Schneider. It is not an overstatement to say that the lesson of Schneider's *Critique of the Study of Kinship* can be more easily and precisely learned from Barnes's short paper.[2]

The Sursurunga organize relationships according to an ordered system, and this system is informed by emic notions that are not incommensurate with what anthropologists call "matriliny" and "kin types." This claim is not "a perversion of the notion of descent, undertaken in the interest of protecting a typology" (Schneider 1965:75; 1968:1–18; also, Wagner 1975), a view in which distrust of observer bias leads to the overcompensatory conclusion that virtually all order reported by an observer is necessarily imposed. The cases included here present real-life examples of people imposing order on their own lives using kinship idioms—structures very similar to those described as the Rivers, Fortes, and Leach notion of descent (Schneider 1965:*passim*).

Among the Sursurunga, enatic relationships are qualitatively different from patrifilial relationships. An analysis that focuses primarily on what the (matrilineal) descent group does or does not do with the means of production, underrepresents—if not ignores—the role of complementary (patri-) filiation in the

---

2. It should be noted that the point of Barnes's paper was narrowly ethnographic and exemplified, rather than argued for, a particular epistemological orientation.

lives of members of descent groups. This is why methodological individualism and the salience of social statuses are useful models: they attend to the choices made by individuals according to the logic of their situations and to the consequences of those choices. The salience of social statuses means that individuals, not groups, make these choices on the basis of understandings that they hold and that status salience can be an outcome, as well as a guide, to social relations. In treating, as Gough does (along with Allen [1984] and Oliver [1993]), the descent unit itself as the locus of investigation, in viewing it as a principally politico-economic unit, and in evaluating its robusticity according to the degree to which the members of the unit conduct their politico-economic social relations with the good of the descent group in mind, an individual's appreciation of and concern for the link of complementary filiation is wrongly perceived as descent-group sabotage.

Matrilineal understandings are made salient in the context of mortuary feasting, and the integrity of these understandings is not appreciably affected by the acquisition of land and/or bridewealth from one's father. Utilizing the link of complementary filiation in matters of land tenure is not the death knell of matrilineal understandings, or of the matrilineal descent group. A corollary is that the complementary filiation relationship suggests that matriliny be seen not as strong or weak, integral or disintegral, but as activated or not activated, salient or not salient. Just as importantly, attention to the salience of the patrifilial link can highlight the ways in which matrilineal understandings are used in social life.

In this monograph, I have contrasted relationships that Sursurunga have with their maternal and paternal kin—those that have been described as relations of descent and filiation, respectively. Anthropological attention to the descent-filiation distinction dates back to Rivers, received elaborate treatment from Fortes (1969), and is well documented in the writings of Harold Scheffler. More than 30 years ago, Scheffler (1966) provided a synopsis of a fractured (and fractious) discussion about anthropological notions of filiation and, especially, descent. He pointed out that useful thinking about descent distinguishes between descent ideology and "social processes" (1966:542), or what I have called activated social relations. The latter are generally construed as group-related behaviors, leading to another of Scheffler's points, the difference between a group and a category. It was, for Scheffler, important to determine whether (1) a set of people who act together utilize an idiom of a descent category to promote solidarity, or (2) people are impelled to cooperate on the basis of shared understandings about descent and the implications of conformity to those understandings.

Scheffler was trying to get to the bottom of the controversy about whether a group might properly be considered a descent group if it did not have a unilineal ideological charter. He represented what he called the Leach-Goody-Fortes position (best articulated in Fortes 1953) as one that too rigidly defined descent groups as only *unilineal* descent groups. Scheffler's view was that Fortes considered a descent group to be both (1) and (2) above; that is, for Fortes, people behave corporately because they are a descent-based group, and they are a descent-based group because they behave corporately. This, for Scheffler, was "inadequate" (1966:548) because groups vary widely in both structure (i.e., the relationship of group membership to genealogical realities) and function (i.e., what groups do). In this regard, Scheffler noted that

It is never sufficient simply to speak of "descent groups." . . . [I]t must always be specified in what way the group is a descent-group, i.e., how a descent-construct or descent-phrased rule relates to it. . . . In this view, to say of a group that it is a descent group . . . is not to say very much. (1966:546)

Twenty years later, Scheffler recanted his criticism of Fortes (1985:1–3; 1986:341), coming to see (an awareness foreshadowed by the above citation) that what is at stake in the formation of a rule of descent is in fact a rule of filiation. There are only two possible types of filiation—matrifiliation and patrifiliation—and it is the relationship between filiation and descent group membership that is to be the object of comparative inquiry. Only if filiation is the necessary and sufficient criterion for membership in a group can the group be properly (and logically) a descent group. On the other hand, if filiation is merely a sufficient condition for group membership, the group cannot properly be considered to be a descent group (Scheffler 1985:17), and to persist in doing so would contribute to an anthropology doomed to a "largely profitless analytical and theoretical discourse" (Scheffler 1985:18).

I have identified Sursurunga matrilineages as descent groups even though matrifiliation is only a sufficient but not necessary condition for matrilineage membership. That this is so is evidenced by three in-married men at Tekedan village who are from another part of Papua New Guinea (the West Sepik [or Sandaun] Province) and who participate in all of the rights and obligations of the groups with which they are affiliated. Of course, Sursurunga matrilineages as descent groups do not exist in the same way at all times.

The existence of the matrilineage in its nonactivated form—when the salience of matrilineally derived social statuses is low—is quite different from those times when the matrilineage is activated, such as during a mortuary ritual event. Just which version of the matrilineage does Scheffler (and, for that matter, Fortes) mean when specifying that matrifiliation is a criterion for membership?

One possible answer to this question is that the relationship between filiation and descent-group membership must be constantly salient—that is, that actors ever and always conduct themselves with the rule of filiation and its relationship to descent-group membership in their consciousnesses. This is untenable on both logical and empirical grounds, since people cannot be assumed to always retain a particular understanding or idea throughout their lives, nor do people always seem to behave according to their membership in a descent group. This, by the way, is the structural idea that social actors have rules that guide their behavior in unwavering ways. Another possibility is that it does not matter; that is, the distinction between matrifiliation and matrilineal descent has no meaning in this context: the logical relationship between filiation and descent group membership is the same regardless of whether the matrilineage is salient or not in the minds of social actors. This, by the way, is The New Kinship idea that concepts as filiation are chimeras and should not be given analytical primacy.

I prefer a third, less extreme alternative: the relationship between filiation and descent-group membership is at times cognitively submerged; that is, an individual has a preconscious awareness of matri- or patrifiliation and the role that that relationship has in his or her membership in a descent group, an awareness that is sometimes salient, and sometimes not.

An example of this sort of fluctuating salience of filiation and the relationship of filiation to the descent group is the Mae Enga case (Meggitt 1965; Salisbury 1956). As long as the genealogy could be remembered, rights to land for individuals construed as nonagnates were negotiable. In other words, the relationship between filiation and descent group membership is not an unchanging one, but one that fluctuates even as individuals' awareness of the group itself fluctuates between dormant and salient. Filiation as a sufficient and necessary criterion for membership in a Sursurunga matrilineage represents the logical relationship between the two when the matrilineage is inactive, but not when the group is activated. This is because in its dormant, not salient form, membership in a Sursurunga matrilineage is an idealization, and the rule is easily articulated, even by those "outsiders" who would not qualify for membership. In its activated form, membership in a Sursurunga matrilineage is accomplished by the conspicuous performance of actions in, as I have described, mortuary ritual. In sum, a shortage of land among the Mae Enga functions in the same way that a mortuary ritual event functions among the Sursurunga: both circumstances bring to the fore—make salient—the statuses of descent group membership and the rules for inclusion in the group. The lesson for the analysis of descent groups is clear; the relationship between filiation and descent as articulated by Scheffler (1985, 1986) needs to be investigated as it is operates in the mind of the individual social actor, not just once and for all, but when descent-based statuses are salient, as well as when they are not.

The case of Pitili from Chapter 7 shows that there is an analytical advantage to thinking of filiation in terms of the salience of descent. The distinction between filiation and descent is made clear by contrasting the Pitili case with the case below, in which a woman felt estranged from her enates. The utility of thinking in terms of salient social statuses is also illustrated by the case.

Some 50 years ago, Tinpai, a woman of the village of Rukaliklik, was estranged from other members of her matrilineage. The circumstances of the estrangement have been lost, but one of the outcomes was that Tinpai, who was pregnant at the time, named her infant boy *Káptebuán*, meaning "without matrikin." Kápte, as he is known today, reports that he remembers very little of his early days, but does recall that his mother inculcated in him a distrust of the matrilineage that he was and is a part of. These days, however, Kápte's relationships with other members of his matrilineage are congenial. He enjoys full rights as a member of his lineage and is even something of a *kabisit* or big man in his lineage. His mother's links to her enates had no appreciable effect on his own links to that same group of enates.

The case shows that Kápte's relationship to his matrigroup is not a function of his mother's relationship to the group, but rather a function of his birth to a woman who occupied the status member of the group (to her apparent dismay). ·It is the fact of Kápte's being born to Tinpai, herself a member of the group, that has made Kápte a full-fledged matrilineage member in spite of his mother's best efforts. Kápte's filial relationship to his mother—again the Fortes-Scheffler distinction is relevant—made him a matrilineage member on the basis of Sursurunga understandings about the relationship between matrifiliation and matrilineal group membership. If he were connected to his enates by virtue of matrifiliation alone, rather than by a rule of descent that employs matrifiliation as a condition for descent group membership, the result might be something like cumulative matrifiliation in which the connecting links are differently important. This is not hairsplitting; confusing statuses with the people who occupy those statuses has generated some very wrong anthropology in the past. In Kápte's case, it was not his mother's connection to her group, but the facts of his birth that constitute the basis for his matrilineage membership. Recall that in the case of Pitili's children, their connection to Pitili's lineage is based on the connection that Pitili himself had with his lineage. In Kápte's case, a mother's links to her enates had no appreciable effect on his own links to that same group of enates. In contrast, Pitili's children's relationships to his enates did determine the relations between his children and his lineage.

The patrifilial link is significant among the Sursurunga, and there is good reason to suppose that it has always been an important aspect of the Sursurunga social order, since people always have some tie both to their own and their siblings' children, and since the attention to one's father is marked in rites that seem to predate contact. The acquisition of land from one's father is but one aspect of complementary filiation, and any threat to the matrilineage is not qualitatively different today. Fathers on New Ireland have provided resources for their children before the appearances of cash and Christianity; the patrifilial link is forged within the crucible of the nuclear family, and is not due to extramural features on the social landscape. Rather than the result of economic cooperation/assistance between a father and his offspring, ego's relationship—both jural and sentimental—to her or his matrilineage is not necessarily affected by what a father does for her or him; that is, ego still retains matrilineage rights even if she or he also exercises patrifilial rights, and, as I noted in Chapter 4, matrilineal allegiance and patrifilial allegiance are not in an either/or, zero-sum relationship.

If nothing else, the cases of Pitili and Kápte show that patrifilial and matrilineal relationships are very different sorts of relationships. Therefore, father-child succor is not a threat to matrilineal understandings, since father-child help (see Jackson 1995:96ff., 112–113) is a function of complementary filiation, and complementary filiation is not in competition with matrilineally informed social relations. There is no evidence that a Sursurunga individual has ever been penalized or sanctioned by his lineage for utilizing the patrifilial link (although this has happened among the land-short Tolai [T. S. Epstein 1968:114–133]). Indeed, the fact that both mothers and fathers intend to pass resources such as land on to their children suggests that there is not a rivalry between patrifilial and matrilineal inheritance. If there were such a rivalry, then one could expect to see, for example, fathers withholding resources if their children were going to be adequately provisioned by their matrilineage. This does not, to my knowledge, happen.

Although evidence shows that there is an increased use of the patrifilial relationship in the transmission of land rights, there is no evidence of a concomitant *decrease* of matrilineal understandings. Complementary filiation is and presumably always has been an inherent part of unilineal societies, but the determinants of what is involved in relationships of complementary filiation have varied. The economic dependence of ego upon the father—for example, among the Sursurunga, often for land and bridewealth—does not logically entail that the matrilineage is weakened, or that matrilineal understandings are weakened. This is because the mortuary feasting complex makes salient individuals' connections to their matrilineages.

Receiving land and/or bridewealth from one's father among the Sursurunga actually, in an indirect way, reinforces matrilineal understandings, since patrifilial help must be acknowledged and compensated for—specifically because it is from outside of the matrilineage. In Chapter 3, I discussed the means by which the transfer of land from father to son is accomplished by a token purchase and a small feast (nominally sponsored by the son, but with cooperation and assistance from the father). This token purchase is a significantly lowered price—generally about 10 per cent of the price that would have to be paid to another buyer. That the land must be purchased rather than freely given, and that the pig must be presented to the land-selling lineage are the consequences of salient matrilineal understandings. Similarly, when a father provides bridewealth for his son, the son recognizes that a debt is incurred and must be paid off in the future—normally in the form of a pig. This pig represents recognition that one's father is provisioning a person outside his own matrilineage by helping his son. Therefore, with every patrifilial land and/or bridewealth grant—and the accompanying debt—matrilineal understandings are reaffirmed.

Discussion

The locus of any social theory must be the individual. It is individuals, not groups, institutions, clans, or lineages who act, behave, and choose. This does not mean that groups do not affect the individuals' behavior. It only means that, insofar as we are concerned with an actor's intentions, we must attend to whether, and how much, the group affects those intentions. Social statuses, such as membership in a matrilineage, can be considered an influence on behavior only if the understandings about the statuses are salient in the decision-making process of individual actors. In this regard, one must bear in mind the distinction between filiation and descent, and attention to the relative salience of the two filial relationships. Gough, in attending only to one function of the descent group, failed to understand its structure—the relationships between matrifiliation and matrilineal descent group membership—as well as other functions of the group, as determined by understandings about the salience for individuals of matrifilial and patrifilial statuses. Schneider, on the other hand, looked at both the structure and function of the matrilineal descent group, but did not account adequately for patrifiliation, nor for the ways in which matrilineal descent group membership may not be salient for an individual.

The outcome(s) of the behaviors of social actors cannot logically be assumed to be (although they may be demonstrated to be) related to the understandings and motivations that impel those actors. Causes need to be distinguished from consequents. The Sursurunga data show that the understandings that cause mortuary feasting are not identical to the matrilineal understandings that become salient as a result of mortuary feasting. The fact that matrilineal descent groups are activated in Sursurunga mortuary feasting strongly suggests the possibility that, inverting Gough, the transfer of land within a matrilineage makes the group salient and seem integrated rather than the other way around. Likewise, Schneider's discussion of the dynamics of matrilineal systems fails to distinguish between, for example, matrifilial understandings that make the status of husband/father ("logically") detachable from the system and the patrifilial understandings that accompany matriliny and that are part of a system in which the status of husband/father *is* necessary.

The salience of social statuses is an important consideration in the study of social relations. Holy suggests as much when he elaborates on how people "act and feel" (the phrase is from Carsten [1995:236]) about relationships (1996:168ff.). This, he says, should be the beginning of the study of relatedness, whether that relatedness is expressed in a Fortes-like idiom of kinship or not. Much of the foregoing has been a description of how Sursurunga "act and feel," and I think the notion of status salience is the key to a more precise understanding of "act and feel." Indeed, the ways in which salience is activated is the most critical variable in the equation of human behavior. For descent theory, it is important to note, as Scheffler (1985, 1986) points out, first, how people treat statuses such as being a child; second, the relationship of filiation to the requirements of descent group membership; and third, the relation between the two. It is also necessary to consider the salience of each of these three components if one is ever to make sense of the relationship between social structure and social relations.

Sursurunga feasting reflects the tension between process and structure, showing how mortuary feasting activates enatic rights and obligations. This analysis is consistent with the processual perspective since the salience of matrilineal understandings and the activation of social relations are in part the product of other, not necessarily matrilineally informed, understandings and social relations. In my view, when individuals participate in feasting, Sursurunga matriliny is more salient than it is when a template for guiding the behaviors entailed in feast participation.

Matrigroups—especially matrilineages and matrimoieties—become "constituted" or activated through the mortuary feast sequence. This is not meant to suggest that the matrilineal descent group does not exist unless or until feasting activates it. The awareness of the status of matrigroup membership is not newly remade with each feasting (or other) event. Rather, the awareness of group membership is salient or not, and nonsalient—dormant or preconscious—understandings are quite different from non-existent ones.

Individuals have reasons for continued participation in Sursurunga mortuary feasting that have little or nothing to do with matrilineal descent understandings. The argument is a functional one: feasting fulfills certain requirements that individuals have—such as avoiding *rumrum*/"feeling shame"—for those who participate in it, and in so doing, unintentionally activates matriliny. It follows, then, that I do not mean to say that individuals somehow know that feasting is "good for matriliny." In other words, feasting is performed and matriliny made salient without the benefit of some ultimate *telos*. This attention to methodological individualism, itself part of the intellectual heritage of The New Melanesian Ethnography, provides the perspective from which the function or utility of feasting has been examined. Individuals experience the various "pressures" to conform to feasting requirements in ways that can be essentially unrelated to the function of these institutions within the larger scheme of things.

Not only is this true for mortuary feasting, but it is also true in other aspects of Sursurunga social life. For example, the pressure to conform to moiety exogamy is experienced as a need to avoid social and economic penalties, and as a wish to avoid the shame of what is perceived to be an incestuous relationship. The societal functions of matrimoiety exogamy, on the other hand, have little to do with the perceived consequences of intramoiety marriage. Matrimoiety exogamy in fact provides a "cross-cutting tie" in which members of different clans of the same moiety are united by, to paraphrase Fortes, an axiom of fraternity, and cross-moiety affinal relationships are unequivocally established.

In Chapter 6, I outlined some of the reasons that individuals participate in mortuary feasting. That list is far from exhaustive. There is also, for example, the biologically rooted need to ingest protein. And there is also the wish to enter into the network of pig debts/transactions that is a worthwhile investment of labor, time, and resources that appreciates at what is, by most standards, a phenomenal rate. The investment is safe in that pigs are never really lost, and they provide access to cash in times of decreasing profits from copra and cacao and an increasing cost of living.

THE NEW MELANESIAN ANTHROPOLOGY

With regard to The New Model Anthropology, I cannot agree that "recent experiments with ethnography as literature and with techniques of montage . . . hold considerable promise for capturing present and past complexities of Melanesian life" (Keesing and Jolly 1992:237). The complexities of life anywhere are difficult enough to convey without trying to be clever about it. I do agree that the goals of anthropologists are undermined, according to Carrier (1992:*passim*), when essentializing the "Other" or "Melanesia" blurs the object of inquiry for the observer, reducing Verstehen. Verstehen is important, but it is at best a means to an end. And that end is, in the words of D'Andrade, "the goal of obtaining a surer understanding of how things work, of what is happening 'out there'" (D'Andrade 1995:408).

In dealing with mortuary feasts and matriliny, I attend to aspects of Melanesian "exotica" (Carrier 1992:7) without treating them as more "authentically" (Carrier 1992:14) Melanesian. Carrier prudently warns against anthropologists of Melanesia who imbue innovations such as cash-cropping and Christianity with a tinge of artificiality. The concern about authenticity and artificiality is reduced if not eliminated by attention to the individual, since for an individual, the fact that a component of a person's set of cultural understandings was new to her or his parents does not, in itself, reduce the influence that that component has on the logic of the person's situation. Since the analysis used in this book attends to the bases of individuals' actions without essentializing the Other, it meets Carrier's criterion of "increasing our knowledge of Melanesian societies" (Carrier 1992:22) nomothetically. Keesing and Jolly (1992:226), on the other hand, argue that "a concern with ritual, exchange, or kinship has become a nostalgic anthropological memory," and suggest that ethnographic treatment of such things may indicate a shortcoming on the part of the ethnographer. Perhaps. But I think they are wrong for two reasons. The first is that, implicitly or not, such a view itself essentializes the "new" and the "traditional" in Melanesia.[3] The second is that it cannot be said that participants in ritual, partakers in an exchange, or users of kinship understandings make choices in a way that is significantly different from sellers of copra or adherents to Christianity. Keesing and Jolly express mild surprise at the "striking disjuncture" of a man attired in long trousers and sunglasses one day and nearly "stark naked" the next (1992:236). Keesing and Jolly, in making the argument against an idealized notion of "Melanesian," still use an adjective such as "striking" when they present evidence that buttresses their argument. The "disjuncture" is far from "striking" if this case is considered in view of the variability of the salience of social statuses and in terms of individuals making choices according to the logic of their situations.[4] Errington and Gewertz (1995) have shown how it is all too easy to imagine that Melanesian societies are to be construed as sites of "inflexible tradition" where such variability is absent.

Carrier (1992:29) says that the New Model Anthropology is part of a corrective to an overessentializing anthropology. But the solution to essentialization is not a New Model or New Kinship or New anything. Rather, distinguishing between causes and effects in social analysis and seeing phenomena such as

---

3. To their credit, Keesing and Jolly acknowledge their own interests in "traditional Melanesia" (1992:227). Furthermore, Keesing has noted that few Pacific Islanders are "interested in the *authentic* ways in which their ancestors actually lived" (Keesing 1993:588; emphasis added).

4. Perhaps the man in question *did* himself experience the situation as a "striking disjuncture." Naturally, emically held inconsistencies in the behavioral environment should be noted by the ethnographer, but not attributed to social actors by the ethnographer.

mortuary ritual and matrilineal descent as both cause and effect is a proven method of getting it more or less right, as I have tried to do.

Glossary

B: BROTHER kin type
BC: BROTHER'S CHILD kin type
bang: men's house
bingbingpul: pig given at a funeral; accompanies **lulsit**
CC: CHILD'S CHILD kin type
D: DAUGHTER kin type
DH: DAUGHTER'S HUSBAND kin type
diar mokos: "the two who mourn"; wife and child(ren) of a deceased man
f.s.: female speaking
FB: FATHER'S BROTHER kin type
FF: FATHER'S FATHER kin type
FM: FATHER'S MOTHER kin type
FZ: FATHER'S SISTER kin type
FZD: FATHER'S SISTER'S DAUGHTER kin type
FZS: FATHER'S SISTER'S SON kin type
H: HUSBAND kin type
HB: HUSBAND'S BROTHER kin type
HM: HUSBAND'S MOTHER kin type
HZ: HUSBAND'S SISTER kin type
kak kokup: (my) cross cousin; a marriageable person
kak pup: (my) husband
kak sinat: (my) affine; especially WZ, WB, HZ, HB
kak tau: (my) aunt/nepote; FZ, BC
kak wák: (my) wife
kakang: my father
kálámul a tataun: man who sponsors a funeral feast
kalik: boy; adolescent (pl. kalilik)
kámlang: my father; m.s. opposite moiety friend
kastam (N-M): tradition, mortuary feasting
kawang: my uncle/nepote; MB, ZC
kebeptai: parental care for children

koko: (my) uncle; term of address for **kawang**

kokos: answer, return, payback; to complete an exchange of pork (see **utngin sál**)

kukung (lik): my opposite-sex sibling

lulsit: money paid at funeral; accompanies **bingbingpul**

M: MOTHER kin type

MB: MOTHER'S BROTHER kin type

MBD: MOTHER'S BROTHER'S DAUGHTER kin type

MBS: MOTHER'S BROTHER'S SON kin type

MF: MOTHER'S FATHER kin type

MM: MOTHER'S MOTHER kin type

MMZS: MOTHER'S MOTHER'S SISTER'S SON kin type

MZ: MOTHER'S SISTER kin type

m.s.: male speaking

mamang: my mother

mis (N-M): shell money from Lihir Island; see **reu**

namnam: food; eating

natung: my child

ngin i pol: second and largest mortuary feast; literally, "drinking the green coconut"

pal: (women's) cooking area/edifice

pupung: my grandfather/grandchild

ratis bu: distribution of betel nut to those who provide pigs at a **ngin i pol** feast

reu: shell money from Lihir Island; see **mis**

S: SON kin type

SW: SON'S WIFE kin type

songsong: my sweat

suka bim: a defunct segment of the mortuary feasting sequence

táptápir: the third and final feast in the mortuary feasting sequence

tata: (my) father; dad

tatalen: traditional ways and customs

tataun: funeral; burial

tinang: to grieve

tuang: same-sex sibling; same-sex enate

turpasi: to purchase a pig

utngin sál: literally "new road"; to initiate an exchange of pork (see **kokos**)

W: WIFE kin type

WB: WIFE'S BROTHER kin type

WF: WIFE'S FATHER kin type

WZ: WIFE'S SISTER kin type

wakang: my grandmother/grandchild

wowo: grandmother/daughter's child; also opposite-sex sibling. See **wakang, kukung(lik)**.

yanang: my mother-/daughter-in-law (HM, SW)

Z: SISTER kin type

ZC: SISTER'S CHILD kin type

References

Albert, Steven M.
  1987   The Work of Marriage and Death: Ritual and Political Process Among the Lak,
          Southern New Ireland, Papua New Guinea. Ph.D. diss. University of Chicago.
Allen, Michael
  1981   Rethinking Old Problems: Matriliny, Secret Societies and Political Evolution.
          In *Vanuatu: Politics, Economics, and Ritual in Island Melanesia,* M. Allen, ed.,
          pp. 9–34. Sydney: Academic Press.
  1984   Elders, Chiefs and Big Men: Authority Legitimation and Political Evolution in
          Melanesia. *American Ethnologist* 11:20–41.
Avruch, Kevin
  1990   Melford Spiro and the Scientific Study of Culture. In *Personality and the Cul-
          tural Construction of Society,* D. K. Jordan and M. J. Swartz, eds., pp. 15–59.
          Tuscaloosa: University of Alabama Press.
Bailey, Frederick G.
  1960   Tribe, Caste, and Nation: A Study of Political Activity and Political Change in
          Highland Orissa. Manchester: Manchester University Press.
Barker, John, ed.
  1990   *Christianity in Oceania: Ethnographic Perspectives.* Lanham, Maryland: Uni-
          versity Press of America.
Barker, John
  1992   Christianity in Western Melanesian Ethnography. In *History and Tradition in
          Melanesian Anthropology,* J. Carrier, ed., pp. 144–173. Berkeley: University
          of California Press.
Barnes, John A.
  1962   African Models in the New Guinea Highlands. *Man* 62:5–9.
Barth, Fredrik
  1987   *Cosmologies in the Making: A Generative Approach to Cultural Variation in
          Inner New Guinea.* Cambridge: Cambridge University Press.
Battaglia, Debbora
  1985   "We Feed Our Fathers": Paternal Nurture Among the Sabarl of Papua New
          Guinea. *American Ethnologist* 12:427–441.

1990   *On the Bones of the Serpent: Person, Memory, and Mortality in Sabarl Island Society.* Chicago: University of Chicago Press.

Beaumont, Clive H.

1972   New Ireland Languages: A Review. In *Papers in Linguistics of Melanesia*, No. 3, S. A. Wurm, ed., pp. 1–41, Australian National University, Pacific Linguistic Series A, No. 35.

1976   Austronesian Languages: New Ireland. In *New Guinea Area Languages and Language Study*, vol. 2, S. A. Wurm, ed., pp. 387–397, Australian National University, Pacific Linguistic Series C, No. 39.

Bell, F.L.S.

1934   A Report on Field Work in Tanga. *Oceania* 4:290–309.

1937   Death in Tanga. *Oceania* 7:316–39.

Birth, Kevin K.

1990   Reading and the Righting of Writing Ethnographies. *American Ethnologist* 17:549-557.

Bolyanatz, Alexander H.

1994a   Defending Against Grief on New Ireland: The Place of Mortuary Feasting in Sursurunga Society. *Journal of Ritual Studies* 8:115–133.

1994b   Legitimacy, Coercion, and Leadership among the Sursurunga of Southern New Ireland. *Ethnology* 33:53-63.

1995   Matriliny and Revisionist Anthropology. *Anthropos* 90:169–180.

1996   Musings on Matriliny: Understandings and Social Relations Among the Sursurunga of New Ireland. In *Gender, Kinship, Power*, M. J. Maynes, A. Waltner, B. Soland, and U. Strasser, eds., pp. 81-97. London: Routledge.

1998a   Economic Cooperatives, Development, and Matriliny in Papua New Guinea. *Notes on Anthropology* 2:31–39.

1998b   Where is Claes Pietersz Bay?: An Episode in the History of the Sursurunga of New Ireland. *Ethnohistory* 45:319–347.

Brown, Donald E.

1991   *Human Universals.* New York: McGraw-Hill.

Brown, George

1908   *Autobiography.* London: Hodder & Stoughton.

1910   *Melanesians and Polynesians.* London: Macmillan and Sons.

Busby, Cecelia

1997   Permeable and Partible Persons: a Comparative Analysis of Gender and Sexuality in South India and Melanesia. *Journal of the Royal Anthropological Institute* (n.s.) 3:261–278.

Capell, Arthur

1971   The Austronesian Languages of Australian New Guinea. In *Current Trends in Linguistics*, T. A. Sebeok, ed., pp 240–340. Vol. 8: Linguistics in Oceania. The Hague: Mouton and Co.

Carrier, James

1992   Introduction. In *History and Tradition in Melanesian Anthropology*, J. Carrier, ed., pp. 1–37. Berkeley: University of California Press.

Carsten, Janet

1995   The Substance of Kinship at the Heart of the Hearth: Feeding, Personhood, and Relatedness among Malays in Pulau Langkawi. *American Ethnologist* 22:223–241.

Chowning, Ann

1969   *The Austronesian Languages of New Britain.* Pacific Linguistics, Series A, 21:17–45.

1991   Proto Oceanic Culture: The Evidence from Melanesia. In *Currents in Pacific Linguistics: Papers on Austronesian Languages and Ethnolinguistics in Honor of George W. Grace,* R. Blust, ed., pp 43–75. Pacific Linguistics Series C No. 117. Canberra: The Australian National University.

Clark, Jeffrey
1995   Shit Beautiful: Tambu and Kina Revisited. *Oceania* 65:195–211.

Clay, Brenda
1975   *Pinikindu: Maternal Nurture, Paternal Substance.* Chicago: University of Chicago Press.

1986   *Mandak Realities: Person and Power in Central New Ireland.* New Brunswick, New Jersey: Rutgers University Press.

1992   Other Times, Other Places: Agency and the Big Man in Central New Ireland. *Man* (N.S.) 27:719–733.

Condra, Ed
1992   Patpatar Background Study. Unpublished manuscript.

Damon, Frederick H.
1989   Introduction. In *Death Rituals and Life in the Societies of the Kula Ring*, F. H. Damon and R. Wagner, eds., pp. 3–19. DeKalb, Illinois: Northern Illinois University Press.

Damon, Frederick H., and Roy Wagner, eds.
1989   *Death Rituals and Life in the Societies of the Kula Ring.* DeKalb, Illinois: Northern Illinois University Press.

D'Andrade, Roy G.
1995   Moral Models in Anthropology. *Current Anthropology* 36:399–408.

Danks, Benjamin
1933   *In Wild New Britain: The Story of Benjamin Danks, Pioneer Missionary.* Sydney: Angus & Robertson.

Davies, Robin, and Elisabeth Fritzell
n.d.   Duke of York Islands Background Study. Unpublished manuscript.

Dumont, Louis
1970   Religion, Politics and Society in the Individualistic Universe. *Proceedings of the Royal Anthropological Institute of Great Britain and Ireland*, pp. 31–41.

Epstein, A. L.
1969   *Matupit: Land, Politics, and Change among the Tolai of New Britain.* Canberra: The Australian National University Press.

1979   Tambu: The Shell Money of the Tolai. In *Fantasy and Symbol*, R. Hook, ed., pp. 149–205. London: Academic Press.

1992   *In the Midst of Life: Affect and Ideation Among the Tolai.* Berkeley: University of California Press.

Epstein, T. Scarlett
1968   *Capitalism, Primitive and Modern: Some Aspects of Tolai Economic Growth.* East Lansing, Michigan: Michigan State University Press.

Errington, Frederick
1974   *Karavar: Masks and Power in a Melanesian Ritual.* Ithaca: Cornell University Press.

Errington, Frederick, and Deborah Gewertz
1994   From Darkness to Light in the George Brown Jubilee: The Invention of Nontradition and the Inscription of a National History in East New Britain. *American Ethnologist* 21:104–122.

1995   *Articulating Change in the "Last Unknown."* Boulder: Westview Press.

Eves, Richard
   1995   Shamanism, Sorcery and Cannibalism: The Incorporation of Power in the
          Magical Cult of Buai. *Oceania* 65:212–233.
   1996   Remembrance of Things Passed: Memory, Body and the Politics of Feasting in
          New Ireland, Papua New Guinea. *Oceania* 66:266–277.
Filer, Colin S., and Richard T. Jackson
   1989   The Social and Economic Impact of a Gold Mine in Lihir: Revised and Ex-
          panded. Unpublished report to the Lihir Liaison Committee.
Fortes, Meyer
   1953   The Structure of Unilineal Descent Groups. *American Anthropologist* 55:17–
          41.
   1957   Malinowski and the Study of Kinship. In *Man and Culture: An Evaluation of
          the Work of Bronislaw Malinowski*, R. Firth, ed., pp. 157–188. London: Rout-
          ledge & Kegan Paul.
   1969   *Kinship and the Social Order.* Chicago: Aldine.
Foster, Robert J.
   1988   Social Reproduction and Value in a New Ireland Society, Tanga Islands, Papua
          New Guinea. Ph.D. diss. University of Chicago.
   1990a Nurture and Force-Feeding: Mortuary Feasting and the Construction of Collec-
          tive Individuals in a New Ireland Society. *American Ethnologist* 17:431–448.
   1990b Value Without Equivalence: Exchange and Replacement in a Melanesian Soci-
          ety. *Man* (NS) 25:54–69.
   1995   *Social Reproduction and History in Melanesia.* Cambridge: Cambridge Uni-
          versity Press.
Fox, Robin
   1983   *Kinship and Marriage.* Cambridge: Cambridge University Press.
Friederici, Georg
   1912   *Wissenschaftliche Ergebnisse einer amtlichen Forschungsreise nach dem Bis-
          marck-Archipel im Jahre 1908.* Band II. Beitrage zur Volker- und Spra-
          chenkunde von Deutsch-Neuguinea. (Mitteilungen aus den Deutschen Schutz-
          gebieten No. 5.) Berlin: Mittler und Sohn.
Gellner, Ernest
   1959   Holism versus Individualism in History and Sociology. In *Theories of History*,
          P. Gardiner, ed., pp. 488–503. Glencoe, Illinois: Free Press.
Godelier, Maurice
   1986[1982] *The Making of Great Men: Male Domination and Power among the New
          Guinea Baruya.* R. Swyer, tran. Cambridge: University Press.
   1998   Transformations and Lines of Evolution. In *Transformations of Kinship*, M.
          Godelier, T. R. Trautmann, and F. E. Tjon Sie Fat, eds., pp. 386–413. Wash-
          ington: Smithsonian Institution Press.
Goody, Jack
   1990   *The Oriental, the Ancient and the Primitive.* Cambridge: Cambridge University
          Press.
Goody, Jack, and S. J. Tambiah
   1973   *Bridewealth and Dowry.* Cambridge Papers in Social Anthropology, No. 7.
          Cambridge: University Press.
Gough, Kathleen
   1961   The Modern Disintegration of Matrilineal Descent Groups. In *Matrilineal
          Kinship*, D. M. Schneider and K. Gough, eds., pp. 631–652. Berkeley and Los
          Angeles: University of California Press.

Gregory, Christopher A.
1982   *Gifts and Commodities*. London: Academic Press.
Groves, William C.
1933   "Divakuzmit"—A New Ireland Ceremony. *Oceania* 3:297–311.
Hallowell, A. Irving
1955   The Self and the Behavioral Environment. In *Culture and Experience*, pp. 75–109. Philadelphia: University of Pennsylvania Press.
Harris, Grace G.
1989   Concepts of Individual, Self, and Person in Description and Analysis. *American Anthropologist* 91:599–612.
Hollyman, K. J.
1990   Personalized and Non-Personalized Possession: Final Consonants in Kumak and Other Languages of Far Northern New Caledonia. In *Currents in Pacific Linguistics: Papers on Austronesian Languages and Ethnolinguistics in Honor of George W. Grace*, R. Blust, ed., pp. 145–154. Pacific Linguistics Series C No. 117. Canberra: The Australian National University.
Holy, Ladislav
1996   *Anthropological Perspectives on Kinship*. London: Pluto Press.
Houseman, Michael, and Douglas R. White
1998   Network Mediation of Exchange Structures. In *Kinship, Networks, and Exchange*, T. Schweizer and D. R. White, eds., pp. 59–89. Cambridge: Cambridge University Press.
Hutchisson, Don
1984   Sursurunga Dialect Survey Report. Unpublished ms.
1986   The Pronomial System in Sursurunga. In *Pronominal Systems*, U. Wiesemann, ed., pp. 1–29. Tubingen: G. Narr.
Jackman, Harry H.
1988   *Copra Marketing and Price Stabilization in Papua New Guinea: A History to 1975*. Pacific Research Monograph No. 17. Canberra: The Australian National University Press.
Jackson, Stephen A.
1995   Exchanging Help: Death, Self-Similarity, and Social Responsibility in a New Ireland Community, Papua New Guinea. Ph.D. diss. University of Virginia.
Jolly, Margaret
1992   Custom and the Way of the Land: Past and Present in Vanuatu and Fiji. *Oceania* 62:330-354.
Jordan, David K.
1990   Eufunctions, Dysfunctions, and Oracles: Literary Miracle-Making in Taiwan. In *Personality and the Cultural Construction of Society: Papers in Honor of Melford E. Spiro*, D. K. Jordan and M .J. Swartz, eds., pp. 98-115. Tuscaloosa, Alabama: University of Alabama Press.
Josephides, Lisette
1991   Metaphors, Metathemes, and the Construction of Sociality: A Critique of the New Melanesian Ethnography. *Man* (NS) 26:145–161.
Kahn, Miriam
1986   *Always Hungry, Never Greedy: Food and the Expression of Gender in a Melanesian Society*. Cambridge: Cambridge University Press.
Kay, Paul, and Willet Kempton
1984   What is the Sapir-Whorf Hypothesis? *American Anthropologist* 86:65–79.

Keesing, Roger M.
1988 *Melanesian Pidgin and the Oceanic Substrate.* Stanford: Stanford University Press.
1993 Kastom Re-examined. *Anthropological Forum* 4(6):587–596.
Keesing, Roger M., and Margaret Jolly
1992 Epilogue. In *History and Tradition in Melanesian Society*, J. Carrier, ed., pp. 224–247. Berkeley: University of California Press.
Lanyon-Orgill, Peter A.
1960 *A Dictionary of the Ralauna Language.* Published by the Author.
Lemonnier, Pierre
1991 From Great Men to Big Men: Peace, Substitution and Competition in the Highlands of New Guinea. In *Big Men and Great Men: Personifications of Power in Melanesia,* M. Godelier and M. Strathern, eds., pp. 7–27. Cambridge: University Press.
Lepowsky, Maria
1993 *Fruit of the Motherland: Gender in an Egalitarian Society.* New York: Columbia University Press.
Levin, Harold Gary
1977 Intracultural Variability and Ethnographic Description: A Decision-Making Analysis of Funerary Behavior Among the New Guinea Kafe. Ph.D. diss. University of Pennsylvania.
Levy, Robert I.
1973 *Tahitians: Mind and Experience in the Society Islands.* Chicago: University of Chicago Press.
Lichtenberk, F.
1985 Possessive Constructions in Oceanic Languages and in Proto-Oceanic. In *Austronesian Linguistics at the 15th Pacific Science Congress* (Pacific Linguistics C-88), A. K. Pawley and L. Carrington, eds., pp. 93–140. Canberra: Australian National University.
Liep, John
1989 The Day of Reckoning on Rossel Island. In *Death Rituals and Life in the Societies of the Kula Ring*, F. H. Damon and R. Wagner, eds., pp. 230–253. DeKalb, Illinois: Northern Illinois University Press.
1991 Great Man, Big Man, Chief: A Triangulation of the Massim. In *Big Men and Great Men: Personifications of Power in Melanesia,* M. Godelier and M. Strathern, eds., pp. 28–47. Cambridge: Cambridge University Press.
Lucy, John A.
1993a *Grammatical Categories and Cognition: A Case Study of the Linguistic Relativity Hypothesis.* Cambridge: University Press.
1993b *Language Diversity and Thought: A Reformulation of the Linguistic Relativity Hypothesis.* Cambridge: Cambridge University Press.
McCarthy, J. Keith
1964 *Patrol Into Yesterday: My New Guinea Years.* London: Angus & Robertson.
Macintyre, Martha
1984 The Problem of the Semi-Alienable Pig. *Canberra Anthropology* 7:109–121.
Malinowski, Bronislaw
1935 *Coral Gardens and Their Magic.* New York: American Book Company.
1955[1927] *Sex and Repression in Savage Society.* New York: Meridian Books.
1961[1922] *Argonauts of the Western Pacific.* New York: E.P. Hutton.

Marriot, McKim
1976   Hindu Transactions: Diversity without Dualism. In *Transactions and Meanings: Directions in the Anthropology of Exchange and Symbolic Behavior*, B. Kapferer, ed., pp. 109–142. Philadelphia: Institute for the Study of Human Values.

Marshall, Mac
1983   Introduction: Approaches to Siblingship in Oceania. In *Siblingship in Oceania: Studies in the Meaning of Kin Relations*, M. Marshall, ed., pp. 1–15. ASAO Monograph No. 8. Lanham, Maryland: University Press of America.

Mauss, Marcel
1967   *The Gift*. I. Cunnison, tran. New York: Norton.

Meggitt, Mervyn
1965   *The Lineage System of the Mae-Enga*. New York: Barnes & Noble.
1974   "Pigs Are Our Hearts!" The Te Exchange Cycle Among the Mae Enga of New Guinea. *Oceania* 44:165–203.

Metcalf, Peter, and Richard Huntington
1991   *Celebrations of Death: The Anthropology of Mortuary Ritual*, 2nd ed. Cambridge: Cambridge University Press.

Mimica, Jadran
1988   *Intimations of Infinity: The Cultural Meanings of the Iqwaye Counting System and Number*. Oxford: Berg.

Montague, Susan
1989   To Eat for the Dead. In *Death Rituals and Life in the Societies of the Kula Ring*, F. H. Damon and R. Wagner, eds., pp. 22–45. DeKalb, Illinois: Northern Illinois University Press.

Mosko, Mark
1995   Rethinking Trobriand Chieftainship. *Journal of the Royal Anthropological Institute* (n.s.) 1:763–785.

Nachman, Steven Roy
1978   In Honor of the Dead, In Defiance of the Living: An Analysis of the Nissan Mortuary Feast. Ph.D. diss. Yale University.

Nash, Jill
1974   *Matriliny and Modernisation: The Nagovisi of South Bougainville*. New Guinea Research Bulletin no. 55. Canberra: The Australian National University.

Neumann, Klaus
1992a   *Not the Way It Really Was: Constructing the Tolai Past*. Pacific Islands Monograph Series, No. 10. Honolulu: University of Hawaii Press.
1992b   Tradition and Identity in Papua New Guinea: Some Observations Regarding Tami and Tolai. *Oceania* 62:295–316.
1997   Nostalgia for Rabaul. *Oceania* 67:177–193.

Oliver, Douglas L.
1993   Rivers (W.H.R.) Revisited: Matriliny in Southern Bougainville. *Pacific Studies* 16(3):1–54, 16(4):1–40.

Ortner, Sherry
1984   Theory in Anthropology Since the Sixties. *Comparative Studies in Society and History* 26:126–166.

Parkinson, Richard
1887   *Im Bismarck Archipel*. Leipzig: Brockhaus.

Pawley, Andrew, and Malcom Ross
1993   Austronesian Historical Linguistics and Culture History. *Annual Review of Anthropology* 22:425–459.

Pawley, Andrew, and Timoci Sayaba
1990   Possessive-Marking in Wayan, A Western Fijian Language: Noun Class or Relational System? In *Pacific Island Languages: Essays in Honour of G. B. Milner*, J. H. C. S. Davidson, ed., pp. 147–171. Honolulu: University of Hawaii Press.

Petersen, Glenn
1982   Ponapean Matriliny: Production, Exchange, and the Ties that Bind. *American Ethnologist* 9:129–144.

Popper, Karl R.
1952   *The Open Society and Its Enemies*, 2nd ed. London: Routledge and Kegan Paul.

Powdermaker, Hortense
1931   Mortuary Rites in New Ireland (Bismarck Archipelago). *Oceania* 2:26–43.

Radcliffe-Brown, A. R.
1924   The Mother's Brother in South Africa. *South African Journal of Science* 21:542–55.

Richards, Audrey I.
1950   Some Types of Family Structure Amongst the Central Bantu. In *African Systems of Kinship and Marriage*, A. R. Radcliffe-Brown and D. Forde, eds., pp. 207–251. London: Oxford University Press.

Sack, Peter, and Dymphna Clark, eds. and trans.
1980   *The Draft Annual Report for 1913-1914*. Canberra: The Australian National University.

Salisbury, Richard F.
1956   Unilineal Descent Groups in the New Guinea Highlands. *Man* 56:2–7.
1970   *Vunamami: Economic Transformation in a Traditional Society*. Berkeley and Los Angeles: University of California Press.

Scheffler, Harold W.
1966   Ancestor Worship in Anthropology: Or, Observations on Descent and Descent Groups. *Current Anthropology* 7:541–551.
1985   Filiation and Affiliation. *Man* (NS) 20:1–20.
1986   The Descent of Rights and the Descent of Persons. *American Anthropologist* 88:339–350.
1991   Sexism and Naturalism in the Study of Kinship. In *Gender at the Crossroads of Knowledge: Feminist Anthropology in the Postmodern Era*, M. di Leonardo, ed., pp. 361–382. Berkeley: University of California Press.

Schlaginhaufen, Otto
1915-16 *Le Maire's Claes Pietersz.-Bucht an der Ostkuste-Neu-Irlands*. Jahresbericht der Geographish-Ethnographischen Gesellschaft in Zurich 17:3–33.
1920-21 *Weitere Bemerkungen zur Claes Pietersz.-Bucht an der Ostkuste Neu-Irlands*. Mitteilung der Geographischen-Ethnographischen Gesellschaft in Zürich 21:49–59.

Schnee, Heinrich
1904   *Bilder aus der Sudsee*. Berlin: D. Reimer (E. Vohsen).

Schneider, David M.
1961   Introduction: The Distinctive Features of Matrilineal Descent Groups. In *Matrilineal Kinship*, D. M. Schneider and K. Gough, eds., pp. 1–32. Berkeley: University of California Press.

1965 Some Muddles in the Models: Or, How the System Really Works. In *The Relevance of Models for Social Anthropology*, M. Banton, ed., pp. 25–86. A.S.A. Monographs No. 1. London: Tavistock.

1968 *American Kinship: A Cultural Account.* Englewood Cliffs, New Jersey: Prentice-Hall.

1983 Conclusions. In *Siblingship in Oceania*, M. Marshall, ed., pp. 389–404. ASAO Mongraph No. 8. Lanham, Maryland: University Press of America.

1984 *A Critique of the Study of Kinship.* Ann Arbor: University of Michigan Press.

1989 Australian Aboriginal Kinship: Cultural Construction, Deconstruction, and Misconstruction. *Man* 24:165–166.

1992 Ethnocentrism and the Notion of Kinship. *Man* 27:629–631.

1995 *Schneider on Schneider: The Conversion of the Jews and Other Anthropological Stories*, R. Handler, ed. Durham: Duke University Press.

Shapiro, Warren
1988 Ritual Kinship, Ritual Incorporation, and the Denial of Death. *Man* 23:275–297.

1989 Untitled Response to David M. Schneider. *Man* 24:166–167.

Shimizu, Akitoshi
1990 Untitled Response to David M. Schneider. *Man* 27:631–633.

Sperber, Dan
1985 *On Anthropological Knowledge.* Cambridge: Cambridge University Press.

1996 *Explaining Culture: A Naturalistic Approach.* Oxford: Blackwell Publishers.

Spiro, Melford E.
1961 Social Systems, Personality, and Functional Analysis. In *Studying Personality Cross-Culturally*, B. Kaplan, ed., pp. 93–127. New York: Harper & Row.

1982 *Oedipus in the Trobriands.* Chicago: University of Chicago Press.

1986 Cultural Relativism and the Future of Anthropology. *Cultural Anthropology* 1:259–286.

1993 Is the Western Conception of the Self "Peculiar" within the Context of the World Cultures? *Ethos* 21:107–153.

1996 Postmodernist Anthropology, Subjectivity, and Science: A Modernist Critique. *Comparative Studies in Society and History* 38:759–780.

Stephan, Emil, and Fritz Graebner
1907 *Neu-Mecklenberg.* Berlin: Dietrich Reimer.

Strathern, Andrew
1969 Descent and Alliance in the New Guinea Highlands: Some Problems of Comparison. *Royal Anthropological Institute Proceedings for 1968:*37–51.

1971 *The Rope of Moka: Big-Men and Ceremonial Exchange in Mount Hagen, New Guinea.* Cambridge: Cambridge University Press.

Strathern, Marilyn
1984 Marriage Exchanges: A Melanesian Comment. *Annual Review of Anthropology* 13:41–73.

1988 *The Gender of the Gift: Problems with Women and Problems with Society in Melanesia.* Berkeley: University of California Press.

1991 Introduction. In *Big Men and Great Men: Personifications of Power in Melanesia,* M. Godelier and M. Strathern, eds., pp. 1–4. Cambridge: University Press.

Swartz, Marc J.
1990 Aggressive Speech, Status, and Cultural Distribution among the Swahili of Mombasa. In *Personality and the Cultural Construction of Society: Papers in*

Honor of Melford E. Spiro, D. K. Jordan and M. J. Swartz, eds., pp. 116–142. Tuscaloosa, Alabama: University of Alabama Press.

1991   *The Way the World Is*. Berkeley: University of California Press

1993   Funneling: How Culture Works Despite Itself. Paper presented to the session "Individual variation and Cultural Models," 92nd Annual Meeting of the American Anthropological Association, Washington, D.C., 17-21 November 1993.

Territory of New Guinea

1933-34 Patrol Report No. 2 of Namatanai Sub-District. Unpublished Patrol Report by H.E. Woodmen.

Territory of Papua and New Guinea

1949-50 Patrol Report No. 1 of Namatanai, New Ireland. Unpublished Patrol Report by F.P. Kaad.

1950-51 Patrol Report No. 2 of Namatanai, New Ireland. Unpublished Patrol Report by G.P. Taylor.

1953-54 Patrol Report No. 3 of Namatanai, New Ireland. Unpublished Patrol Report by D. Permezel.

1955-56 Patrol Report No. 2 of Namatanai, New Ireland. Unpublished Patrol Report by G.D. Collins.

1958-59a Patrol Report No. 1 of Namatanai, New Ireland. Unpublished Patrol Report by F.E. Haviland.

1958-59b Patrol Report No. 6 of Namatanai, New Ireland. Unpublished Patrol Report by F.E. Haviland.

1966-67 Patrol Report No. 15 of Namatanai, New Ireland. Unpublished Patrol Report by John D. Brady.

1968-69a Patrol Report No. 2 of Namatanai, New Ireland. Unpublished Patrol Report by N. Liosi.

1968-69b Patrol Report No. 13 of Namatanai, New Ireland. Unpublished Patrol Report by W. Noel Levi.

1970-71a Patrol Report No. 2 of Namatanai, New Ireland. Unpublished Patrol Report by Volo Vele.

1970-71b Patrol Report No. 13 of Namatanai, New Ireland. Unpublished Patrol Report by J. Amoroso.

1971-72a Patrol Report No. 9a of Namatanai, New Ireland. Unpublished Patrol Report by Gregory W. O'Brien.

1971-72b Patrol Report No. 9b of Namatanai, New Ireland. Unpublished Patrol Report by P.R. Owens and Gregory W. O'Brien.

Thurnwald, H.

1938   *Ehe und Mutterschaft in Buin*. Archiv fur Anthropologie und Völkerforschung (NS) 24:214–226.

Tooby, John, and Leda Cosmides

1992   The Psychological Foundations of Culture. In *The Adapted Mind*, J. H. Barkow, L. Cosmides, and J. Tooby, eds., pp. 19-136. New York: Oxford University Press.

Tuzin, Donald F.

1976   *The Ilahita Arapesh: Dimensions of Unity*. Berkeley and Los Angeles: University of California Press.

1997   *The Cassowary's Revenge: The Life and Death of Masculinity in a New Guinea Society*. Chicago: University of Chicago Press.

Wagner, Roy

1975   *The Invention of Culture*. Englewood Cliffs, New Jersey: Prentice-Hall.

1986   *Asiwinarong*. Princeton: Princeton University Press.
1989   Conclusion: The Exchange Context of the Kula. In *Death Rituals and Life in the Societies of the Kula Ring*, F. H. Damon and R. Wagner, eds., pp. 254–274. DeKalb, Illinois: Northern Illinois University Press.

Watkins, James W. N.
1962   Historical Explanations in the Social Sciences. In *Theories of History*. P. Gardiner, ed., pp. 503–514. Glencoe, Illinois: Free Press.

Watson-Franke, Maria-Barbara
1992   Masculinity and the "Matrilineal Puzzle." *Anthropos* 87:475–488.

Weiner, Annette
1976   *Women of Value, Men of Renown: New Perspectives in Trobriand Exchange*. Austin: University of Texas Press.
1992   *Inalienable Possessions*. Berkeley and Los Angeles: University of California Press.

Weiner, James F.
1988   *The Heart of the Pearlshell: The Mythical Dimensions of Foi Sociality*. Berkeley: University of California Press.

Yanigasako, Sylvia, and Jane Collier
1987   *Gender and Kinship: Essays Toward a Unified Analysis*. Stanford: Stanford University Press.

Young, Michael
1971   *Fighting with Food: Leadership, Values and Social Control in a Massim Society*. Cambridge: Cambridge University Press.

Index

About the Author

ALEXANDER H. BOLYANATZ is Assistant Professor of Anthropology, Wheaton College, Illinois.

DATE DUE